Teaching Jesus

What & How Jesus Taught

How We Teach Jesus

compiled by Mark Standley, PhD
foreword by H. Fred Brown, JD, M. Div.

Copyright 2023 by Standby Media.
All rights reserved. No part of this book may be reproduced or utilized in any form or by electronic, mechanical or other means without the prior written permission of the copyright holder.

Compiled by Mark Standley, PhD using ChatGPT and other print and human resources

Printed in the United States.
First edition, August, 2023
Book Cover Design: Luis M. Ramirez
www.luisramirezweb.com
ISBN (paperback): 979-8-9888093-0-2
V. 5.3

Other Books by Mark Standley

- Digital Storytelling: iMovie (2010), PowerPoint (2010) (Visions)
- Technology Standards (2008) (Visions)
- Global Project-based Learning (2010) (Visions)
- Our Museum of Us: Curating Your Family's Stuff into a Digital Future (2020)

Book of Questions:
- Handheld Leader (2011)
- Teaching Powerful Storytelling (2012)
- Unmanned Aerial Systems for Schools (2016)
- Drone Essential Knowledge and Skills (DEKS) (2019)
- Fishing on Kayaks (2021)
- Touring on Bikes (with David Plaskett) (2020)
- Learning to Become an Old Man with Dr Jim Giles and Dr. Scott Hoyer (2021)

(at Amazon)

Table of Contents

Foreword..Page 5

How This Book is Organized..................Page 7

Introduction ....Page 10

Section I
What and How Jesus Taught..................Page 13

Section II
Teaching Jesus..Page 96

Section III
How We Teach Jesus Today..................Page 128

Section IV .
The Bible Teaching Jesus......................Page 169

Section V
How Other Religions Teach About Jesus..............Page 187

Glosssary..Page 204

Index ....Page 234

About the Authors..................................Page 237

How Jesus Taught -
Sermon on the Mount

"And why do you
worry about clothes? See how the
flowers of the field grow. They do not
labor or spin. Yet I tell you that not
even Solomon in all his splendor was
dressed like one of these. If that is
how God clothes the grass of the field,
which is here today and tomorrow is
thrown into the fire, will he not much
more clothe you—you of little faith."

Jesus
Matthew 6:28-30) (NIV)

Foreword

My congratulations to Dr. Standley for his excellent book - 'Teaching Jesus.' I find it quite informative. It is an introductory course on the Bible, comparative religion, and the teachings of Jesus.

Jesus' brilliant three year ministry was and is today a commentary upon loving your neighbor. His ministry incurred the wrath of the Temple lawyers (pharisees) because it included women, children, foreigners (gentiles), Samaritans (Jewish outcasts), lepers and anyone else considered "unclean" by Jewish law. Jesus connected his teaching to the Hebrew Bible which Christians call the Old Testament today. This "Teaching Jesus" inspired the New Testament of the Christian Bible and he continues to inspire me and hundreds of millions of Christians world wide to this day.

As I read the book, I was excited by the comparison between 'Teaching About Jesus' and 'Teaching Jesus.' It took me back to age five at Vacation Bible School in an Episcopal Church in Memphis, TN. My Father was an Army officer in advanced training in Memphis for deployment to the South Pacific for the invasion of the Phillipine Islands with General Douglas McArthur. My Mother was one of the teachers of the class of about 20 five year old children. "Teaching About Jesus" was a coloring book depicting Jesus who held a Shepard's crook to protect us from any enemy, like a Shepard protecting his sheep. "Teaching Jesus" was the assurance that Jesus was with each of us and did not want us to be afraid. We memorized the 23rd Psalm which we recited before the entire congregation at a Sunday service. My Father spent over one year in the Phillipine Island invasions and returned home safely at the end of World War Two.

Twenty years later in 1963, I was in critical condition in a Navy Hospital Intensive Care Unit (ICU) in Long Island N.Y. During a Navy deployment to Europe, I was involved in a near fatal motorcycle accident and fire.

As I emerged from a coma, an ICU nurse said she overheard me muttering about a "valley of shadow of death" and she wondered if it was from the Bible. "Yes", I answered, it is from the 23rd Psalm. That verse goes, "Yea, though I walk through the valley of the shadow of death, I will fear no evil: for thou art with me: thy rod and thy staff, they comfort me."

My Mother, who was at my bedside said, "Freddie learned that Psalm 20 years ago during World War Two".

The "Teaching About Jesus" and "Teaching Jesus" will be with me forever.

Fred Brown
JD, M. Div.

How this Book is Organized

This book comes from my profound respect and love for Jesus as teacher and His teachings. My whole life I have had a faith in God underinformed of the facts of Jesus's life and teachings despite years of church and Sunny school. Had I paid better attention then, I might not need this book today. And gratefully, the more facts I have discovered and collected here, the more informed my faith becomes. I wrote this book for people who look for the facts of Jesus teachings, His methods, and how people who knew Him then and know Him now teach Jesus.

To sort through the literary, academic, and commentary of Jesus's teaching, I'm tapped into the computer intelligence of ChatGPT. I'm impressed how this jumble of bits and bytes can bring back 'factual' information and knowledge. Because it is artificial information gathering, I encourage myself and anyone reading this book to check the facts, verify them, and chat (your own Chat GPT - God, Preachers, Teachers) with other resources to check whether the information in this book adheres to your collective knowledge and understanding of Jesus teachings.

The book title, 'Teaching Jesus,' uses the word 'teaching' as an adjective and verb. Teaching (adjective) Jesus is what and how He taught. In education we have a three-dollar word, 'andragogy' (from Greek ἀνδρ-, meaning "man", and ἀγωγός, 'leading'- thus, 'leading men'), to describe how a teacher teaches adults. Section I uncovers and explores Jesus's teaching content and methods. It includes content recorded in the Gospels and ways He taught. We explore His parables, questions, miracles, sermons, metaphors, and teachable moments. You should find commonly held knowledge about what and how He taught.

What's the grammatical difference between teaching about Jesus and teaching Jesus?

"The difference between "teaching about Jesus" and "teaching Jesus" lies in the structure and the object of the verb "teaching."

1. "Teaching about Jesus": In this phrase, "about Jesus" functions as a prepositional phrase that modifies the verb "teaching." The focus is on imparting knowledge or providing information concerning Jesus. It involves teaching others about the life, teachings, and significance of Jesus, without necessarily promoting personal belief or faith in Him.

2. "Teaching Jesus": In this phrase, "Jesus" serves as the direct object of the verb "teaching." The emphasis is on instructing or imparting knowledge directly related to Jesus Himself. It often implies a more personal and experiential approach, where the teachings of Jesus are the primary focus of instruction, with the aim of encouraging faith, discipleship, and adherence to His teachings." (from ChatGPT, Open AI)

Essentially, "teaching about Jesus" refers to imparting knowledge or information about Jesus, while "teaching Jesus" refers to instructing or sharing directly the teachings of Jesus.

The phrase 'teaching Jesus' describes how people who knew Him (directly or indirectly over the past two thousand plus years) teach about Him. In Section II we explore how Jesus, God, the twelve Disciples, John the Baptist, other followers gave so much to 'teach Jesus' through inspired methods and through writings that became the New Testament and Gospels. This Section reports how people who never met Jesus such as Paul, and others wrote the New Testament,

We continue to use the verb 'teaching Jesus' to look at other forms of teaching Jesus in Section III. This includes 'how people teach Jesus today (and in the past) - in chruch sermons, personal evangelism, Bible studies, social media, Christian literature, education, workshops theological institutions, retreats, art, music, poetry, TV, movies, and conferences today to the present 'teach Jesus' - His life, and His teachings. You will also find recommendations and organizing guidelines to "teach Jesus" in each for these formats today at church, education, theological institutions, personal evangelism, Bible studies, workshops, conferences, or retreats. Use these for references in building your own curriculum and events and build on the questions here to help to know and understand Jesus's messages.

Section IV is focused on the Bible itself. The book has such a storied and important history, that many books have been written to share its history. Since it is nearly impossible to understand 'teaching Jesus' without knowing about the Bible, specifically the Old and New Testament, I have created this Section to review some of the facts of the Bible's history, authors, and evolution from Koine Greek to present day English and other languages. The Bible (especially New Testament) gives us the words and descriptions of Jesus's teachings; our faith takes us the rest of the way.

Jesus was so known across the world and time. Other religions have had to make sense of this divine teacher. Section V compares religions and how each teaches 'about' or refers to Jesus in either a spiritual, historical, or referential manner. It's revealing to see how he was viewed among members of Judaism, Hinduism, Islam, Buddhism, and other non-Christian religions.

You will find a descriptive Glossary with phrases, concepts, places, and events related to Teaching Jesus (again generated from the computer to help clear up basic terms or phrases in English and their root languages)(i.e.Aramaic, Greek, Hebrew) common in Christianity. It's helpful to have a basic knowledge of these concepts and events to help build your understanding of Teaching Jesus.

You will find this book filled with a basic collection of the facts of Teaching Jesus - what and how He taught and how we teach Him in the past and in today's world. There's plenty here for the beginner Christian, a Jesus scholar, to Chritian schools to gain knowledge, encourage more research, and start building a solid foundation for on insights and faith in your own path to Teaching Jesus.

Introduction

Jesus was a gifted and divine teacher. How He taught is as important as what He taught. He was referred to as a 'rabbi' ('divine teacher') by His disciples because of His message and methods. This book, Teaching Jesus, explores the content and methods He used to teach wisdom. And the people and their media who have been teaching Jesus since.

Teachers know their content area. Typically, they know the past and present of their subject matter, and if they master their craft, they know both extremely well. Jesus was unique among teachers. As a divine teacher, He knew intimately the past, present, and future of His material. This gave Him a profound knowledge that was and is sometimes difficult for mere mortals to understand. So, He used a variety of unique and seemingly spontaneous teaching methods to communicate. We are in complete awe considering what and how He taught.

Jesus taught through a variety of methods, including sermons, parables, miracles, teachable moments, metaphors and questions. He used parables -'short stories with a moral or spiritual lesson,' to illustrate complex concepts in simple, relatable and memorable ways. He performed miracles, such as healing the sick and feeding the hungry to demonstrate His power and compassion. In addition, Jesus taught directly through sermons and talks with His disciples and other followers. He emphasized love, forgiveness, and the importance of putting others before one's self. Through His teachings, Jesus challenged the social and religious norms of His time and inspired many people then and now.

Thomas Jefferson, third President of the United States, compiled a similar book to Teaching Jesus. Like this book, 'The Moral Teachings of Jesus of Nazareth,' Jefferson's work focused on the moral lessons and literal teachings of Jesus. Jefferson studied the canonical Gospels in French, Greek, Latin and the King James

Version of the Bible for his source materials. He cut and pasted the content into a chronological order of Jesus's teachings. Unlike this book Jefferson left out descriptions of Jesus's miracles and supernatural elements. This book, Teaching Jesus, includes all of those elements, and importantly holds onto Jesus's divinity. I wonder - 'what if' - Thomas Jefferson had ChatGPT (Open AI) at his disposal. Would his book look anything like this book, 'Teaching Jesus'?

While compiling this book and doing my own research (talking with scholars, reading books, and employing computer knowledge (ChatGPT)), I was driven by a singular thought. I wished I had learned the contents of this Teaching Jesus book when I was a younger person. As a teenager, I attended Vacation Bible School. Throughout the hot and humid East Texas week, we were given instruction and encouragement by our Sunday School teachers. Today I look at their names signed in a small New Testament they gifted us with great respect for their kindness and teachings. Their faith and love was clear, but I needed more. Even then, I did not feel I knew Jesus.

Later that summer I attended a Bible Camp in the East Texas woods. I met Jesus there among the hymns, humidity, and mosquitoes. It was the most pure feeling of connection to a higher being I have ever known. I felt so calm and peaceful. Upon returning home, I shared my excitement. I was told I didn't really know the facts or truth about God. It was a time I knew what I knew about God and Jesus by my faith, but not being able to match the facts with my faith. Putting together this book, 'Teaching Jesus,' and studying the contents helps me know more of Jesus's ministry - what I did not know then, but know now.

So, with Jesus there is always more to learn. We can study all the teachings, study His words and actions, but we can never truly come to know the essence of Jesus other than through faith and profound appreciation for His teachings, His life, and Him. I wish every young person and adult would receive this book to help them open their blossuming flowers of faith.

A petal here. A stamen there. Jesus provides us with Himself as the ultimate metaphor of a living flower. We can take in parts of the flower - this most gifted of all teachers, what and how He taught. In His teachings, Jesus asks us to consider the flowers of the field in their beauty and simple perfection (Matthew, 6: 28-30). Now and in this book, let us consider Jesus and His teachings in the same light.

Mark Standley
August, 2023

Section I
What and How did Jesus Teach

1. Who was Jesus - His Divinity
2. Gift Teacher - 'Rabbi'
3. How and what Jesus taught
4. Questions to know and understand what and how Jesus taught

Who was Jesus - His Divinity

How is Jesus God?

The belief that Jesus is God is a central tenet of Christianity. This concept, known as the divinity of Jesus or the doctrine of the Incarnation, asserts that Jesus Christ was both fully human and fully divine. Understanding how Jesus was God requires exploring several key Christian beliefs:

    1. The Trinity: The doctrine of the Trinity teaches that God exists in three persons: the Father, the Son (Jesus Christ), and the Holy Spirit. These three persons are distinct from one another but share the same divine essence, making them one God. According to This doctrine, Jesus, as the Son, is eternally and fully divine.

    2. The Incarnation: The doctrine of the Incarnation holds that Jesus, the divine Son of God, took on human flesh and was born of the Virgin Mary. While Jesus was fully human, He did not lose His divine nature. This belief is based on passages such as John 1:14, which states, "The Word became flesh and made His dwelling among us."

    3. Jesus' teachings and actions: The Gospels contain numerous instances where Jesus made divine claims about Himself, forgave sins, and demonstrated His authority over the natural and spiritual world through miracles and healings. These events and statements are interpreted by Christians as evidence of Jesus' divine nature.

    4. The Resurrection: Christians believe that Jesus was crucified, died, and was buried, but on the third day, He rose

from the dead. The Resurrection is seen as a confirmation of Jesus' divinity, as it demonstrated His victory over sin and death.

    5. The early Church: The belief in Jesus' divinity can be traced back to the early Church, as evidenced by the writings of the apostles and early Church leaders. The early Church formulated creeds, such as the Nicene Creed, which affirmed the belief in Jesus as "God from God, Light from Light, true God from true God."

It is important to note that the belief in Jesus as God is a matter of faith, and interpretations may differ among various Christian denominations and individual believers. However, the divinity of Jesus remains a central and foundational doctrine in Christianity.

Why is Jesus God?

The belief that Jesus is God is based on the understanding of Jesus' identity as revealed in the New Testament of the Bible. It is important to note that different Christian denominations may have variations in their specific theological interpretations, but I will provide a general explanation.

Christians believe that Jesus is God for several reasons:

    1. Divine Revelation: According to Christian belief, God has revealed Himself to humanity through Jesus Christ. In the New Testament, Jesus is described as the Son of God who came to Earth in human form. He claimed to be one with the Father (God) and referred to Himself as the "I Am," which is associated with God's self-revelation in the Old Testament (Exodus 3:14).

    2. Incarnation: Christians believe in the doctrine of the Incarnation, which teaches that Jesus is both fully human and fully divine. It is believed that in Jesus, God took on human flesh and became man, while still retaining His divine nature. This union of divinity and humanity in Jesus is seen as unique and points to His divine nature.

    3. Miracles and Authority: Jesus' ministry included performing miracles, such as healing the sick, raising the dead, and calming storms. These extraordinary acts were seen as evidence of His divine power and authority over creation.

4. Resurrection: Christians believe in the resurrection of Jesus. According to the New Testament, Jesus was crucified, died, and rose from the dead on the third day. The resurrection is seen as a validation of Jesus' claims, including His divine nature and His victory over sin and death.

5. Early Christian Beliefs: From the earliest days of Christianity, the belief in Jesus as God was held by the early Christian community. The New Testament writings and the early creeds, such as the Nicene Creed, affirm Jesus' divinity.

It is important to note that the concept of Jesus' divinity and the specific theological explanations vary among different Christian denominations. However, the belief in Jesus as God is foundational to the Christian faith based on the teachings and accounts found in the Bible.

The Difference between Jesus as a Human and Jesus as God

In Christian theology, Jesus is both fully human and fully divine, possessing two natures united in one person. This concept, known as the hypostatic union, seeks to explain the relationship between Jesus' humanity and divinity. Here are some differences between Jesus' human nature and divine nature:

Jesus the human:

1. Birth and growth: Jesus was born of the Virgin Mary and experienced physical growth and development like any other human being (Luke 2:40, 52).

2. Human emotions and experiences: Jesus experienced human emotions such as joy, sorrow, and anger (John 11:33-35, Mark 3:5, Luke 10:21). He also felt hunger (Matthew 4:2) and thirst (John 19:28).

3. Temptation: Jesus was tempted by the devil in the wilderness but did not give in to temptation (Matthew 4:1-11). This demonstrates His capacity to experience human trials and temptations.

4. Suffering and death: Jesus underwent physical suffering during His crucifixion and ultimately died on the cross (Matthew 27, Mark 15, Luke 23, John 19). Death is a central aspect of the

human experience.

Jesus as God:
1. Divine origin: Jesus is described as the eternal Son of God who existed before His earthly incarnation (John 1:1-14, Philippians 2:6-8).
2. Miracles and authority: Jesus performed miracles, such as healing the sick, raising the dead, and calming storms, which demonstrated His divine power and authority (Matthew 8:23-27, John 11:38-44, Mark 5:21-43).
3. Forgiveness of sins: Jesus forgave sins, an action that, according to Jewish belief, only God can perform (Mark 2:5-12, Luke 7:47-50).
4. Divine claims: Jesus made claims about Himself that pointed to His divinity, such as the "I am" statements in the Gospel of John (e.g., "I am the way, the truth, and the life" in John 14:6 and "I am the resurrection and the life" in John 11:25).
It is essential to recognize that, according to Christian belief, Jesus' human and divine natures were not separate entities but were united in one person. This unity allowed Jesus to experience and understand the human condition fully while also possessing the divine power to accomplish His mission as the Messiah and the savior of humanity. The hypostatic union is a complex and mysterious concept that has been the subject of much theological reflection and debate throughout Christian History.

What's the Difference between God, Jesus and Holy Spirit?

In Christian theology, God, Jesus, and the Holy Spirit are distinct entities that together make up the Holy Trinity, a central doctrine in Christianity. The concept of the Trinity states that there is one God who exists in three persons: God the Father, God the Son (Jesus Christ), and God the Holy Spirit. While each person is distinct, they are all co-equal, co-eternal, and of the same substance. Here's a brief description of each:
1. God the Father: Often simply referred to as "God," the Father is the first person of the Trinity. He is the creator of the

universe and everything in it. God the Father is all-powerful, all-knowing, and all-loving. He is often depicted as the ultimate authority figure and the source of divine providence.

2. Jesus Christ (God the Son): Jesus is the second person of the Trinity, the Son of God, who became incarnate (took on human form) through the Virgin Mary. Jesus lived a sinless life, preached about the Kingdom of God, performed miracles, and was crucified for the sins of humanity. He rose from the dead three days later and ascended into heaven, demonstrating His divine nature and role as the Savior. Jesus acts as the mediator between God the Father and humanity, and it is through faith in Him that Christians believe they can obtain salvation.

3. Holy Spirit (God the Holy Spirit): The Holy Spirit is the third person of the Trinity and is often associated with God's presence and activity in the world. The Holy Spirit is said to have descended on Jesus's disciples at Pentecost, empowering them to spread the Gospel and perform miracles. The Holy Spirit is believed to be active in the lives of believers today, guiding, comforting, convicting, and empowering them to live a Christ-centered life.

The concept of the Trinity can be challenging to fully comprehend, as it is a complex theological idea. However, in essence, the Trinity expresses the belief that there is one God who exists in three persons, each with distinct roles and functions, yet all united in essence, power, and purpose.

Why do we Capitalize the Names of God and Jesus?

Capitalizing the names of God and Jesus in English is often done out of respect and reverence. It is a convention that has developed over time within English-speaking Christian traditions. Capitalizing these names is seen as a way to acknowledge their divine nature and to give them special significance.
Additionally, capitalizing these names helps to distinguish them

from regular nouns and to highlight their importance in religious contexts. It serves as a visual indicator that these words refer to specific religious figures and not just generic terms.

It's important to note that not all English translations or versions of the Bible consistently capitalize these names. The capitalization practice may vary among different religious traditions, translations, and individual preferences.

Gifted Teacher - 'rabbi'

How was Jesus such a gifted teacher?

Jesus was considered a gifted teacher for several reasons, which contributed to the impact of His teachings and the lasting influence He has had on the world. Some of these reasons include:

    1. His divine wisdom: As the Son of God, Jesus had divine wisdom and a deep understanding of human nature, which allowed Him to communicate profound truths in an accessible and relatable manner.

    2. Use of parables: Jesus frequently used parables – simple, illustrative stories – to convey complex spiritual concepts. Parables made His teachings more engaging and memorable, helping people understand His message more easily.

    3. Connection with the audience: Jesus was able to connect with people from various backgrounds and social standings. He showed empathy and understanding, which made His listeners feel valued and respected.

    4. Asking thought-provoking questions: Jesus often asked questions that challenged people's assumptions and encouraged them to think deeply about their beliefs and actions. This approach engaged His audience and stimulated critical thinking.

    5. Teaching with authority: Jesus taught with confidence and authority, demonstrating a profound understanding of Scripture and its implications. His authoritative teaching style commanded respect and left a lasting impression on His listeners.

    6. Use of everyday examples: Jesus used examples from

daily life and nature to illustrate His teachings, making them relatable and easily understandable. This approach helped His audience grasp complex spiritual truths by connecting them to familiar experiences.

7. Focus on practical application: Jesus emphasized the practical application of His teachings, urging His followers to live out their faith through acts of love, compassion, and service. This focus on action made His teachings relevant and transformative.

8. Adaptability: Jesus adapted His teaching methods to suit the needs of His audience. He used different techniques, such as storytelling, dialogue, and direct instruction, depending on the situation and the people He was addressing.

9. Encouragement of personal reflection: Jesus's teachings often encouraged personal reflection and introspection. He challenged His listeners to examine their own beliefs, actions, and motivations, promoting spiritual growth and self-improvement.

10. Timeless and universal message: The core message of Jesus's teachings – love, forgiveness, and the importance of a personal relationship with God – transcends cultural and Historical boundaries, making it relevant and compelling to people across time and place.

Jesus's unique combination of divine wisdom, relatability, and effective teaching methods made Him an exceptional teacher, and His teachings continue to inspire and guide people worldwide.

Why did His Disciples call Jesus 'rabbi'?

The term "rabbi" is a Hebrew word that means "teacher" or "master." ('rabbouni' in Aramaic - ܪܒܘܢܝ in Syriac script). In the context of first-century Judaism, a rabbi was a respected religious leader who taught and interpreted the Scriptures, often having a group of followers or disciples who learned from them. The disciples called Jesus 'rabbi' because they recognized Him as their spiritual teacher and leader.

Jesus had a profound understanding of the Scriptures and taught with authority, which drew people to listen to His teachings. The Gospels frequently mention Jesus teaching in synagogues, public places, and private gatherings. His wisdom and insight, along with the miracles He performed, convinced many of His divine origin and authority. Consequently, His followers addressed Him as "Rabbi" to show their respect and acknowledge Him as their guide and teacher.

Additionally, by calling Jesus "rabbi," the disciples acknowledged their position as His students, willing to learn from Him and follow His teachings. This title emphasized the relationship between Jesus and His followers, reflecting their commitment to follow and learn from Him in their spiritual journey.

How did Jesus Teach?

Jesus taught in a variety of ways, utilizing different methods to convey His message and make His teachings accessible and understandable to His audience. Some of the ways Jesus taught include:

    1. Parables: Jesus often used parables, which are simple stories that convey moral or spiritual lessons. Parables used familiar, everyday situations and objects to teach deeper truths, making them relatable and easy to remember. Examples of Jesus' parables include the Good Samaritan, the Prodigal Son, and the Sower.

    2. Sermons - Direct Instruction: Jesus delivered sermons, such as the Sermon on the Mount (found in Matthew 5-7), which provided moral guidance and instructions on how to live a righteous life. The Sermon on the Mount contains key teachings like the Beatitudes, the Lord's Prayer, and the Golden Rule.

    3. Question and Answer: Jesus often engaged in discussions and used questions to challenge the understanding of His listeners and provoke thought. He answered questions from His disciples, religious leaders, and others who sought His wisdom.

    4. Teachable Moments: Jesus used events and situations He encountered as opportunities to teach. For example, when He saw

a widow giving her last coins to the temple treasury, He used the moment to teach about the true nature of generosity (Mark 12:41-44).

5. Miracles and Healings: Jesus performed miracles and healings, which demonstrated His divine power and compassion.

6. Metaphors: Jesus taught using metaphors to make complex spiritual concepts more accessible to His listeners and to convey His message in memorable and impactful ways.

Parables

Why did Jesus Teach using Parables?

Jesus taught using parables for:

1. Relatability: Parables are simple, easy-to-understand stories that often draw from everyday life experiences. By using parables, Jesus made His teachings accessible and relatable to a wide range of people, regardless of their background, education, or social status.

2. Engagement: Parables are engaging and memorable, making it easier for listeners to remember the message. By telling stories that captured the imagination, Jesus ensured that His teachings would be shared, discussed, and passed down through generations.

3. Encourage deeper thinking: Parables often contain a hidden or symbolic message that invites listeners to reflect on the deeper meaning. Jesus used parables to encourage His followers to think more critically about spiritual concepts, moral values, and their relationship with God.

4. Convey complex ideas: Parables allow the expression of complex ideas and abstract concepts through simple, relatable stories. Jesus used parables to teach about the kingdom of God, forgiveness, love, and other essential spiritual principles without overwhelming His audience.

5. Discretion: In some instances, Jesus used parables to convey His message discreetly to avoid direct confrontation with religious leaders or opponents. This approach allowed Him

to teach His followers without drawing too much attention or inciting conflict.

Overall, parables were an effective and versatile teaching method that allowed Jesus to communicate His message.

Describe the Number and Type of Parables from Jesus

Jesus is known for using parables in His teachings, and the Gospels record many of these stories. The number and type of parables varies somewhat depending on which Gospel is being consulted, but here is a general overview:

1. In the Gospel of Matthew, Jesus is recorded as telling 23 parables, including the Parable of the Sower, the Parable of the Wheat and the Tares, and the Parable of the Talents.

2. In the Gospel of Mark, Jesus is recorded as telling 13 parables, including the Parable of the Mustard Seed, the Parable of the Wicked Tenants, and the Parable of the Growing Seed.

3. In the Gospel of Luke, Jesus is recorded as telling 28 parables, including the Parable of the Prodigal Son, the Parable of the Good Samaritan, and the Parable of the Rich Fool.

4. In the Gospel of John, Jesus is not recorded as telling any parables, but He does use metaphors and other figurative language in His teachings.

The types of parables that Jesus tells in the Gospels vary widely in subject matter and structure, but they all use simple, everyday situations to convey deeper spiritual truths. Some parables are focused on the nature of God and His kingdom, while others address themes of repentance, forgiveness, and the importance of faith.

The parables of Jesus have been a central part of Christian teaching and worship for centuries, and continue to be studied and appreciated by people of all faiths and backgrounds.

How many Parables did Jesus Teach?

It is difficult to determine an exact number of parables Jesus taught, as the count may vary depending on the source and interpretation. Generally, there are around 30-40 parables attributed to Jesus in the Gospels. In the New Testament, Jesus' teachings are primarily found in the Gospels of Matthew, Mark, and Luke. These three Gospels, known as the Synoptic Gospels, contain most of Jesus' parables.

Here are some of the most famous parables:
1. The Good Samaritan (Luke 10:25-37)
2. The Prodigal Son (Luke 15:11-32)
3. The Sower (Mark 4:1-20, Matthew 13:1-23, Luke 8:4-15)
4. The Mustard Seed (Mark 4:30-32, Matthew 13:31-32, Luke 13:18-19)
5. The Talents or Minas (Matthew 25:14-30, Luke 19:12-27)
6. The Lost Sheep (Matthew 18:12-14, Luke 15:3-7)
7. The Wise and Foolish Builders (Matthew 7:24-27, Luke 6:46-49)

The parables use everyday situations and objects to teach moral and spiritual lessons, making them easily relatable and memorable for Jesus' audience.

The Parable of the Good Samaritan

The Parable of the Good Samaritan is a story told by Jesus in the New Testament of the Bible, found specifically in the book of Luke (10:25-37). This parable is told in response to a question posed by a lawyer about how to inherit eternal life and who exactly counts as a neighbor.

Here is the parable:
A man was going down from Jerusalem to Jericho and fell among robbers, who stripped him and beat him, leaving him half dead. A priest happened to be going down the same road, but when he saw the man, he passed by on the other side. Likewise, a Levite, when he came to the place and saw the man, also passed by on the other side. But a Samaritan, as he journeyed, came to where the man was, and when he saw him, He had compassion. He went to him and bound up his wounds, pouring on oil and wine.

Then he set him on his own animal, brought him to an inn, and took care of him. The next day, he took out two denarii, gave them to the innkeeper, and said, 'Take care of him, and whatever more you spend, I will repay you when I come back.'

After telling the parable, Jesus asked the lawyer which of these three – the priest, the Levite, or the Samaritan – proved to be a neighbor to the man who fell among the robbers. The lawyer replied, "The one who showed him mercy." Jesus then told him to go and do likewise.

In the story:
- The injured man represents anyone in need.
- The priest and the Levite represent individuals who fail to act with kindness and compassion despite their religious standing.
- The Samaritan, a member of a group often despised by the Jewish population, represents the one who shows true compassion and mercy. he acts as a neighbor should, despite ethnic, religious, or societal differences.

The Parable of the Good Samaritan illustrates the principle of loving one's neighbor and showing mercy to those in need, regardless of their background or status. It underscores the idea that a 'neighbor' is not just someone who lives near us or is part of our social group, but anyone who needs our kindness and help.

The Parable of the Lost Son

The Parable of the Lost (Prodigal) Son is a well-known story told by Jesus, found in the Gospel of Luke 15:11-32. It conveys the themes of forgiveness, redemption, and the unconditional love of God. Here is a summary of the parable:

A man had two sons, and the younger son asked His father for His share of the inheritance. The father agreed and divided His property between them. Soon after, the younger son gathered His belongings and traveled to a distant country, where he

squandered His wealth in wild living.
After he had spent everything, a severe famine hit the country, and he began to be in need. he found work feeding pigs, and he became so hungry that he longed to fill his stomach with the pods the pigs were eating, but no one gave him anything. Finally, the younger son came to his senses and realized that even his father's hired servants had food to spare, while he was starving. He decided to return to His father and confess his wrongdoings, saying he was no longer worthy to be called his son and asking to be treated like one of the hired servants.

When the son was still a long way off, his father saw him coming and was filled with compassion. He ran to his son, embraced him, and kissed him. The son confessed his sins and acknowledged his unworthiness, but the father immediately called for the best robe, a ring, and sandals to be put on his son. He also ordered a fattened calf to be killed for a feast, declaring that his son was dead and is now alive again, lost and now found.
Meanwhile, the older son was working in the field, and as he approached the house, he heard the music and dancing. He asked a servant what was happening, and the servant informed him that his brother had returned and his father was celebrating. The older son became angry and refused to go in.

The father came out and pleaded with the older son, who expressed his frustration, claiming that he had always been obedient and never received a celebration. The father told him that everything he had was already his, but they had to rejoice and celebrate because the younger brother was dead and now alive, lost and now found.
The Parable of the Lost Son highlights the themes of forgiveness, redemption, and God's unconditional love. It emphasizes the joy of reconciliation and the importance of celebrating when someone who was lost turns back and finds their way home.

The Parable of the Sower

The Parable of the Sower is a story told by Jesus in the New Testament of the Bible, specifically found in the books of Matthew (13:1–23), Mark (4:1–20), and Luke (8:4–15). It's one of the many parables used by Jesus to teach His followers about various aspects of life, faith, and the Kingdom of God. Here is the parable as it is presented in the Book of Matthew:
"A sower went out to sow. And as he sowed, some seeds fell along the path, and the birds came and devoured them. Other seeds fell on rocky ground, where they did not have much soil, and immediately they sprang up, since they had no depth of soil, but when the sun rose they were scorched. And since they had no root, they withered away. Other seeds fell among thorns, and the thorns grew up and choked them. Other seeds fell on good soil and produced grain, some a hundredfold, some sixty, some thirty. He who has ears, let him hear."
In This parable, the sower represents those who spread the teachings of God, while the seed symbolizes the Word of God. The different types of soil represent the various ways that people receive the Word of God:

    1. The seed that fell along the path represents those who hear the Word of God but don't understand it, and the evil one (often interpreted as Satan) comes and snatches away what has been sown in their heart.

    2. The seed falling on rocky ground represents those who hear the Word and immediately receive it with joy, but since they have no root, they endure for a while, but when tribulation or persecution arises on account of the Word, they immediately fall away.

    3. The seed falling among thorns refers to those who hear the Word, but the cares of the world and the deceitfulness of riches choke the Word, and it proves unfruitful.

    4. The seed falling on good soil refers to the person who hears the Word and understands it. He indeed bears fruit and yields, in one case a hundredfold, in another sixty, and in another thirty.

This parable illustrates how the Word of God may be accepted or rejected in various ways, and it encourages individuals to be like the "good soil," receptive and fruitful in response to God's Word.

The Parable of the Mustard Seed

The Parable of the Mustard Seed is another one of Jesus' teachings, found in the New Testament books of Matthew (13:31-32), Mark (4:30-32), and Luke (13:18-19). It's used to illustrate the Kingdom of God's humble beginnings and its potential for vast growth. Here's the version from Matthew:

"He put another parable before them, saying, 'The kingdom of heaven is like a grain of mustard seed that a man took and sowed in His field. It is the smallest of all seeds, but when it has grown it is larger than all the garden plants and becomes a tree, so that the birds of the air come and make nests in its branches.'"

The mustard seed in the parable represents the Kingdom of God, which begins small—in the teachings and ministry of Jesus, for instance—but grows into something much larger and influential, reaching out and offering refuge, like the birds nesting in its branches.

While a mustard seed isn't actually the smallest of all seeds, it was a common expression in Jewish culture to illustrate something very small. Similarly, a mustard plant doesn't grow into the largest of all trees but can reach a significant size for a garden plant—up to 10 feet tall. These elements of the parable are hyperbolic expressions meant to emphasize the contrast between humble beginnings and impressive growth.

The parable essentially encourages faith, patience, and hope, illustrating that even seemingly small, insignificant beginnings can lead to substantial, impactful outcomes in the context of faith and the spread of the Kingdom of God.

The Parable of Talents or Minas

The Parable of the Talents is found in the New Testament of the Bible in the book of Matthew (25:14-30). A similar but slightly different parable, known as the Parable of the Minas, can be found in the book of Luke (19:11-27). Both parables are about stewardship, accountability, and the expectation of productivity for the Kingdom of God.

In the Parable of the Talents, a master going on a journey entrusts His property to His servants. He gives one servant five talents (a large sum of money), another two talents, and another one talent, each according to His ability. The servant who received five talents went and traded with them and made five more. Likewise, the servant with two talents gained two more. But the servant who received one talent went and dug in the ground and hid His master's money.

When the master returned and settled accounts with them, the first two servants reported their gains and were praised as "good and faithful" servants. They were rewarded by being put in charge of many things and invited to share in their master's happiness.

The servant with one talent, however, explained that he hid the money because he was afraid of the master, whom he perceived as a harsh man. The master rebuked This servant as "wicked and lazy," took His talent, and gave it to the servant who had ten talents. The master explained that everyone who has will be given more, but those who have not, even what they have will be taken away. The unprofitable servant was then cast into the outer darkness.

In the Parable of the Minas in Luke, the circumstances are somewhat different. A nobleman going to a distant country to get royal power for Himself gave ten of His servants one mina each (a smaller sum than a talent) and instructed them to do business until he comes back. Upon His return, he rewarded the servants who had gained more money and punished the servant who had simply hidden the mina.

These parables underscore the importance of using one's resources or gifts wisely to produce positive outcomes. They highlight the concept that God expects us to make the most of what we're given, whether it's wealth, abilities, or opportunities. Furthermore, they convey that there will be an accountability for how we use what we're given.

The Parable of the Lost Sheep

The Parable of the Lost Sheep appears in two of the books of the New Testament in the Bible: Matthew (18:12-14) and Luke (15:3-7). It's a story that Jesus tells to illustrate the joy in finding something (or someone) that was lost, symbolizing the joy in heaven when a sinner repents.
Here's the version from the book of Luke:
"Then Jesus told them This parable: 'Suppose one of you has a hundred sheep and loses one of them. Doesn't he leave the ninety-nine in the open country and go after the lost sheep until he finds it? And when he finds it, he joyfully puts it on His shoulders and goes home. Then his calls his friends and neighbors together and says, 'Rejoice with me; I have found my lost sheep.' I tell you that in the same way there will be more rejoicing in heaven over one sinner who repents than over ninety-nine righteous persons who do not need to repent.'"
In This parable, the shepherd represents God, or Jesus Himself as the "Good Shepherd." The hundred sheep represent all of humanity, and the lost sheep represents a person who has strayed away or become lost in sin. The joyous act of the shepherd finding the lost sheep and celebrating mirrors the joy in heaven when a lost soul is found or when a sinner repents.
This parable is often used to emphasize God's love and care for every individual, the importance of every single person to God, and His desire to bring everyone to repentance and salvation.

The Parable of the Wise and Foolish Builder

The Parable of the Wise and Foolish Builders, also known as the Parable of the Two Foundations, is a story told by Jesus in the New Testament of the Bible, specifically found in Matthew 7:24-27 and Luke 6:46-49. It serves as a metaphor for the importance of building one's life on a solid foundation, which represents following Jesus' teachings.
Here is the parable as presented in Matthew:
"Everyone then who hears these words of mine and does them

will be like a wise man who built His house on the rock. And the rain fell, and the floods came, and the winds blew and beat on that house, but it did not fall, because it had been founded on the rock. And everyone who hears these words of mine and does not do them will be like a foolish man who built His house on the sand. And the rain fell, and the floods came, and the winds blew and beat against that house, and it fell, and great was the fall of it."

In the parable:
- The wise builder represents those who hear Jesus' teachings and put them into practice. Their efforts are compared to a house built on a solid, reliable foundation—the rock—which withstands various trials and tribulations represented by the storm.
- The foolish builder, on the other hand, represents those who hear Jesus' teachings but do not put them into practice. Their neglect is compared to a house built on a weak, unreliable foundation—the sand—which collapses in the face of trials and tribulations, represented by the storm.

The main message of the parable is the importance of not just hearing, but also applying Jesus' teachings in one's life. Such action is likened to building one's life on a sturdy foundation that can weather the difficulties and challenges of life.

Compare Jesus's Parables and those in the Old Testament

The parables of Jesus and those found in the Old Testament share some similarities, but also have some notable differences.

Similarities:
1. Both the parables of Jesus and those found in the Old Testament use stories and metaphors to convey important spiritual truths.
2. Both types of parables often draw on everyday situations and objects to make their points, such as farming, fishing, or family relationships.
3. Both types of parables are intended to provoke thought

and inspire listeners to reflect on their own lives and relationship with God.

Differences:
　　1. Jesus's parables are more focused on the coming of the Kingdom of God, while many of the parables in the Old Testament are focused on themes like justice, mercy, and the importance of obedience to God's commands.
　　2. The parables of Jesus are often more metaphorical and symbolic than those found in the Old Testament, using imagery like seeds, sheep, or vines to represent deeper spiritual truths.
　　3. The parables of Jesus are often more open-ended than those found in the Old Testament, leaving listeners to interpret and apply the story's meaning to their own lives and situations. Overall, both the parables of Jesus and those found in the Old Testament are powerful tools for conveying important spiritual truths in a memorable and relatable way. While they differ somewhat in focus and style, both types of parables continue to inspire and challenge listeners to This day.

Sermons - Direct Instruction

The Sermon on the Mount

The Sermon on the Mount is a collection of teachings by Jesus, found in the Gospel of Matthew, chapters 5 through 7. It is one of the most famous and influential discourses in the Christian faith, presenting core moral and ethical principles for followers of Jesus.
Here is an overview of the key components of the Sermon on the Mount:
　　1. The Beatitudes (Matthew 5:3-12): These are a series of blessings that describe the qualities and virtues of those who are considered true disciples of Jesus. They emphasize humility, mercy, purity of heart, peacemaking, and the willingness to endure persecution for the sake of righteousness.
　　2. Salt and Light (Matthew 5:13-16): Jesus uses the

metaphors of salt and light to illustrate the role of His followers in the world. They are to preserve goodness and righteousness (like salt) and shine as a beacon of hope and guidance (like light) to others.

3. The Fulfillment of the Law (Matthew 5:17-20): Jesus declares that He has come to fulfill the Law and the Prophets, not to abolish them. He emphasizes the importance of righteousness and teaches that His followers must exceed the righteousness of the religious leaders of that time.

4. Moral Teachings (Matthew 5:21-48): Jesus expands on various commandments, offering deeper insights into their meaning and application. He addresses topics such as anger, adultery, divorce, oaths, retaliation, and love for enemies.

5. Acts of Righteousness (Matthew 6:1-18): Jesus teaches about the proper attitudes and motives when engaging in acts of righteousness, such as giving to the needy, praying, and fasting. He encourages His followers to practice these deeds in secret, seeking the Father's approval rather than human praise.

6. The Lord's Prayer (Matthew 6:9-13): Jesus provides a model prayer that emphasizes the reverence of God, the importance of forgiveness, and the reliance on God's provision and guidance.

7. Treasures in Heaven (Matthew 6:19-24): Jesus warns against materialism and the pursuit of earthly wealth, advising His followers to seek treasures in heaven, where they are eternal and secure.

8. Do Not Worry (Matthew 6:25-34): Jesus encourages His followers to trust in God's provision and care, rather than worrying about material needs.

9. Judging Others (Matthew 7:1-6): Jesus teaches that one should not judge others hypocritically, but instead focus on addressing one's own faults and shortcomings.

10. Ask, Seek, Knock (Matthew 7:7-12): Jesus encourages persistence in prayer and seeking God's guidance, promising that those who ask, seek, and knock will receive, find, and have doors opened for them.

11. The Narrow and Wide Gates (Matthew 7:13-14): Jesus speaks of the choice between the narrow gate leading to life and

the wide gate leading to destruction, emphasizing the importance of choosing the path of righteousness.

    12. False Prophets and Discernment (Matthew 7:15-20): Jesus warns against false prophets and teachers, advising His followers to discern their authenticity by examining their fruits (actions and teachings).

    13. True and False Disciples (Matthew 7:21-23): Jesus emphasizes that only those who truly do the will of the Father will enter the kingdom of heaven, not merely those who profess His name.

    14. The Wise and Foolish Builders (Matthew 7:24-27): Jesus concludes the sermon with a parable about two builders, illustrating the importance of building one's life on the solid foundation of His teachings.

The Sermon on the Mount is a comprehensive teaching that provides guidance for living a righteous life, emphasizing the importance of inner transformation, practical piety, and adherence to Jesus's teachings.

The Sermon on the Plain

The Sermon on the Plain is a discourse given by Jesus, found in the Gospel of Luke, chapter 6, verses 17-49. While it shares similarities with the Sermon on the Mount in Matthew, the Sermon on the Plain is shorter and has its own unique elements. It primarily focuses on moral teachings, social justice, and the conduct expected of Jesus's followers. Some of the key components of the Sermon on the Plain include:

    1. Blessings and Woes (Luke 6:20-26): Jesus begins the sermon with a series of blessings, similar to the Beatitudes in Matthew. He pronounces blessings on the poor, the hungry, those who weep, and those who are persecuted. In contrast, He also pronounces woes on the rich, the well-fed, those who laugh, and those who are well-regarded, highlighting the reversal of fortunes in God's kingdom.

2. Love for Enemies (Luke 6:27-36): Jesus teaches His followers to love their enemies, do good to those who hate them, bless those who curse them, and pray for those who mistreat them. He emphasizes the need to be merciful, just as God is merciful.

3. Judging Others (Luke 6:37-42): Jesus warns against judging others and teaches the principle of reciprocity: "Give, and it will be given to you." He also reiterates the lesson about removing one's faults before trying to correct others, using the analogy of a speck in a brother's eye and a plank in one's own eye.

4. A Tree and Its Fruit (Luke 6:43-45): Similar to the Sermon on the Mount, Jesus teaches that a good tree produces good fruit and a bad tree produces bad fruit. People's actions reveal the true condition of their hearts.

5. The Wise and Foolish Builders (Luke 6:46-49): Jesus concludes the sermon with a parable that highlights the importance of putting His teachings into practice. Those who hear His words and act upon them are like a wise builder who constructs His house on a solid foundation, while those who hear but do not act are like a foolish builder who builds on unstable ground.

The Sermon on the Plain emphasizes moral teachings, social justice, and the expectations Jesus has for His followers. It invites listeners to examine their lives and align their actions with the values of God's kingdom.

Lord's Prayer

The Lord's Prayer is important for several reasons:

1. It is a model of how to pray: The Lord's Prayer provides a model for how to pray, with its focus on acknowledging God's sovereignty, asking for daily needs, seeking forgiveness, and ending with praise and recognition of God's power.

2. It is a shared tradition: The Lord's Prayer is a shared tradition among Christians and is often recited as part of church services or other religious ceremonies. It provides a sense of unity

and shared purpose among believers.

    3. It reminds us of our relationship with God: The Lord's Prayer reminds us of our relationship with God and our dependence on Him for our daily needs and forgiveness. It helps us to stay grounded and focused on what is truly important in life.

    4. It teaches us important values: The Lord's Prayer teaches us important values, such as forgiveness, humility, and trust in God. It provides a moral framework for how we should live our lives and treat others.

Overall, the Lord's Prayer is an important part of Christian tradition and provides a framework for prayer and spiritual growth. It reminds us of our relationship with God and teaches us important values that can help us to live meaningful and fulfilling lives.

In Aramaic
the Lord's Prayer translated into Aramaic, the language spoken by Jesus:

ܐܒܘܢ ܕܒܫܡܝܐ
ܢܬܩܕܫ ܫܡܟ
ܬܐܬܐ ܡܠܟܘܬܟ
ܢܗܘܐ ܨܒܝܢܟ
ܐܝܟܢܐ ܕܒܫܡܝܐ ܐܦ ܒܐܪܥܐ
ܗܒ ܠܢ ܠܚܡܐ ܕܣܘܢܩܢܢ ܝܘܡܢܐ
ܘܫܒܘܩ ܠܢ ܚܘܒܝܢ
ܐܝܟܢܐ ܕܐܦ ܚܢܢ ܫܒܩܢ ܠܚܝܒܝܢ
ܘܠܐ ܬܥܠܢ ܠܢܣܝܘܢܐ
ܐܠܐ ܦܨܢ ܡܢ ܒܝܫܐ
ܡܛܠ ܕܕܝܠܟ ܗܝ ܡܠܟܘܬܐ ܘܚܝܠܐ ܘܬܫܒܘܚܬܐ
ܠܥܠܡ ܥܠܡܝܢ

In Koine Greek
(the form of Greek used during the time of Jesus and early gospels from the Aramaic)

Πάτερ ἡμῶν ὁ ἐν τοῖς οὐρανοῖς·

ἁγιασθήτω τὸ ὄνομά σου·
ἐλθέτω ἡ βασιλεία σου·
γενηθήτω τὸ θέλημά σου
ὡς ἐν οὐρανῷ καὶ ἐπὶ γῆς·
τὸν ἄρτον ἡμῶν τὸν ἐπιούσιον δὸς ἡμῖν σήμερον·
καὶ ἄφες ἡμῖν τὰ ὀφειλήματα ἡμῶν,
ὡς καὶ ἡμεῖς ἀφήκαμεν τοῖς ὀφειλέταις ἡμῶν·
καὶ μὴ εἰσενέγκῃς ἡμᾶς εἰς πειρασμόν,
ἀλλὰ ῥῦσαι ἡμᾶς ἀπὸ τοῦ πονηροῦ.
Ὅτι σοῦ ἐστιν ἡ βασιλεία καὶ ἡ δύναμις καὶ ἡ δόξα εἰς τοὺς αἰῶνας.
Ἀμήν.

In Greek:

Πάτερ ημών, ὁ ἐν τοῖς οὐρανοῖς·
ἁγιασθήτω τὸ ὄνομά σου·
ἐλθέτω ἡ βασιλεία σου·
γενηθήτω τὸ θέλημά σου,
ὡς ἐν οὐρανῷ καὶ ἐπὶ γῆς·
τὸν ἄρτον ἡμῶν τὸν ἐπιούσιον δὸς ἡμῖν σήμερον·
καὶ ἄφες ἡμῖν τὰ ὀφειλήματα ἡμῶν,
ὡς καὶ ἡμεῖς ἀφίεμεν τοῖς ὀφειλέταις ἡμῶν·
καὶ μὴ εἰσενέγκῃς ἡμᾶς εἰς πειρασμόν,
ἀλλὰ ῥῦσαι ἡμᾶς ἀπὸ τοῦ πονηροῦ.
Ὅτι σοῦ ἐστιν ἡ βασιλεία καὶ ἡ δύναμις καὶ ἡ δόξα εἰς τοὺς αἰῶνας.
Ἀμήν.

In Latin:

Pater noster, qui es in caelis,
sanctificetur nomen tuum;
adveniat regnum tuum;
fiat voluntas tua,
sicut in caelo et in terra.

Panem nostrum cotidianum da nobis hodie;
et dimitte nobis debita nostra,
sicut et nos dimittimus debitoribus nostris;
et ne nos inducas in tentationem,
sed libera nos a malo.
Amen.

In English:

"Our Father, who art in heaven,
hallowed be thy Name,
thy kingdom come,
thy will be done,
on earth as it is in heaven.
Give us This day our daily bread.
And forgive us our trespasses,
as we forgive those who trespass against us.
And lead us not into temptation,
but deliver us from evil.
For thine is the kingdom, the power, and the glory,
forever and ever. Amen."

In Spanish:

"Padre nuestro que estás en los cielos,
santificado sea tu Nombre;
venga tu reino;
hágase tu voluntad,
así en la tierra como en el cielo.
Danos hoy el pan nuestro de cada día;
perdona nuestras ofensas,
como también nosotros perdonamos a los que nos ofenden;
no nos dejes caer en la tentación,
y líbranos del mal.
Amén."

What's the Difference between 'Forgive us Our Trespasses' and 'Forgive us Our Debts'?

In the context of the Lord's Prayer, "forgive us our trespasses" and "forgive us our debts" are two different translations of the same phrase in different versions of the Bible.

In the traditional English version, "forgive us our trespasses" is commonly used in Christian denominations such as the Anglican, Episcopal, and some Protestant churches. This version focuses on the idea of seeking forgiveness for our wrongdoings, our moral and spiritual trespasses against God and others.

On the other hand, "forgive us our debts" is an alternative translation found in the Catholic and some Protestant denominations, such as the Lutheran tradition. This version emphasizes the concept of debts or sins as a form of spiritual indebtedness, reflecting the idea that our sins create a debt that needs to be forgiven.

Both versions convey the same fundamental meaning: a plea for forgiveness of our sins or wrongdoings. The difference lies in the specific wording used, reflecting the variations in translation and interpretation among different Christian traditions.

Questions and Answers

Describe the Variety of Questions Jesus used in His Teaching

Jesus employed a variety of questions in His teaching methods to engage with His listeners, stimulate critical thinking, and clarify spiritual truths. The different types of questions He used include:

1. Rhetorical questions: These questions were posed to make a point or provoke thought rather than to solicit an answer. For example, in Matthew 7:3-4, Jesus asks, "Why do you see the speck in your brother's eye, but do not notice the log in your own eye?"

2. Challenging questions: Jesus often asked questions that challenged conventional wisdom, religious leaders, or societal norms. These questions pushed listeners to reevaluate their

beliefs and assumptions. For instance, in Matthew 22:41-45, Jesus asks the Pharisees about the identity of the Messiah, leading them to reconsider their understanding of the Scriptures.

3. Open-ended questions: These questions encouraged reflection and introspection, allowing listeners to explore their thoughts and beliefs more deeply. In Mark 8:27, Jesus asks His disciples, "Who do people say that I am?" This question prompts the disciples to consider popular opinions before affirming their own belief in Jesus's identity.

4. Clarifying questions: Jesus used questions to clarify or emphasize a point, helping His listeners understand His teachings more fully. In Luke 10:36, after sharing the Parable of the Good Samaritan, Jesus asks, "Which of these three, do you think, proved to be a neighbor to the man who fell among the robbers?" This question guides the listener to the intended lesson of the parable.

5. Hypothetical questions: Jesus sometimes presented hypothetical situations to illustrate a point or teach a lesson. In Matthew 18:12-14, He asks, "If a man has a hundred sheep, and one of them has gone astray, does he not leave the ninety-nine on the mountains and go in search of the one that went astray?" This question sets the stage for a lesson on God's love for the lost. By using these diverse types of questions, Jesus engaged His listeners, fostered critical thinking, and conveyed spiritual truths in a memorable and thought-provoking manner.

Why did Jesus ask the Question "Who Do You Say I Am?"

The question "Who do you say I am?" is a crucial moment in the New Testament of the Christian Bible, appearing in the gospels of Matthew (16:15), Mark (8:29), and Luke (9:20). This question occurs when Jesus is talking to His disciples. He was seeking to understand their perception of His identity and to encourage them to reflect on their beliefs about Him. This question followed His initial inquiry, "Who do people say that I am?" which was aimed at understanding the various opinions about Jesus held by the general public.

In a broader context, Jesus had been performing miracles, teaching, and gathering followers. However, there were varying opinions about who Jesus was. Some thought he was a prophet, others John the Baptist returned from the dead, or Elijah. So, Jesus asked His disciples first, "Who do people say the Son of Man is?" (Matthew 16:13) After hearing their responses, Jesus then made the question personal: "But who do you say I am?"

In asking This question, Jesus was prompting His disciples to consider their personal beliefs, beyond the rumors and popular opinion. The disciples, especially Simon Peter, affirmed their belief that Jesus was the Messiah, the Son of the living God. When Peter responded to Jesus's question by proclaiming, "You are the Christ, the Son of the living God" (Matthew 16:16), he demonstrated his understanding of Jesus's true identity. This confession of faith played a pivotal role in the development of the early Christian movement and remains a cornerstone of Christian belief to This day.

From a theological perspective, the question has several implications:

1. It stresses the importance of personal faith and understanding. It's not enough to simply follow the crowd's belief; each person must make a personal decision about who Jesus is.

2. It helps to distinguish Jesus' true identity as the Messiah, not just another prophet or religious teacher.

3. Elicit a personal confession of faith from the disciples. It was essential for them to recognize Jesus as the Messiah and the Son of God, as This understanding would form the foundation of their faith and future ministry.

4. It sets the stage for the rest of Jesus' ministry, His crucifixion, and resurrection, as well as the establishment of the Christian Church.

This question remains important in Christian theology and evangelism today, as it encourages individuals to personally consider who Jesus is to them.

Teachable Moments

Describe Jesus Teaching at the Last Supper

The Last Supper was a meal that Jesus shared with His disciples on the night before His crucifixion. It is a significant event in Christian History and is often depicted in art and literature. According to the Bible, Jesus and His disciples gathered in an upper room in Jerusalem to celebrate the Jewish holiday of Passover. During the meal, Jesus broke bread and gave it to His disciples, saying, "This is my body, which is given for you. Do This in remembrance of me." He then took a cup of wine and said, "This cup that is poured out for you is the new covenant in my blood."

This event is often referred to as the institution of the Eucharist or Communion in Christian theology, which is the practice of sharing bread and wine as a symbol of Jesus' sacrifice. During the Last Supper, Jesus also predicted that one of His disciples would betray Him. This led to a discussion among the disciples, with each one denying that they would be the one to betray Jesus. Later that night, Judas Iscariot, one of Jesus' disciples, did betray Him by leading the Roman authorities to arrest Him.
The Last Supper is significant in Christian theology as it is seen as the final meal that Jesus shared with His disciples before His death. It has become an important symbol of Christian faith and is celebrated in various ways, including through the Eucharist or Communion.

The Last Supper is an event that is highly significant for Christians for several reasons:

    1. It is a representation of Christ's sacrifice: During the Last Supper, Jesus shared bread and wine with His disciples and instructed them to do the same in remembrance of Him. Christians believe that the bread and wine represent Christ's body and blood, which were sacrificed for the forgiveness of sins.

    2. It is a symbol of unity: The Last Supper is also a symbol of unity among Christians. The act of sharing bread and wine

together represents the idea of the community of believers coming together as one body in Christ.

3. It is a source of spiritual nourishment: The Last Supper is a source of spiritual nourishment for Christians. The act of receiving the bread and wine during the Eucharist is seen as a way of receiving the grace and love of Christ into one's life.

4. It is a reminder of Christ's teachings: The Last Supper is also a reminder of the teachings of Christ, such as humility, love, and service to others. Christians are called to follow Christ's example and live their lives in accordance with His teachings.

Overall, the Last Supper is a highly significant event for Christians, representing Christ's sacrifice, unity among believers, spiritual nourishment, and a reminder of Christ's teachings.

What Other 'Teachable Moments' did Jesus Use to Teach?

Jesus often used significant events and actions in His life as teaching moments. Apart from the Last Supper, here are some other key events where Jesus used actions and circumstances to convey deeper spiritual truths:

1. Washing the Disciples' Feet (John 13:1-17): During the Last Supper, Jesus performed the act of washing His disciples' feet, which was typically a task for a servant. This unexpected act served as a lesson in humility and servant leadership. Jesus taught that just a He, being their Master and Lord, washed their feet, they should also wash one another's feet, indicating the importance of humble service to others in His kingdom.

2. The Transfiguration (Matthew 17:1-9, Mark 9:2-9, Luke 9:28-36): Jesus took Peter, James, and John to a high mountain where he was transfigured before them, appearing in radiant glory with Moses and Elijah. This event served to confirm Jesus' identity as the Son of God and emphasized the fulfillment of the Law and Prophets in Him.

3. Calming the Storm (Mark 4:35-41, Matthew 8:23-27, Luke 8:22-25): As Jesus and His disciples were crossing a lake, a storm arose. Jesus calmed the storm, demonstrating His power

over nature and teaching His disciples about faith and trust in Him, even in times of danger and uncertainty.

    4. Feeding the Five Thousand (Matthew 14:13-21, Mark 6:30-44, Luke 9:10-17, John 6:1-15): When a large crowd gathered to listen to Jesus, He miraculously fed them with five loaves of bread and two fish provided by a boy. This miracle not only showcased Jesus' divine power but also taught about God's provision and the significance of sharing.

    5. Raising Lazarus from the Dead (John 11:1-44): The raising of Lazarus was one of the most dramatic signs of Jesus' power over life and death. It served as a clear demonstration of His divine authority and a foreshadowing of His own resurrection.

    6. Jesus' Triumphal Entry into Jerusalem (Matthew 21:1-11, Mark 11:1-11, Luke 19:28-44, John 12:12-19): As Jesus rode into Jerusalem on a donkey, the crowds hailed Him as the coming King. This event symbolically communicated Jesus' role as the Messiah and was a fulfillment of Old Testament prophecy.

    7. Jesus' Death and Resurrection (Matthew 27-28, Mark 15-16, Luke 23-24, John 19-20): The crucifixion and resurrection of Jesus are central to Christian belief and teaching. Through these events, Jesus taught about the depths of God's love, the gravity of human sin, the promise of forgiveness, and the hope of eternal life.

In all these instances, Jesus used real-life situations to illustrate spiritual truths, making them more accessible and relatable to His disciples and followers. His teachings continue to inspire and guide believers today.

Describe Jesus Teaching by Washing the Disciples' Feet

The washing of the disciples' feet is a significant event that takes place in the New Testament of the Christian Bible, specifically in the Gospel of John, Chapter 13:1-17. This event happens during the Last Supper, the final meal Jesus shares with His disciples before His crucifixion. It is a powerful demonstration of Jesus's humility and servant leadership, and it conveys a crucial lesson about what it means to follow Him.

The story goes like this:

Jesus and His disciples were having their meal. In the culture of that time, the washing of feet was a common practice because of the dusty roads and the sandals worn by people. It was typically a task carried out by a servant, given the feet were considered the lowest and dirtiest part of the body.

Knowing that His hour had come to depart from This world, Jesus stood up from the table, removed His outer robe, and tied a towel around Himself. Then He poured water into a basin and began to wash the disciples' feet and to wipe them with the towel that was tied around Him.

When He came to Simon Peter, Peter initially refused, saying, "Lord, are you going to wash my feet?" Jesus replied, "You do not know now what I am doing, but later you will understand." Peter then responded, "You will never wash my feet." Jesus answered, "Unless I wash you, you have no share with me." Then Simon Peter said to Him, "Lord, not my feet only but also my hands and my head!"

After washing their feet, Jesus put on His robe again and sat down, asking them, "Do you know what I have done to you? You call me Teacher and Lord—and you are right, for that is what I am. So, if I, your Lord and Teacher, have washed your feet, you also ought to wash one another's feet. For I have set you an example, that you should do as I have done to you."

The washing of the disciples' feet is a powerful act of humility and service. It's a clear demonstration of Jesus's teaching that leadership is about serving others, not lording over them.

The washing of the feet is so significant that some Christian denominations have included the foot-washing ceremony or "Maundy Thursday" services as part of their Holy Week observances.

Describe Jesus Teaching through the Transfiguration

The Transfiguration of Jesus is a significant event narrated in the New Testament, specifically in the Gospels of Matthew (17:1–8),

Mark (9:2–8), and Luke (9:28–36). It's also mentioned in the Second Epistle of Peter (1:16–18).

In This event, Jesus takes three of His closest disciples—Peter, James, and John—to a high mountain, often believed to be Mount Tabor or Mount Hermon. As they reach the summit, the disciples witness a miraculous transformation:

    1. Jesus's Appearance Transforms: The disciples see Jesus transfigure before them. His face shines like the sun, and His clothes become dazzling white, showing His divine glory. This visible transformation underscores Jesus's divine nature and His glory as the Son of God.

    2. Moses and Elijah Appear: Moses (representing the Law) and Elijah (representing the Prophets) appear and converse with Jesus. This event signifies that Jesus is the fulfillment of both the Law and the Prophets, the two primary components of the Hebrew Scriptures (Old Testament).

    3. The Divine Voice: A bright cloud overshadows them, and a voice from heaven declares, "This is my Son, whom I love; with Him I am well pleased. Listen to Him!" This voice, understood to be God's, reinforces Jesus's divine sonship and authoritative teaching.

    4. After the Transfiguration: When the disciples hear the voice, they fall to the ground in fear. Jesus touches them and tells them not to be afraid. When they look up, they see no one except Jesus.

The Transfiguration was a pivotal moment in Jesus's life and a transformative experience for the disciples. It confirmed Jesus's identity as the Son of God, prepared them for His upcoming death and resurrection, and gave them a glimpse of the heavenly glory. This event is considered a bridge between Jesus's public ministry and His passion, marking the point at which the focus of the Gospel narratives starts to turn more towards His death and resurrection.

The Transfiguration continues to be an important event in Christian theology and tradition, celebrated as the Feast of the Transfiguration in many Christian denominations.

Describe Jesus Teaching by Calming of the Storm

The calming of the storm is a miracle attributed to Jesus in the Christian New Testament, recounted in the Gospels of Matthew (8:23-27), Mark (4:35-41), and Luke (8:22-25). The event serves as a significant demonstration of Jesus' divine authority over the natural world, as well as a metaphorical teaching about faith during difficult circumstances.

The story unfolds as follows:

Jesus and His disciples decide to cross the Sea of Galilee in a boat. As they embark on their journey, Jesus, tired from a day of teaching, falls asleep. While Jesus is sleeping, a sudden and violent storm arises, with fierce winds and waves that threaten to capsize the boat.

The disciples, some of whom are seasoned fishermen and thus familiar with the sea's unpredictability, are terrified. In their fear and desperation, they wake Jesus, saying, "Lord, save us! We're going to drown!" (Matthew 8:25) or "Teacher, don't you care if we drown?" (Mark 4:38)

Jesus, upon waking, rebukes the disciples for their lack of faith. Then, demonstrating His divine authority, He commands the wind and the waves to be still: "Quiet! Be still!" (Mark 4:39). Immediately, the storm ceases, and the sea becomes completely calm.

Upon witnessing This, the disciples are awestruck and filled with wonder. They ask each other, "Who is This? Even the wind and the waves obey Him!" (Mark 4:41). This miracle deepens their understanding of Jesus's divine nature and power.

The event of Jesus calming the storm is often interpreted as a demonstration not only of Jesus's authority over nature but also of His power to bring peace and safety in the midst of life's metaphorical storms. It encourages believers to have faith in Jesus during challenging times, trusting in His ability to bring calm and order amidst chaos and turbulence.

Describe Jesus Teaching by Feeding the Crowd of 5000 People

The Feeding of the 5000 is one of the miracles attributed to Jesus in the New Testament of the Christian Bible. It is the only miracle (apart from the resurrection) that is recorded in all four Gospels: Matthew 14:13-21, Mark 6:30-44, Luke 9:10-17, and John 6:1-15.

Here is a summary of the event:
Jesus had been teaching a large crowd of people in a remote location. As the day wore on, the disciples approached Jesus and suggested He send the crowd away to nearby villages to find food, as they were in a remote place and the people were growing hungry.
Jesus responded, "They do not need to go away. You give them something to eat." The disciples, bewildered, pointed out they only had five loaves of bread and two fish - far from enough to feed such a crowd.
Jesus instructed them to bring the loaves and fish to Him. He then ordered the crowd to sit down on the grass. Taking the five loaves and the two fish, Jesus looked up to heaven, gave thanks, and broke the loaves. He then gave them to the disciples to distribute to the people.
All the people ate and were satisfied. And when the disciples gathered up the leftovers, there were twelve baskets full of broken pieces that were leftover, more than they started with. The total number of those who ate was about five thousand men, besides women and children.
The Feeding of the 5000 has significant symbolism and teaching:

    1. Jesus as the Provider: This miracle is seen as a demonstration of Jesus' divine authority and compassion, showing His power to provide for physical needs.

    2. Symbolism of the Bread: The miracle also foreshadows the Last Supper, where Jesus breaks bread and gives it to His disciples, symbolizing His body given for the salvation of humanity.

    3. Eucharistic Overtones: The actions of Jesus in This miracle - taking, blessing, breaking, and giving the bread - are the same actions He performs at the Last Supper, which became the

basis for the Christian practice of the Eucharist (Communion).

4. Lesson of Sharing: Some interpretations of the story suggest a lesson about the power of sharing, as a small amount of food is shared among many, resulting in abundance.

The Feeding of the 5000 is one of the most well-known miracles of Jesus and continues to be a key story in Christian teaching.

Describe Jesus Teaching by Raising Lazarus from the Dead

The story of Jesus raising Lazarus from the dead is a powerful narrative found in the New Testament of the Christian Bible, specifically in John 11:1-44. This event is unique to the Gospel of John and is considered one of the most dramatic signs of Jesus's divinity and His power over life and death.

Here is a summary of the event:

1. Illness and Death of Lazarus: Jesus receives a message from Mary and Martha, who are sisters living in Bethany, stating that their brother Lazarus, whom Jesus loves, is ill. Instead of going immediately to Bethany, Jesus stays where He is for two more days. By the time He decides to go to Bethany, Lazarus has already been dead for four days.

2. Jesus's Interaction with Martha and Mary: Upon His arrival, Jesus is met by Martha, who expresses her faith in Him, stating, "Lord, if you had been here, my brother would not have died. But I know that even now God will give you whatever you ask." Jesus assures her that Lazarus will rise again and asserts, "I am the resurrection and the life. The one who believes in me will live, even though they die."

3. Jesus Weeps: After speaking with Martha, Jesus asks to see Mary. When He sees her weeping, and the others who had come with her also weeping, He is deeply moved and troubled. He asks where Lazarus has been laid, and then Jesus weeps, showing His compassion and empathy. This moment is captured in the famous verse John 11:35, "Jesus wept," which is the shortest verse in the Bible.

4. The Miracle of Resurrection: Jesus goes to the tomb,

which is a cave with a stone laid across the entrance. Despite Martha's objection about the odor since Lazarus has been dead for four days, Jesus insists they remove the stone. After praying aloud to God, Jesus calls out in a loud voice, "Lazarus, come out!" To the amazement of all present, Lazarus comes out, His hands and feet wrapped with strips of linen, and a cloth around His face. Jesus instructs them to take off the grave clothes and let Him go.

The raising of Lazarus showcases Jesus's power over death, foreshadows His own resurrection, and serves as a significant sign leading up to the climax of the Gospel of John. It not only establishes Jesus as the giver of life but also evokes faith in the witnesses, reinforcing the idea that belief in Jesus leads to eternal life.

Describe Jesus's Triumphant Entry into Jerusalem

Jesus's triumphant entry into Jerusalem, often referred to as Palm Sunday, is an event recorded in all four Gospels: Matthew 21:1-11, Mark 11:1-11, Luke 19:28-44, and John 12:12-19. This event marks the beginning of Holy Week, the final week of Jesus's life leading up to the crucifixion.

Here's a summary of the event:

    1. Preparation for the Entry: As Jesus and His disciples approach Jerusalem, coming from Bethphage and Bethany at the Mount of Olives, He sends two disciples ahead, instructing them to find a donkey (Matthew and Mark specify a colt) tied up in the village. He tells them to bring it to Him, and if anyone questions them, they are to say, "The Lord needs it."

    2. Acclamation of the Crowds: The disciples find the donkey and bring it to Jesus. They put their cloaks on the donkey, and Jesus sits on it. As Jesus enters Jerusalem, a great multitude of people spread their cloaks on the road, while others cut branches from trees (John specifies palm branches) and spread them on the road.

    3. Praise and Worship: The crowds ahead of and behind Jesus shout, "Hosanna to the Son of David!" "Blessed is he

who comes in the name of the Lord!" "Hosanna in the highest heaven!" (Matthew 21:9). In the Gospel of Luke, some of the Pharisees in the crowd tell Jesus to rebuke His disciples, to which Jesus replies, "I tell you, if they keep quiet, the stones will cry out."

4. Arrival in Jerusalem: As He approaches Jerusalem and sees the city, Jesus weeps over it (Luke 19:41), prophesying its destruction. Upon arrival in the city, all of Jerusalem is stirred, asking, "Who is This?" The crowds answer, "This is Jesus, the prophet from Nazareth in Galilee."

The triumphant entry into Jerusalem serves as a significant point in Jesus's ministry. It is His official presentation to the nation as the Messianic King. The use of a donkey, the spreading of cloaks and branches, and the acclamations of the crowd are all loaded with symbolism from the Old Testament and associated with the arrival of the Messiah. However, the joy and celebration of This event are soon followed by Jesus's passion and crucifixion, underscoring the profound tension and drama of Holy Week.

Describe Jesus's Death and Resurrection

Jesus's death and resurrection is a central event in Christian belief and theology. The account is recorded in the New Testament, in the Gospels of Matthew (chapters 27-28), Mark (chapters 15-16), Luke (chapters 23-24), and John (chapters 19-20).

Death: Crucifixion

1. The Trial: Jesus is arrested in the Garden of Gethsemane after being betrayed by one of His disciples, Judas Iscariot. He is then brought before the Jewish council (Sanhedrin) and later Pontius Pilate, the Roman governor. Despite finding no guilt in Him, Pilate yields to the crowd's demand to crucify Jesus to prevent a potential riot.

2. The Crucifixion: Jesus is forced to carry His own cross to the site of His execution, a place called Golgotha (meaning "the place of the skull"). He is crucified between two thieves. Above His head, a sign reads "Jesus of Nazareth, the King of the Jews."

3. The Death: On the cross, Jesus experiences great suffering. He cries out, "My God, My God, why have you forsaken me?" (Matthew 27:46) before declaring "It is finished" (John 19:30) and then giving up His spirit. The Gospels describe supernatural events that occur upon His death, including an earthquake and the curtain of the temple being torn in two.

4. The Burial: Joseph of Arimathea, a secret disciple of Jesus, asks Pilate for Jesus's body. He takes it down from the cross, wraps it in a clean linen shroud, and lays it in His own new tomb, hewn out of the rock. A large stone is rolled in front of the entrance of the tomb.

Resurrection

1. The Empty Tomb: On the first day of the week, after the Sabbath, Mary Magdalene (and in some accounts other women) visits the tomb at dawn and finds the stone rolled away and the tomb empty.

2. The Angelic Announcement: An angel (or two, according to some Gospels) appears to the women, announcing that Jesus is not there but has risen. They are instructed to go and tell the disciples.

3. Jesus's Appearances: Jesus appears to Mary Magdalene and later to His disciples and others, showing them His wounds and eating with them, confirming that He is not a ghost but has truly risen from the dead. These post-resurrection appearances happen over a period of 40 days.

4. The Ascension: After 40 days, Jesus leads His disciples to the Mount of Olives, where He blesses them and then is taken up into heaven.

Jesus's death is seen by Christians as an atoning sacrifice for the sins of the world, fulfilling Old Testament prophecy about the Messiah. His resurrection is viewed as a triumphant victory over sin and death, solidifying the promise of eternal life for believers. This foundational event gives meaning to the Christian faith and is commemorated each year during Holy Week and Easter.

Describe Jesus Teaching on the Walk to Emmaus

The story of the Walk to Emmaus is a post-resurrection account found in the Gospel of Luke (24:13-35) in the New Testament of the Christian Bible.

Here's a summary of the event:

1. The Journey Begins: On the day of Jesus's resurrection, two of His followers were walking to Emmaus, a village about seven miles from Jerusalem. They were discussing all the recent events that had taken place, notably Jesus's crucifixion and reports of His resurrection.

2. The Unrecognized Stranger: While they were discussing these things, Jesus Himself approached and began walking with them. However, their eyes were "kept from recognizing Him."

3. Discussion of Recent Events: Jesus asked them what they were discussing, and they shared their disappointment about Jesus's death. They had hoped He would be the one to redeem Israel. They also mentioned how some women from their group had found Jesus's tomb empty that morning and had seen angels who said He was alive.

4. Jesus's Response: Jesus responded by saying, "How foolish you are, and how slow to believe all that the prophets have spoken! Did not the Messiah have to suffer these things and then enter His glory?" He then explained the Scriptures to them, beginning with Moses and all the Prophets, showing them how these writings pointed to Him.

5. Recognition at the Breaking of Bread: As they approached Emmaus, Jesus acted as though He were going further. But the two followers urged Him to stay with them as it was nearly evening. At the table, Jesus took bread, gave thanks, broke it, and began to give it to them. At This point, their eyes were opened and they recognized Him, but He disappeared from their sight.

6. Return to Jerusalem: The followers, filled with joy and amazement, returned to Jerusalem that same night to share their experience with the other disciples. They recounted how they had recognized Jesus when He broke the bread.

The Emmaus narrative is significant for several reasons:

- It reinforces the reality of Jesus's resurrection, showing Jesus appearing in a physical, though transformed, body.
- It underscores the importance of the Scriptures in understanding who Jesus is and the necessity of His suffering and death.
- It demonstrates the way in which Jesus is revealed through the breaking of bread, a central element of the Christian Eucharist.
- It exemplifies the joy and urgency of sharing the Good News of the Resurrection with others.

Describe Jesus Teaching through His Confrontations at the Temple

Jesus's confrontations at the Temple are significant events in His life and ministry, demonstrating His authoritative teachings and His critique of certain religious practices of His time. Two main confrontations are described in the New Testament: the cleansing of the Temple and various debates with religious leaders.

1. Cleansing of the Temple: This is a dramatic episode reported in all four Gospels (Matthew 21:12-17, Mark 11:15-19, Luke 19:45-48, John 2:13-16). Jesus enters the Temple in Jerusalem and finds it being used as a marketplace for selling animals for sacrifices and changing currency. He overturns the tables of the money changers and the seats of those selling doves, quoting the Old Testament prophets Isaiah and Jeremiah, saying, "My house shall be called a house of prayer, but you have made it a den of robbers." This event illustrates Jesus's strong disapproval of commercial activity in the Temple, which should be a place of worship, not profit. It also foreshadows the conflicts that lead to His crucifixion.

2. Debates with Religious Leaders: Jesus had numerous encounters and debates with religious authorities—Pharisees, Sadducees, scribes, and priests—often within the Temple complex. These confrontations typically centered on issues of religious law and authority. For instance:
- Paying Taxes to Caesar (Matthew 22:15-22): The

Pharisees and Herodians tried to trap Jesus into taking a side on whether it was lawful to pay taxes to the Roman Emperor. Jesus responded by asking for a denarius (a Roman coin), asked whose likeness and inscription it bore (Caesar's), and famously stated, "Render therefore unto Caesar the things which are Caesar's; and unto God the things that are God's." This wise answer left His opponents amazed.

- The Greatest Commandment (Matthew 22:34-40): Asked by a Pharisee which commandment in the law was the greatest, Jesus quoted Deuteronomy and Leviticus to summarize the law into two commandments: Love God with all your heart, soul, and mind, and love your neighbor as yourself.
- Question about the Messiah's lineage (Matthew 22:41-46): Jesus confounds the Pharisees by asking them how the Messiah could be both David's son and David's Lord, referring to a Psalm attributed to David. His question left them unable to answer.
- Seven Woes (Matthew 23:1-39): Jesus criticized the scribes and Pharisees for their hypocrisy and self-righteousness, highlighting the discrepancy between their teachings and their actions.

Through these confrontations, Jesus challenged established norms and presented radical reinterpretations of religious practices and teachings, emphasizing the spirit of the law over the letter. They also demonstrate Jesus's role as a reformer and a prophet, and His authority as the Messiah.

Jesus and the Disciples at the Garden of Gethsemane

Jesus did not actually teach in the Garden of Gethsemane according to the New Testament in the Bible. Instead, the Garden of Gethsemane is famously known as the place where Jesus went to pray on the night before His crucifixion. This is described in the Gospels of Matthew (26:36-46), Mark (14:32-42), and Luke (22:39-46).

While Jesus was in the Garden of Gethsemane, He prayed earnestly to God and expressed His deep distress over the events that were to come. It was in This moment of intense emotional

anguish that Jesus said, "Father, if you are willing, take This cup from me; yet not my will, but yours be done." (Luke 22:42).
His followers, Peter, James, and John were with Him but they kept falling asleep. Jesus asked them to "watch and pray so that you will not fall into temptation. The spirit is willing, but the flesh is weak." (Matthew 26:41).
While This event isn't typically classified as a teaching moment, one could interpret Jesus's actions as teaching by example about prayer, submission to God's will, and spiritual vigilance. However, explicit teaching as He did in parables or sermons did not occur in the Garden of Gethsemane, based on the biblical accounts.

Miracles and Healings

Describe Key Miracles and Healings Performed by Jesus

Jesus is reported to have performed numerous miracles and healings according to the New Testament in the Bible. Here are some of the key miracles and healings attributed to Jesus:

1. Turning Water into Wine (John 2:1-11): During a wedding at Cana, when the wine ran out, Jesus converted six jars of water into wine.

2. Healing of the Official's Son (John 4:46-54): Jesus healed a royal official's son in Capernaum just by saying the words, "Go, your son will live".

3. Healing of the Paralytic at Bethesda (John 5:1-15): Jesus healed a man who had been invalid for 38 years.

4. Feeding of the 5,000 (Matthew 14:13-21, Mark 6:31-44, Luke 9:10-17, John 6:1-15): Jesus miraculously fed 5,000 men, not including women and children, from five loaves of bread and two fish.

5. Walking on Water (Matthew 14:22-33, Mark 6:45-52, John 6:16-21): Jesus walked on the Sea of Galilee to reach a boat carrying His disciples.

6. Healing of the Blind Man in Bethsaida (Mark 8:22-26): Jesus healed a blind man by putting spit on His eyes and laying hands on him.

7. Healing of the Man Born Blind (John 9:1-41): Jesus healed a man born blind by making mud with saliva, putting it on the man's eyes, and instructing him to wash in the Pool of Siloam.

8. Raising of Lazarus (John 11:1-44): Jesus resurrected Lazarus who had been dead and buried for four days.

9. Healing of a Woman with Hemorrhage (Matthew 9:20–22, Mark 5:25–34, Luke 8:43–48): A woman suffering from bleeding for 12 years touched Jesus's cloak and was healed instantly.

10. Healing the Ten Lepers (Luke 17:11-19): Jesus healed ten men suffering from leprosy.

11. Healing the Centurion's Servant (Matthew 8:5–13, Luke 7:1–10): The servant of a centurion was healed by Jesus.

12. Casting Out an Unclean Spirit (Mark 1:21-28): Jesus expelled a demon from a man in Capernaum.

13. Curing a Deaf Man with a Speech Impediment (Mark 7:31-37): In the region of Decapolis, Jesus healed a man who was deaf and had a speech impediment.

14. Restoring a Man's Withered Hand (Matthew 12:9–13, Mark 3:1–6, Luke 6:6–11): On the Sabbath, Jesus healed a man with a withered hand.

15. Resurrection of Jairus' Daughter (Matthew 9:18–26, Mark 5:21–43, Luke 8:40–56): Jesus brought a girl, the daughter of Jairus, back to life.

These are just some of the many miracles and healings associated with Jesus in the New Testament.

Turning Water into Wine (John 2:1-11) during a Wedding at Cana

Jesus and His disciples were in attendance. At the wedding, the hosts ran out of wine, which was considered a significant embarrassment and social faux pas in that culture. Jesus' mother, Mary, approached Him and informed Him of the situation.
In response, Jesus told the servants to fill six large stone jars with water. Each jar could hold about 20 to 30 gallons. After they filled the jars, Jesus instructed them to draw some out and take it to the

master of the banquet, who was responsible for overseeing the wedding feast.

When the master of the banquet tasted the water that had been turned into wine, he was amazed. He called the bridegroom and remarked that usually, the best wine is served first, followed by the lower quality wine after the guests have had too much to drink. However, in This case, the master of the banquet was surprised because the newly served wine was of exceptional quality. He praised the bridegroom for saving the best wine for last.

This miraculous event is commonly known as the first miracle of Jesus, where He turned water into wine. It is significant because it showcases Jesus' divine power and serves as a symbol of the abundance and joy that He brings into people's lives. The miracle also highlights Jesus' concern for the host's embarrassment and His willingness to provide for their needs.

Healing of the Official's Son (John 4:46-54)

In the story of the healing of the official's son, Jesus returned to Cana in Galilee after His encounter with the Samaritan woman at the well. There, a certain royal official approached him, desperate for Jesus to heal His son who was gravely ill.

The official pleaded with Jesus to come and heal his son before he died. Jesus responded by telling the official, "Unless you see signs and wonders, you will not believe." The official, undeterred, begged Jesus once more, saying, "Sir, come down before my child dies."

In response to the official's plea, Jesus said, "Go; your son will live." The official believed Jesus' words and departed for His home. On His way back, His servants met him and informed him that His son was indeed alive and recovering. The official inquired about the time when His son's condition began to improve, and the servants revealed that it occurred at the exact moment Jesus had said, "Your son will live."

As a result of This miraculous healing, the official and His entire household came to believe in Jesus. This story demonstrates

Jesus' ability to heal from a distance, without physically being present or laying hands on the person in need. It also highlights the importance of faith in Jesus' words and the transformative power it can have in a person's life.

Healing of the Paralytic at Bethesda (John 5:1-15):

The healing of the paralytic at Bethesda is a notable miracle performed by Jesus, as recorded in the Gospel of John, specifically in John 5:1-15.
In Jerusalem, near the Sheep Gate, there was a pool called Bethesda, surrounded by five covered colonnades. It was believed that an angel would occasionally stir the waters of the pool, and the first person to enter the water afterward would be healed from their ailments.
At This pool, Jesus encountered a man who had been paralyzed for 38 years. Jesus noticed him lying there and asked if he wanted to get well. The paralyzed man explained that he had no one to help him into the pool when the water was stirred, so he never had the opportunity to receive healing.
In response, Jesus said to the man, "Get up, pick up your mat, and walk." Instantly, the man was healed and regained the ability to walk. he picked up His mat and walked away.
The healing of the paralytic at Bethesda is significant for several reasons. Firstly, it demonstrates Jesus' compassion and willingness to heal those who are suffering. The man had been paralyzed for a significant portion of His life, and Jesus showed him mercy and restored His ability to walk.
Secondly, the miracle challenges the legalistic understanding of healing associated with the pool of Bethesda. Instead of relying on the water's stirring or the assistance of others, Jesus directly healed the man through His divine power, bypassing any human intermediaries.
Lastly, This miracle provoked controversy among the Jewish religious leaders because it occurred on the Sabbath. They criticized the man for carrying His mat on the Sabbath, as it was considered work. This incident led to a discussion about Jesus'

authority and His relationship with the Father, further revealing His divine identity and mission.

Overall, the healing of the paralytic at Bethesda serves as a powerful demonstration of Jesus' compassion, divine power, and His ability to bring about profound physical healing.

Feeding of the 5,000
(Matthew 14:13-21, Mark 6:31-44, Luke 9:10-17, John 6:1-15):

The feeding of the 5,000 is one of the most well-known miracles performed by Jesus, and it is recorded in all four of the Gospels: Matthew 14:13-21, Mark 6:31-44, Luke 9:10-17, and John 6:1-15. Jesus and His disciples had been ministering to large crowds, teaching and healing the sick. On This occasion, a vast multitude had gathered to hear Jesus, and it was getting late in the day. The disciples approached Jesus and suggested sending the crowd away to nearby villages to find food for themselves.

However, Jesus responded by telling the disciples, "You give them something to eat." The disciples were puzzled and replied that they only had five loaves of bread and two fish. Jesus instructed the disciples to bring the loaves and fish to Him. Taking the loaves and fish, Jesus looked up to heaven, blessed the food, and then began distributing it to the crowd through His disciples. Miraculously, the small amount of food multiplied, and everyone in the crowd ate their fill. Afterward, the disciples collected twelve baskets full of leftover fragments.

The feeding of the 5,000 is significant for several reasons. Firstly, it demonstrates Jesus' divine power to provide for the physical needs of people in a miraculous way. The multiplication of the bread and fish reveals His authority over the natural elements and His ability to perform extraordinary acts.

Secondly, the miracle serves as a demonstration of Jesus' compassion and concern for the crowd. Instead of sending them away hungry, Jesus desired to meet their needs and ensure that they were cared for.

Furthermore, the feeding of the 5,000 foreshadows the Eucharist or the Lord's Supper, where Jesus takes bread, blesses it, and shares it with His disciples. It emphasizes the spiritual truth that Jesus is the bread of life, providing sustenance and nourishment for all who come to Him in faith.

This miracle also had an impact on the people who witnessed it. They recognized that Jesus was a prophet and some even proclaimed Him as the long-awaited Messiah. However, it's important to note that Jesus withdrew to a mountain afterward because He did not want people to misunderstand His mission as solely a political one.

Overall, the feeding of the 5,000 is a significant miracle that showcases Jesus' power, compassion, and provision. It reveals His divine nature and highlights His ability to meet both the physical and spiritual needs of those who seek Him.

Walking on Water
(Matthew 14:22-33, Mark 6:45-52, John 6:16-21)

The account of Jesus walking on water is found in three of the Gospels: Matthew 14:22-33, Mark 6:45-52, and John 6:16-21. After the feeding of the 5,000, Jesus instructed His disciples to get into a boat and go ahead of Him to the other side of the Sea of Galilee while He dismissed the crowds. Jesus then went up to a mountainside to pray.

Meanwhile, the disciples were in the boat, and the sea became rough due to strong winds. They were struggling to make progress. During the fourth watch of the night, which is between 3 a.m. and 6 a.m., Jesus came to the disciples walking on the water.

When the disciples saw Jesus, they were terrified, thinking they were seeing a ghost. However, Jesus reassured them, saying, "Take courage! It is I. Don't be afraid."

Peter, one of the disciples, responded to Jesus, "Lord, if it's you, command me to come to you on the water." Jesus granted His request, and Peter stepped out of the boat and began walking on the water toward Jesus. However, when Peter saw the strong wind, he became afraid and began to sink. He cried out to Jesus, "Lord, save me!"

Jesus immediately reached out His hand and caught Peter, saying, "You of little faith, why did you doubt?" After they got into the boat, the wind ceased, and the disciples worshiped Jesus, declaring Him the Son of God.

The account of Jesus walking on water carries significant spiritual and symbolic meaning. It demonstrates Jesus' power over the natural elements, revealing His divinity. Jesus' ability to walk on water defies the laws of nature and establishes His authority over creation.

Furthermore, Peter's brief walk on the water highlights the importance of faith and trust in Jesus. Initially, Peter displayed great faith by stepping out of the boat and walking toward Jesus. However, when His focus shifted to the storm instead of Jesus, he faltered. Jesus used This moment to teach Peter about the significance of unwavering faith and trust in Him, even amidst challenging circumstances.

This event also serves as a reminder that Jesus is present with His disciples even in the midst of life's storms. When the disciples were struggling against the wind and waves, Jesus came to them, assuring them of His presence and providing them comfort. Overall, the account of Jesus walking on water serves to strengthen the disciples' faith, reveal Jesus' divine power, and teach important lessons about trust and focus.

Healing of the Blind Man in Bethsaida (Mark 8:22-26):

The healing of the blind man in Bethsaida is a unique miracle recorded only in the Gospel of Mark, specifically in Mark 8:22-26. Jesus and His disciples arrived in Bethsaida, where some people brought a blind man to Jesus, begging Him to touch and heal the man. Jesus took the blind man by the hand and led him outside the village. In a private and intimate setting, Jesus spat on the man's eyes and laid His hands on him.

After doing This, Jesus asked the blind man if he could see anything. The man responded that he saw people but they looked like trees walking around. It seemed that the man's sight was partially restored, but His vision was not yet clear.

Jesus placed His hands on the man's eyes again, and This time the man's sight was fully restored. He could see everything clearly. Jesus then instructed the man not to go back into the village or tell anyone about the healing.

The healing of the blind man in Bethsaida is distinctive because it occurred in two stages. Initially, the man's sight was partially restored, but His vision was blurry, perceiving people as walking trees. However, after the second touch by Jesus, His sight was completely restored, and he could see clearly.

This miracle serves as a reminder that Jesus' miracles are not always instantaneous, and healing can happen progressively or in stages. It highlights Jesus' compassion and willingness to work patiently with individuals according to their specific needs. Additionally, the location of the healing outside the village and Jesus' instruction not to tell anyone about it suggest that Jesus desired to avoid unnecessary attention and to focus on the individual's well-being rather than seeking public recognition. The healing of the blind man in Bethsaida underscores Jesus' power and authority over physical ailments. It demonstrates His ability to restore sight to the blind and serves as a testament to His divine nature as the Son of God.

Overall, This unique healing account emphasizes the compassionate nature of Jesus, His ability to bring progressive healing, and the importance of obedience to His instructions.

Healing of the Man Born Blind (John 9:1-41)

The healing of the man born blind is a remarkable miracle found in the Gospel of John, specifically in John 9:1-41. This story provides profound insight into the spiritual significance of Jesus' miraculous works.

As Jesus and His disciples were passing by, they encountered a man who had been blind from birth. His condition presented an opportunity for Jesus to reveal God's power and glory.

The disciples asked Jesus, "Rabbi, who sinned, this man or his parents, that he was born blind?" Jesus responded that neither the man nor His parents sinned, but rather His blindness would be an occasion for God's work to be displayed.

To heal the man, Jesus spat on the ground, made clay with His saliva, and applied it to the blind man's eyes. He then instructed the man to go and wash in the pool of Siloam. The man obeyed, and as he washed, His sight was miraculously restored.

The news of this extraordinary healing quickly spread throughout the community, and people were amazed. The man's neighbors, as well as the religious authorities, questioned him about the healing. Some were skeptical and doubted that he was truly the man who had been blind.

The Pharisees, the religious leaders of the time, were particularly interested in This case. They interrogated the man and His parents, seeking to undermine the significance of the miracle and discredit Jesus. They accused Jesus of being a sinner because He performed the healing on the Sabbath.

The man who had been healed boldly testified about His experience, stating that Jesus was a prophet and marveling at the fact that no one had ever healed a person born blind before. He challenged the Pharisees' unbelief and their refusal to acknowledge Jesus as the source of His healing.

Ultimately, the Pharisees cast out the man who had been blind from the synagogue, rejecting His testimony and clinging to their own self-righteousness. But Jesus sought out the man and revealed Himself to be the Son of God. The man believed in Jesus and worshiped Him.

The healing of the man born blind holds profound spiritual meaning. It symbolizes Jesus as the light of the world, who brings spiritual illumination and reveals the truth to those who were spiritually blind. The physical healing serves as a metaphor for the greater healing of spiritual blindness and the restoration of relationship with God through faith in Jesus.

This miracle also highlights the reactions of different individuals to Jesus' works. Some were open to belief and marveled at His power, while others clung to their own religious traditions and refused to acknowledge the truth.

Overall, the healing of the man born blind showcases Jesus' divine power, His ability to bring both physical and spiritual healing, and the responses of various individuals to His miraculous works. It challenges us to examine our own spiritual blindness and embrace the light of Christ.

Raising of Lazarus (John 11:1-44)

The raising of Lazarus is one of the most profound and significant miracles performed by Jesus, recorded in the Gospel of John, specifically in John 11:1-44. This extraordinary event demonstrates Jesus' power over death and reveals His true identity as the resurrection and the life.

The story begins with Jesus receiving news that His dear friend Lazarus, the brother of Mary and Martha, was seriously ill. However, Jesus delayed His departure for two days, stating that Lazarus' sickness would not end in death but would bring glory to God.

When Jesus and His disciples arrived in Bethany, Lazarus had already been in the tomb for four days. Martha and Mary, grieving the loss of their brother, expressed their faith in Jesus but also questioned why He had not arrived earlier to prevent Lazarus' death.

Moved by their sorrow, Jesus was deeply troubled. He asked where Lazarus had been laid, and upon reaching the tomb, Jesus wept. Witnessing His genuine compassion and sorrow, the people around remarked, "See how He loved Him!"

Jesus then commanded the stone covering the tomb to be removed. Martha, expressing concern due to the length of time since Lazarus' death, warned about the odor that would arise from the decaying body. Jesus reminded her that if she believed, she would see the glory of God.

With the stone removed, Jesus prayed to the Father, thanking Him for hearing His prayer and expressing that He knew the Father always heard Him. In a loud voice, Jesus called out, "Lazarus, come out!" Astonishingly, Lazarus, who had been dead and wrapped in burial clothes, emerged from the tomb, still bound by the graveclothes.

Jesus commanded the bystanders to unbind Lazarus and let Him go. This miracle astounded many who witnessed it, and it led to the belief and faith in Jesus as the Son of God.

The raising of Lazarus holds profound theological significance. It serves as a foreshadowing of Jesus' own resurrection and victory over death. It demonstrates Jesus' power and authority over life and death, showcasing Him as the source of eternal life.

Furthermore, this miracle challenges people's perceptions and deepens their understanding of Jesus' identity. Jesus explicitly declares, "I am the resurrection and the life. The one who believes in me will live, even though they die; and whoever lives by believing in me will never die."

The raising of Lazarus also reveals Jesus' compassion for His friends and His ability to empathize with human suffering. Even though He knew He would raise Lazarus from the dead, Jesus wept alongside those who mourned, demonstrating His deep love and understanding of human pain.

Overall, the raising of Lazarus is a remarkable and transformative miracle that showcases Jesus' power over death, His divine identity, and His promise of eternal life for all who believe in Him. It invites us to place our faith in Jesus as the resurrection and the life, assuring us that even in the face of death, there is hope and victory through Him.

Healing of a Woman with Hemorrhage
(Matthew 9:20–22, Mark 5:25–34, Luke 8:43–48)

The healing of a woman with a hemorrhage is a significant miracle performed by Jesus and is recorded in the Gospels of Matthew 9:20–22, Mark 5:25–34, and Luke 8:43–48.

The story revolves around a woman who had been suffering from a hemorrhage for twelve years. She had spent all her resources seeking medical help but had only grown worse. In her desperation, she came to believe that if she could just touch Jesus' clothes, she would be healed.

In a large crowd surrounding Jesus, the woman reached out and touched the edge of His cloak. Immediately, her bleeding stopped, and she felt in her body that she was healed of her affliction. Jesus, perceiving that power had gone out from Him, turned around and asked who had touched Him.

Trembling with fear, the woman came forward, fell at Jesus' feet, and confessed her act and her healing. Jesus responded with compassion and told her, "Daughter, your faith has healed you. Go in peace and be freed from your suffering."

This miracle holds several significant lessons. Firstly, it highlights the woman's faith and her belief in Jesus' healing power. Her faith was so strong that she was willing to reach out and touch Jesus, despite societal norms and her own condition.

Secondly, the miracle demonstrates Jesus' ability to heal even in cases that seem hopeless. The woman had been suffering for a long time, and medical treatments had failed to provide any relief. However, through her touch and her faith, Jesus brought about her complete healing.

Furthermore, the story reveals Jesus' compassion and willingness to acknowledge and affirm the woman's faith. Jesus took the time to engage with her, listen to her testimony, and offer words of comfort and assurance.

Symbolically, the healing of the woman with a hemorrhage represents more than just physical healing. It signifies restoration, both physically and spiritually. In the Jewish context, the woman's condition made her ritually unclean and socially isolated. Jesus not only healed her physically but also restored her to the community, granting her peace and freedom from suffering.

Overall, the healing of the woman with a hemorrhage serves as a powerful example of faith, Jesus' compassion, and the transformative power of encountering Him. It encourages us to approach Jesus with trust, knowing that He is capable of bringing healing and restoration to all aspects of our lives.

Healing the Ten Lepers (Luke 17:11-19)

The healing of the ten lepers is a powerful miracle performed by Jesus, and it is specifically recorded in the Gospel of Luke, in Luke 17:11-19.

As Jesus was on His way to Jerusalem, He entered a village and encountered ten lepers standing at a distance. Leprosy was a dreadful disease that carried social and religious stigma, and those afflicted with it were considered unclean and isolated from society.

The lepers called out to Jesus, pleading for mercy and healing. Recognizing their desperate condition, Jesus instructed them to go and show themselves to the priests. In the Jewish culture, it was the priests who had the authority to declare a person clean from leprosy and reintegrate them into society.

As the ten lepers obeyed Jesus and began their journey to the priests, they were miraculously healed. Their leprosy vanished, and they were made clean. However, only one of them, a Samaritan, turned back, praising God with a loud voice and falling at Jesus' feet, expressing gratitude for His healing.

Jesus, surprised and disappointed that the other nine lepers did not return to give thanks, asked, "Were not all ten cleansed? Where are the other nine? Has no one returned to give praise to God except This foreigner?" Jesus then declared to the grateful Samaritan, "Rise and go; your faith has made you well."

This healing account carries profound significance beyond the physical healing of the lepers. It highlights the themes of faith, gratitude, and salvation.

Firstly, the faith of the ten lepers is demonstrated in their cry for mercy and their obedience to Jesus' command. Their faith and willingness to follow His instructions led to their healing.

Secondly, the story underscores the importance of gratitude and acknowledging God's work in our lives. The Samaritan leper's act of returning to give thanks and praise to Jesus emphasized the significance of expressing gratitude for God's blessings.

Additionally, Jesus' remark about the one leper being a foreigner, a Samaritan, highlights the universality of salvation. It illustrates that faith and gratitude transcend cultural and religious boundaries, and God's healing and salvation are available to all who believe.

The healing of the ten lepers serves as a reminder for us to cultivate an attitude of gratitude, recognizing and expressing thanks for the blessings we receive from God. It encourages us to have faith, obey God's commands, and return to Him with gratitude for the work He has done in our lives.

Ultimately, this miracle points to the transformative power of Jesus, both physically and spiritually, and the importance of faith, gratitude, and salvation in our relationship with Him.

Healing the Centurion's Servant (Matthew 8:5–13, Luke 7:1–10)

The healing of the Centurion's servant is a remarkable miracle performed by Jesus, as recorded in both Matthew 8:5–13 and Luke 7:1–10. This event showcases the faith of the Centurion and demonstrates Jesus' authority and power over sickness and distance.

A Centurion, a Roman military officer, approached Jesus, requesting help for His servant who was paralyzed and in great distress. The Centurion displayed deep humility and expressed His unworthiness to have Jesus come under His roof. Instead, he believed that if Jesus would only speak the word, His servant would be healed.

Jesus marveled at the Centurion's faith and declared that He had not found such great faith in all of Israel. He affirmed the Centurion's belief and granted His request, saying, "Go! Let it be done just as you believed it would." The servant was healed at that very moment.

This miracle is significant for several reasons. Firstly, it demonstrates the extraordinary faith of the Centurion. Despite being a Gentile, he displayed profound trust in Jesus' authority and power. The Centurion recognized Jesus' ability to heal without physically being present, and he believed in the power of Jesus' spoken word.

Secondly, the healing of the Centurion's servant reveals the inclusive nature of Jesus' ministry. Jesus showed compassion and granted healing to someone outside of the Jewish community, emphasizing that God's grace and power extend to all who have faith, regardless of their background or nationality.

Furthermore, This miracle highlights the authority and power of Jesus over sickness and physical afflictions. By healing the servant from a distance, Jesus demonstrated that He is not limited by geographical or physical boundaries.

The story also emphasizes the importance of humility and recognition of Jesus' authority. The Centurion recognized His own unworthiness and acknowledged Jesus' superior authority as a military officer would to a commanding officer.

Ultimately, the healing of the Centurion's servant serves as a testament to the power of faith and the comprehensive nature of Jesus' ministry. It reveals His authority over sickness, His ability to heal from a distance, and His willingness to extend grace to all who approach Him with faith.

This miracle challenges us to approach Jesus with humble faith, trusting in His authority and power to bring healing and restoration to our lives, as well as to acknowledge His inclusive and compassionate nature as the Savior of all people.

Casting Out an Unclean Spirit (Mark 1:21-28)

The account of Jesus casting out an unclean spirit is recorded in Mark 1:21-28. This event took place early in Jesus' ministry in the town of Capernaum.

On the Sabbath day, Jesus entered the synagogue in Capernaum and began teaching the people. His teaching astonished them because He taught with authority, unlike the scribes.

During His teaching, a man with an unclean spirit was present in the synagogue. The unclean spirit recognized Jesus and cried out, saying, "What have you to do with us, Jesus of Nazareth? Have you come to destroy us? I know who you are—the Holy One of God!"

Jesus, displaying His authority over the unclean spirit, rebuked it, saying, "Be silent and come out of him!" The unclean spirit convulsed the man and then left him with a loud cry.

The people in the synagogue were amazed and questioned among themselves, "What is This? A new teaching with authority! He commands even the unclean spirits, and they obey Him."

This event demonstrated several important aspects. Firstly, it showcased Jesus' authority over spiritual forces of darkness. The unclean spirit recognized Jesus as the Holy One of God and was compelled to obey His command to leave the possessed man. Secondly, Jesus' authority in teaching was contrasted with the

scribes of the time. The people recognized the uniqueness of Jesus' teaching and were amazed at His authority, in contrast to the scribes who relied on traditional interpretations.
Additionally, This miracle served as an early revelation of Jesus' identity and mission. The declaration of the unclean spirit, acknowledging Jesus as the Holy One of God, foreshadowed His role as the Messiah, the one sent by God to bring deliverance and salvation.
Furthermore, the casting out of the unclean spirit emphasized Jesus' power and victory over evil. It demonstrated that He was not only a teacher but also a deliverer who could set people free from the influence and oppression of evil spirits.
Overall, this account of Jesus casting out an unclean spirit highlights His authority, power, and the revelation of His identity as the Holy One of God. It reveals His mission to bring deliverance and salvation, and it encourages us to recognize His authority and trust in His power to overcome the forces of darkness in our lives.

Curing a Deaf Man with a Speech Impediment (Mark 7:31-37)

The healing of a deaf man with a speech impediment is a powerful miracle performed by Jesus, and it is described in Mark 7:31-37.
Jesus traveled to the region of the Decapolis, where a group of people brought to Him a man who was deaf and had difficulty speaking. They pleaded with Jesus to lay His hands on him and heal him.
Jesus took the man aside privately, away from the crowd. He put His fingers into the man's ears, spat and touched the man's tongue. Then Jesus looked up to heaven, sighed, and said to the man, "Ephphatha," which means "Be opened!"
Instantly, the man's ears were opened, and His speech impediment was removed. He began to hear and speak clearly. Jesus instructed those present not to tell anyone about the healing, but the more He tried to keep it quiet, the more the news spread.
This miracle demonstrates Jesus' compassion for those who

are suffering and His ability to bring complete restoration. By touching the man's ears and tongue, Jesus showed His personal involvement in the healing process. His sighing and looking up to heaven indicated His dependence on the Father's power and the divine source of healing.

The significance of This miracle extends beyond physical healing. The man's restoration of hearing and speech symbolizes the restoration of communication and connection. The man was no longer isolated and excluded due to His impairment. Jesus restored not only His physical abilities but also His social and emotional well-being.

The act of "Ephphatha," meaning "Be opened," carries spiritual symbolism as well. It represents the opening of one's heart, mind, and ears to receive the message of the Gospel. This miracle highlights Jesus' role as the one who opens hearts and enables people to understand and respond to the truth.

Furthermore, the spreading of the news despite Jesus' request for silence reflects the profound impact of His miracles on the lives of people. The more Jesus performed miracles, the more His fame grew, and people could not help but share what they had witnessed.

The healing of the deaf man with a speech impediment illustrates Jesus' authority over physical limitations and His desire to restore individuals to wholeness. It reminds us of His power to open closed doors, restore brokenness, and enable us to hear and proclaim the good news.

Ultimately, this miracle encourages us to approach Jesus with our limitations, trusting in His compassion and power to bring healing and restoration to our lives, both physically and spiritually

Restoring a Man's Withered Hand
(Matthew 12:9–13, Mark 3:1–6, Luke 6:6–11)

The restoration of a man's withered hand is a significant miracle performed by Jesus, and it is recorded in the Gospels of Matthew 12:9–13, Mark 3:1–6, and Luke 6:6–11.

On the Sabbath day, Jesus entered a synagogue, and there was a man present with a withered hand. The Pharisees and religious leaders were watching Jesus closely to see if He would heal on the Sabbath, as they considered it a violation of their strict interpretation of the Sabbath laws.

Knowing their thoughts, Jesus called the man with the withered hand forward and asked the people, "Which is lawful on the Sabbath: to do good or to do evil, to save life or to kill?" The Pharisees remained silent.

Filled with compassion, Jesus said to the man, "Stretch out your hand." As the man obediently stretched out His hand, it was completely restored, becoming as healthy as His other hand.

This miraculous healing caused the Pharisees to become even more hardened in their hearts. They were filled with rage and began to plot with the Herodians against Jesus, seeking to destroy Him.

This healing account holds several significant lessons. Firstly, it reveals Jesus' compassion for those who were suffering. Despite the controversy surrounding healing on the Sabbath, Jesus prioritized the well-being and restoration of the man with the withered hand.

Secondly, it exposes the religious leaders' legalistic mindset and their lack of understanding concerning the purpose of the Sabbath. Jesus challenged their rigid interpretation of the law, emphasizing that acts of goodness and mercy should not be hindered, even on the Sabbath.

Furthermore, This miracle highlights Jesus' authority over physical limitations and His power to restore what has been broken. The man's withered hand symbolizes brokenness and disability, and Jesus restored it to full health, illustrating His ability to bring wholeness and restoration to all areas of life.

Lastly, this healing event served as a catalyst for the growing opposition against Jesus by the religious establishment. It further escalated the conflict between Jesus and the Pharisees, revealing their hardened hearts and resistance to His ministry.

The restoration of the man's withered hand demonstrates Jesus' compassion, His authority over physical limitations, and His challenge to legalistic interpretations of religious laws. It encourages us to prioritize acts of goodness and mercy and to recognize Jesus as the one who brings wholeness and restoration to our brokenness.

Resurrection of Jairus' Daughter
(Matthew 9:18–26, Mark 5:21–43, Luke 8:40–56)

The resurrection of Jairus' daughter is a remarkable and widely known miracle performed by Jesus, and it is recorded in the Gospels of Matthew 9:18–26, Mark 5:21–43, and Luke 8:40–56. Jairus, a synagogue leader, approached Jesus in distress, pleading for Him to come and heal His dying daughter. Jesus agreed to accompany Jairus to His house, and as they made their way through the crowd, a woman who had been suffering from a hemorrhage for twelve years touched the edge of Jesus' cloak and was healed. While This interaction took place, messengers arrived from Jairus' house, informing Him that His daughter had died and urging him not to trouble Jesus any longer.
However, Jesus responded to Jairus, saying, "Do not fear; only believe, and she will be well." Upon arriving at Jairus' house, Jesus allowed only Peter, James, and John, along with the girl's parents, to enter the room. Jesus assured them that the girl was not dead but only sleeping. The people in the room laughed at Him, knowing that she was indeed dead.
Undeterred, Jesus took the girl's hand and commanded her to rise. Immediately, the girl came back to life and began to walk. Her astonished parents were instructed to provide her with food and to keep the miraculous event quiet.
The resurrection of Jairus' daughter demonstrates Jesus' power over death and His ability to bring life to the dead. It illustrates His compassion for the desperate father and reveals His authority as the Son of God.
The miracle also highlights the importance of faith and trust in Jesus' words. Despite the grim report of the girl's death, Jesus encouraged Jairus to have faith and believe in Him. Through This miracle, Jesus taught that faith is essential for experiencing the power and life-giving work of God.
Furthermore, the story parallels the healing of the hemorrhaging

woman, illustrating that Jesus has power over both chronic illnesses and death. It emphasizes the significance of Jesus' personal interaction, His touch, and His command in bringing about healing and restoration.

The resurrection of Jairus' daughter provides hope and reassurance to believers that Jesus has power over death and offers eternal life to all who believe in Him. It reminds us of His compassion, His ability to restore life, and His invitation to trust Him in all circumstances.

Overall, This miracle is a powerful demonstration of Jesus' authority and ability to conquer death, offering hope, healing, and new life to those who place their faith in Him.

Metaphors

Why did Jesus Teach using Metaphors

Jesus' use of metaphors, parables, and similes in His teachings is a distinctive feature of His ministry. There are several reasons why He chose this method of teaching:

- Accessibility and Relatability: By using everyday images and scenarios—like farming, shepherding, baking, and fishing—Jesus made His teachings accessible to the people of His time. These metaphors and stories were rooted in the daily experiences of His listeners, making them more understandable and relatable.
- Memory and Retention: Stories and metaphors are easier to remember than abstract principles. By using vivid imagery and narratives, Jesus ensured that His teachings would be remembered and passed down through generations.
- Engaging the Listener: Parables and metaphors often require the listener to think more deeply and engage with the teaching. They invite reflection and exploration, allowing individuals to find meaning in them over time and in different life situations.
- Revealing and Concealing: Jesus Himself explained that He used parables to both reveal and conceal truths. To those

genuinely seeking, parables provided profound insights. But to those who were indifferent or hostile, the deeper meanings could remain hidden. Jesus says in Matthew 13:11-13 (NIV): "The knowledge of the secrets of the kingdom of heaven has been given to you, but not to them. Whoever has will be given more, and they will have an abundance. Whoever does not have, even what they have will be taken from them. This is why I speak to them in parables: 'Though seeing, they do not see; though hearing, they do not hear or understand.'"

- Challenge to Transformation: Many of Jesus' parables challenged the status quo and provoked listeners to re-examine their beliefs and behaviors. By presenting these challenges in story form, Jesus could invite reflection and transformation without direct confrontation.
- Cultural and Educational Context: Storytelling was a common method of conveying truths in many ancient cultures, including Jewish culture. Given the predominantly oral culture of the time, with limited literacy, stories were an effective medium of communication and education.
- Universality: While rooted in the cultural and societal contexts of His time, the themes of Jesus' parables are universal, transcending time and place. Their truths are applicable to various cultures and eras, allowing people from different backgrounds and periods to derive meaning from them.

In essence, Jesus' use of metaphors and parables reflects His profound understanding of human nature, psychology, and culture. His teachings, conveyed through these means, have resonated deeply across ages, cultures, and backgrounds, revealing His timeless wisdom and divine insight.

Examples of the Metaphors used by Jesus

Jesus often used metaphors, parables, and similes to communicate profound spiritual truths in ways that were relatable and understandable to His listeners. Jesus frequently used metaphors, similes, and parables in His teaching. These served to make complex spiritual concepts more accessible to His listeners and to convey His message in memorable and impactful ways.

While it's challenging to provide an exact number for all the metaphors Jesus used (since this depends on how one defines and categorizes "metaphors" and because some of them can overlap or have variations in different Gospel accounts), here are some of the more prominent metaphors employed by Jesus: Here's a list of some of the metaphors used by Jesus, though this is not exhaustive:

- Good Shepherd: "I am the good shepherd. The good shepherd lays down his life for the sheep." (John 10:11)
- Vine and Branches: "I am the vine; you are the branches. Whoever abides in me and I in him, he it is that bears much fruit, for apart from me you can do nothing." (John 15:5)
- Light of the World: "I am the light of the world. Whoever follows me will not walk in darkness, but will have the light of life." (John 8:12)
- Bread of Life: "I am the bread of life; whoever comes to me shall not hunger, and whoever believes in me shall never thirst." (John 6:35)
- Door of the Sheep: "I am the door. If anyone enters by me, he will be saved and will go in and out and find pasture." (John 10:9)
- Living Water: To the Samaritan woman, He said, "Whoever drinks of the water that I will give him will never be thirsty again. The water that I will give him will become in him a spring of water welling up to eternal life." (John 4:14)
- The Way, the Truth, and the Life: "I am the way, and the truth, and the life. No one comes to the Father except through me." (John 14:6)
- Salt of the Earth: "You are the salt of the earth, but if salt has lost its taste, how shall its saltiness be restored?" (Matthew 5:13)
- Light on a Hill: "You are the light of the world. A city set on a hill cannot be hidden." (Matthew 5:14)
- New Wine in Old Wineskins: "And no one puts new wine into old wineskins. If he does, the new wine will

burst the skins and it will be spilled, and the skins will be destroyed." (Luke 5:37)
- Leaven: "The kingdom of heaven is like leaven that a woman took and hid in three measures of flour, till it was all leavened." (Matthew 13:33)
- Mustard Seed: "The kingdom of heaven is like a mustard seed that someone took and sowed in his field; it is the smallest of all the seeds, but when it has grown it is the greatest of shrubs and becomes a tree, so that the birds of the air come and make nests in its branches." (Matthew 13:31-32)
- A Splinter in your Brothers Eye: "A splinter in your brother's eye and a log in your own." (Matthew 7:3-5)
- Camel and Eye of a Needle: "it is easier for a camel to go through the eye of a needle than for a rich person to enter the kingdom of God" (Matthew 19:24, Mark 10:25, and Luke 18:25)

These metaphors, among others, provide profound insights into the nature of God, the kingdom of heaven, and the spiritual journey of believers. Through these, Jesus conveyed the mysteries of faith in tangible ways, illustrating abstract truths using everyday objects and experiences familiar to His listeners.

Given this extensive use of metaphorical language, it's evident that metaphor was a primary tool in Jesus' teaching toolkit, allowing Him to reach a wide range of audiences and communicate profound truths in accessible ways.

Jesus as the Good Shepherd Metaphor

The metaphor of Jesus as the "Good Shepherd" is one of the most well-known and cherished images used in the New Testament to describe Jesus' relationship with His followers and His self-sacrificial role for humanity. This metaphor is primarily drawn from John 10, where Jesus elaborates on it in detail.
Here's a breakdown of the metaphor:

- The Shepherd and His Sheep: In ancient Palestine, the role of a shepherd was a common and crucial one. Shepherds tended, protected, and guided their sheep, ensuring they had food, water, and safety. Sheep, being defenseless and often not very discerning, relied heavily on their shepherd. The relationship was intimate; shepherds knew their sheep, and the sheep recognized the voice of their shepherd.
- Jesus as the Good Shepherd: When Jesus says, "I am the good shepherd" (John 10:11), He's emphasizing His loving care, guidance, and protective role over His followers. Just as a shepherd knows his sheep, Jesus knows each believer personally.
- Sacrificial Love: Jesus says, "The good shepherd lays down his life for the sheep" (John 10:11). This points to His sacrificial love and foreshadows His crucifixion, where He would lay down His life for humanity's sins. This contrasts with the "hired hand" who runs away when danger approaches because he doesn't truly care for the sheep (John 10:12-13).
- One Flock and One Shepherd: Jesus speaks of other sheep that are not of the current fold, and He must bring them in, so there will be "one flock, one shepherd" (John 10:16). This hints at the inclusion of the Gentiles (non-Jews) into the community of believers, emphasizing the universality of His mission.
- The Relationship: "My sheep hear my voice, and I know them, and they follow me" (John 10:27). This underscores the relationship between Jesus and His followers. They recognize His guidance, trust Him, and follow His lead. The shepherd-sheep relationship implies trust, intimacy, and dependence.
- Eternal Life: In the same passage, Jesus promises, "I give them eternal life, and they will never perish, and no one will snatch them out of my hand" (John 10:28). This emphasizes Jesus' power and authority to grant eternal life and the security believers have in Him.

The "Good Shepherd" metaphor resonates deeply because it paints a picture of Jesus' unyielding love, commitment, sacrifice, and care for humanity. Over time, it has become an iconic representation in Christian art, theology, and liturgy, symbolizing the protective and nurturing nature of Christ.

The Wine and the Branches Metaphor

The "vine and the branches" metaphor is another profound teaching of Jesus that's primarily found in the Gospel of John, specifically John 15:1-8. Through this metaphor, Jesus illuminates the intimate relationship between Himself and His followers, as well as the source of spiritual life and fruitfulness.
Here's a breakdown of the metaphor:
- Jesus as the True Vine: Jesus starts by saying, "I am the true vine" (John 15:1). By identifying Himself as the "true" vine, Jesus may be contrasting Himself with other "vines" that people might rely upon, like the religious systems, cultural identities, or other sources of life and sustenance that prove unreliable. In this metaphor, God the Father is the vinedresser or the gardener.
- Believers as the Branches: Followers of Jesus are described as the branches attached to the vine. As branches, believers are meant to bear fruit, which is indicative of a life lived in accord with Jesus' teachings and the transformative power of the Holy Spirit.
- The Need for Pruning: "Every branch in me that does not bear fruit he takes away, and every branch that does bear fruit he prunes, that it may bear more fruit" (John 15:2). Pruning, in the agricultural sense, involves cutting back parts of a plant to allow for more vigorous and fruitful growth. Spiritually, this pruning can represent God's refining process in a believer's life, which might involve challenges, discipline, or letting go of certain things, all aimed at spiritual growth and greater fruitfulness.
- Abiding in Jesus: A recurring word in this discourse is "abide" or "remain." Jesus emphasizes the necessity for believers to remain in Him: "Abide in me, and I in you. As the branch cannot bear fruit by itself, unless it abides in the vine, neither can you, unless you abide in me" (John 15:4). This speaks to a deep, ongoing relationship of trust, dependency, and connection to Jesus as the source of spiritual life and strength.
- The Consequence of Not Abiding: Jesus warns that branches that don't bear fruit and don't abide in Him will be cut off, wither, and be thrown into the fire (John 15:6). This underscores the importance of a genuine, living relationship with

Jesus, rather than a superficial or merely nominal connection.
- The Fruit: While the text does not define the "fruit" explicitly, other New Testament passages, like Galatians 5:22-23, talk about the "fruit of the Spirit," which includes love, joy, peace, patience, kindness, goodness, faithfulness, gentleness, and self-control. Fruitfulness, then, can be seen as a life that reflects the character of Christ and has a transformative impact on the world.
- The Role of Prayer: Abiding in Jesus is also linked to effective prayer: "If you abide in me, and my words abide in you, ask whatever you wish, and it will be done for you" (John 15:7). This suggests that as one aligns with Jesus and His desires, one's prayers align with God's will, resulting in answered prayers.

In summary, the "vine and the branches" metaphor speaks to the interconnectedness of believers with Jesus, the importance of spiritual dependency on Him for life and vitality, and the transformative potential of a life deeply rooted in Christ.

The Light of the World Metaphor

The "Light of the World" metaphor is another foundational teaching of Jesus that offers insight into both His identity and the mission of His followers. The metaphor is primarily found in the Gospel of John, though it reverberates throughout the New Testament.
Here's a breakdown of the metaphor:
- Jesus as the Light of the World: In John 8:12, Jesus declares, "I am the light of the world. Whoever follows me will not walk in darkness, but will have the light of life." By identifying Himself as the "light," Jesus emphasizes His unique role in dispelling spiritual darkness. Light is often associated with knowledge, clarity, goodness, and life, whereas darkness is linked to ignorance, confusion, evil, and death. Jesus, as the Light, brings understanding of God, righteousness, and offers eternal life.
- Contrast with Darkness: The metaphor of light contrasts starkly with darkness. Darkness in the Bible frequently symbolizes sin, evil, and separation from God. By presenting Himself as the light, Jesus is distinguishing Himself from the

forces of darkness and the spiritual blindness that characterizes the world.

- Life-giving Light: The phrase "light of life" (John 8:12) alludes to the life-giving, transformative power of Jesus' teachings and His sacrificial act on the cross. To follow the light is to receive spiritual awakening and life in its fullest sense.
- Believers as Light: While Jesus is the primary "Light of the World," He also commissions His followers to be lights. In the Sermon on the Mount, Jesus tells His listeners: "You are the light of the world. A city set on a hill cannot be hidden... Let your light shine before others, so that they may see your good works and give glory to your Father who is in heaven" (Matthew 5:14-16). Here, believers are called to reflect Jesus' light through their lives and actions, thereby drawing others towards God.
- Rejection of the Light: In John 3:19-21, Jesus touches on humanity's reaction to the light: "And this is the judgment: the light has come into the world, and people loved the darkness rather than the light because their works were evil." This passage acknowledges that not everyone will embrace or accept the light Jesus offers; some prefer the "darkness" due to their deeds and unwillingness to come to the truth.
- vCosmic Significance: The metaphor's backdrop can be traced to the creation narrative in Genesis, where the first act of creation is God saying, "Let there be light." John's Gospel also starts with a nod to this cosmic dimension, describing Jesus as the Word through whom all things were made and in whom "was life, and that life was the light of all mankind" (John 1:4). In summary, the "Light of the World" metaphor encapsulates Jesus' role as the divine revealer, savior, and source of spiritual enlightenment and life. It also underscores the responsibility of His followers to reflect His light in a world often characterized by spiritual darkness.

The Bread of Life Metaphor

The "Bread of Life" metaphor is a powerful image presented by Jesus in the Gospel of John, specifically in John 6. Through this metaphor, Jesus communicates His unique role as the sustainer of spiritual life and the sole source of eternal salvation. The metaphor unfolds after the feeding of the five thousand, a miracle where Jesus fed a large crowd with only five loaves of bread and two fish.

Here's a breakdown of the metaphor:

- The Setting: After the feeding of the five thousand, the crowd seeks Jesus, likely wanting more miraculous provisions. Jesus redirects their focus from earthly bread to spiritual sustenance: "Do not work for food that perishes, but for the food that endures to eternal life, which the Son of Man will give to you" (John 6:27).

- Jesus as the Bread of Life: In John 6:35, Jesus declares, "I am the bread of life; whoever comes to me shall not hunger, and whoever believes in me shall never thirst." With this, Jesus identifies Himself as the ultimate source of spiritual nourishment. Just as bread (a staple in ancient diets) sustains physical life, Jesus sustains spiritual life.

- The Contrast with Manna: The conversation evolves with the crowd mentioning the manna their ancestors ate in the wilderness (an event from Exodus in the Old Testament). Manna was the miraculous provision from God to the Israelites during their 40 years in the desert. Jesus distinguishes Himself from manna, noting that while those who ate manna eventually died, whoever eats the bread He offers will live forever (John 6:49-51).

- Eating His Flesh and Drinking His Blood: As the discourse progresses, Jesus introduces a more challenging concept: "Unless you eat the flesh of the Son of Man and drink his blood, you have no life in you. Whoever feeds on my flesh and drinks my blood has eternal life, and I will raise him up on the last day" (John 6:53-54). This imagery, while shocking, emphasizes the depth of union and commitment required of His followers. In Christian tradition, this passage is often linked with the Last Supper and the institution of the Eucharist, where bread and wine symbolize Jesus' body and blood.

- Eternal Life: Central to the "Bread of Life" discourse is the promise of eternal life. By coming to and believing in Jesus, believers are assured of eternal sustenance and resurrection:

"This is the bread that comes down from heaven, so that one may eat of it and not die" (John 6:50).
* The Source of Spiritual Nourishment: The metaphor underscores the idea that just as our bodies require food for sustenance, our souls require spiritual nourishment. Jesus offers Himself as the answer to humanity's deepest spiritual hunger and thirst.

In summary, the "Bread of Life" metaphor emphasizes Jesus' role as the unique and ultimate source of spiritual sustenance and eternal life. It calls believers to a profound union with Him, challenging them to find their true nourishment and purpose in Him rather than in temporary, worldly provisions.

The Door of the Sheep Metaphor

The "door of the sheep" or "gate for the sheep" metaphor is one of the "I am" statements of Jesus found in the Gospel of John, specifically in John 10. Through this metaphor, Jesus depicts His role as the sole, legitimate access point to spiritual safety, sustenance, and salvation for His followers.
Here's a breakdown of the metaphor:
* Jesus as the Door: In John 10:7, Jesus states, "Truly, truly, I say to you, I am the door of the sheep." Then again in verse 9, He declares, "I am the door. If anyone enters by me, he will be saved and will go in and out and find pasture." By identifying Himself as the "door," Jesus is illustrating His role as the entranceway to a life of security, nourishment, and relationship with God.
* Safety from Thieves and Robbers: Earlier in the chapter, Jesus contrasts His role as the door with those of "thieves and robbers" who do not enter the sheepfold by the door but climb in another way. These figures represent false prophets, leaders, or any other path that promises salvation or enlightenment apart from Jesus. Such paths, according to Jesus, come to steal, kill, and destroy (John 10:10).
* Life and Abundance: Not only does Jesus promise safety and protection to those who enter through Him, but He also promises abundance: "I came that they may have life and have it

abundantly" (John 10:10). This abundant life isn't merely about material or temporal blessings but signifies a full, meaningful, and eternal relationship with God.

• Role of the Shepherd: The "door" metaphor transitions into another metaphor where Jesus identifies Himself as the "good shepherd." While the door metaphor emphasizes access, safety, and entrance into God's kingdom, the good shepherd metaphor focuses on the care, guidance, protection, and self-sacrificial love that Jesus offers.

• The Exclusivity of the Door: The metaphor underscores the exclusive claim of Jesus as the legitimate and only way to true spiritual safety and salvation. In John 14:6, this exclusivity is echoed when Jesus says, "I am the way, and the truth, and the life. No one comes to the Father except through me."

In summary, the "door of the sheep" metaphor provides a powerful image of Jesus as the sole gateway to spiritual safety and true life with God. It speaks to the protection from spiritual harm, the provision of abundant life, and the exclusivity of Jesus' claim as the legitimate path to a relationship with God.

The Living Water Metaphor

The "Living Water" metaphor is a profound illustration used by Jesus in the Gospel of John to convey the idea of spiritual sustenance and eternal life that only He can provide. This metaphor is particularly rich given the cultural and geographical context of the time. In an arid region like ancient Palestine, water was a crucial and often scarce resource, making its symbolism deeply resonant with Jesus' audience.

Here's a detailed look at the metaphor:

• Encounter with the Samaritan Woman: The primary use of this metaphor is found in John 4, where Jesus engages in a conversation with a Samaritan woman at Jacob's well. When she comes to draw water, Jesus says to her, "If you knew the gift of God, and who it is that is saying to you, 'Give me a drink,' you would have asked him, and he would have given you living water" (John 4:10).

- Water that Satisfies Permanently: As the conversation progresses, Jesus contrasts the water from the well with the water He provides: "Everyone who drinks of this water will be thirsty again, but whoever drinks of the water that I will give him will never be thirsty again. The water that I will give him will become in him a spring of water welling up to eternal life" (John 4:13-14). Here, physical thirst symbolizes spiritual longing. While earthly water provides temporary relief, the "living water" Jesus offers satisfies the soul eternally.
- Spiritual Implications: The term "living water" traditionally referred to flowing water, like that in a river or stream, as opposed to stagnant water in a pond or cistern. When Jesus uses this term, He's implying something fresh, revitalizing, and life-giving. The "living water" is often understood to represent the Holy Spirit – the active presence of God in the believer's life, providing constant guidance, refreshment, and growth.
- Connection to Old Testament Imagery: The concept of living water is rooted in Old Testament scriptures. For instance, in Jeremiah 2:13, God rebukes Israel, saying: "For my people have committed two evils: they have forsaken me, the fountain of living waters, and hewed out cisterns for themselves, broken cisterns that can hold no water." In this context, God is depicted as the source of "living waters," and turning away from Him leads to spiritual drought and emptiness.
- The Feast of Tabernacles Context: In John 7:37-39, during the Feast of Tabernacles, Jesus stands and cries out, "If anyone thirsts, let him come to me and drink. Whoever believes in me, as the Scripture has said, 'Out of his heart will flow rivers of living water.'" The Feast had a water-pouring ceremony, which makes Jesus' proclamation deeply symbolic. The "rivers of living water" flowing from the believer's heart indicate the transformative and overflowing nature of the Spirit.

In summary, the "Living Water" metaphor is a beautiful and powerful illustration of the eternal spiritual sustenance, refreshment, and life that only Jesus can provide. It emphasizes the inadequacy of worldly solutions to satisfy our deepest spiritual longings and underscores Jesus' unique role as the answer to those longings.

The Way, the Truth and the Light Metaphor

Certainly. The phrase you're referencing is actually "I am the way, and the truth, and the life," and it is one of the most famous "I am" statements made by Jesus in the Gospel of John. Here's the full context from John 14:6, where Jesus tells His disciple Thomas, "I am the way, and the truth, and the life. No one comes to the Father except through me."

Let's break down this profound declaration:

- "The Way": In this context, "way" signifies a path or direction. By identifying Himself as "the way," Jesus is positioning Himself as the exclusive pathway to salvation and a relationship with God the Father. This is a direct counter to any belief that there are multiple routes to eternal life or God's favor. It's also worth noting that early Christianity was sometimes referred to as "The Way" (see Acts 9:2; 19:9, 23; 22:4; 24:14, 22).

- "The Truth": In a world filled with relative truths, shifting philosophies, and multiple religious perspectives, Jesus' claim to be "the truth" is significant. He's not just speaking of having truth or teaching truth; He embodies truth itself. This is an affirmation of His divine nature, the veracity of His teachings, and the reliability of His promises.

- "The Life": Jesus doesn't merely give life or point the way to life; He is life itself. This statement underscores His power over death, His role as the creator and sustainer of life, and His promise to grant eternal life to those who believe in Him. This is further emphasized in John 10:10, where He states that He came to give life "abundantly."

- Exclusivity of Access to the Father: The latter part of the statement — "No one comes to the Father except through me" — underscores the exclusivity of Jesus' claim. It reinforces the idea that salvation and a right relationship with God aren't achievable through any other means, philosophy, or religious figure. Jesus is the sole mediator between humanity and God (see also 1 Timothy 2:5).

The metaphorical statement of "the way, the truth, and the life" serves as a powerful declaration of Jesus' unique and unparalleled role in salvation history. It emphasizes His divine nature, the reliability of His teachings, and the promise of eternal life through Him. It's also a call to faith, encouraging believers to put their trust wholly in Him and His redemptive work.

Light on the Hill Metaphor

The metaphor "light on a hill" or more commonly referred to as a "city on a hill" is derived from Jesus' Sermon on the Mount. This metaphor is used to illustrate the visible role and the influence that His followers should have in the world. The specific passage is found in the Gospel of Matthew:
"You are the light of the world. A city set on a hill cannot be hidden. Nor do people light a lamp and put it under a basket, but on a stand, and it gives light to all in the house. In the same way, let your light shine before others, so that they may see your good works and give glory to your Father who is in heaven." - Matthew 5:14-16 (ESV)
Here's a breakdown of the metaphor:
- Visibility and Influence: A city set on elevated ground cannot be hidden. Similarly, a lamp is meant to be placed in a position where its light can be most effective, not hidden under a container. Jesus is conveying that His followers should be like that city or lamp, visible and influential, not hidden or ineffective.
- Purpose of the Light: The light represents the righteous deeds and godly character of believers. The aim isn't for believers to showcase themselves, but for others to see their good works and, as a result, give glory to God. It's an outward manifestation of an inward faith.
- Contrast with Darkness: Light in the Bible often represents goodness, truth, and God's presence, while darkness can symbolize evil, deception, or the absence of God. By calling His followers the "light of the world," Jesus is highlighting their role as a contrast to the spiritual darkness around them.
- Responsibility of Believers: The metaphor underscores

the responsibility of believers to live out their faith in tangible, visible ways. They are to set a moral and spiritual example, illuminating the path to God and righteousness.

- Historical and Modern Usage: Outside its biblical context, the "city on a hill" imagery has been used in political and cultural discourse, particularly in America. It's been employed to convey the idea of America having a special destiny or role as an exemplar nation. John Winthrop, an early Puritan leader, famously used the phrase in a sermon aboard the Arbella, referring to the Massachusetts Bay Colony as a "city upon a hill" with the eyes of all people upon them.

In essence, the "light on a hill" or "city on a hill" metaphor serves as a call for believers to live out their faith in a way that's both visible and impactful, guiding others toward God and righteousness.

Salt of the Earth Metaphor

The "salt of the earth" metaphor is another teaching from Jesus' Sermon on the Mount. Just after referring to His followers as the "light of the world," Jesus says:

"You are the salt of the earth, but if salt has lost its taste, how shall its saltiness be restored? It is no longer good for anything except to be thrown out and trampled under people's feet." - Matthew 5:13 (ESV)

This metaphor carries several layers of meaning:

- Preservation: In ancient times, salt was primarily used as a preservative. Before the advent of refrigeration, salt was one of the main ways to keep food, particularly meat, from spoiling. When Jesus calls His followers the "salt of the earth," He implies that they have a preserving effect on the world, counteracting moral decay and degradation.
- Flavor: Salt is also used to enhance the flavor of food. In this sense, Christians, by living out their faith and values, bring a positive flavor to life and society, adding meaning, hope, and love to a world that often feels tasteless or bland.
- Value: In the ancient world, salt was highly valued.

There were times when it was even used as a form of currency. By likening His followers to salt, Jesus is indicating their immense value in the world.

- Potential Loss of Value: The latter part of the verse raises a cautionary point. Just as salt can lose its flavor and thereby its usefulness, believers can lose their distinctiveness and influence if they become too assimilated into the surrounding culture or neglect their spiritual disciplines.
- Distinctiveness: The metaphor also implies that followers of Jesus should be distinct from the world in terms of their character, values, and actions. If they lose this distinctiveness (or "saltiness"), they lose their ability to influence and positively impact the world around them.
- Healing and Purification: While not directly implied in this particular teaching, it's worth noting that salt was also used for medicinal purposes in ancient times, adding another potential layer of meaning. Followers of Jesus can bring healing and purification to situations and relationships by embodying His teachings and grace.

In summary, the "salt of the earth" metaphor emphasizes the essential role that Jesus' followers play in the world. They are called to preserve, enhance, and bring healing, all while maintaining their distinctiveness and influence. If they lose their "saltiness," they risk becoming ineffective in their purpose.

New Wine in Old Wineskins Metaphor

The metaphor of the "New Wine in Old Wineskins" is one of Jesus' teachings that illustrates the incompatibility between His new teachings and the old ways of religious thinking and practice.

Here's the context in which Jesus presents this metaphor, as found in the Gospel of Matthew:

"Neither do people pour new wine into old wineskins. If they do, the skins will burst; the wine will run out and the wineskins will be ruined. No, they pour new wine into new wineskins, and both are preserved." - Matthew 9:17 (NIV)

Let's break down the metaphor:

- **New Wine:** This represents the teachings and the new covenant that Jesus introduced. It encompasses His message of grace, love, the coming of the Kingdom of God, and a new way of relating to God—not through ritualistic law but through faith in Him.

- **Old Wineskins:** Wineskins were containers made from animal hides, used in ancient times to store liquids, especially wine. As they aged, wineskins would become rigid and lose their elasticity. The old wineskins symbolize the old religious system, primarily represented by the Pharisaic interpretation of the Mosaic Law and the traditions that had been added to it.

- **The Bursting of the Wineskins:** When new wine is put into wineskins, it continues to ferment. As fermentation progresses, gases are produced, causing the wine to expand. Old wineskins, having lost their flexibility, would burst under the pressure of this expansion. This illustrates the idea that the old religious structures and paradigms were not capable of containing or sustaining the dynamic and transformative message of Jesus. The core message of the metaphor is about adaptability and the recognition that new things often require new structures or paradigms to contain and express them. Jesus was introducing a radical shift in understanding one's relationship with God, moving away from legalism and ritual to a heart-based, faith-driven approach. The established religious institutions and mindsets of His day were not equipped to handle or accommodate this shift.

In a broader application, this teaching can serve as a reminder about the dangers of rigidity and being stuck in old ways of thinking, especially when faced with new revelations, ideas, or movements. It underscores the importance of openness and adaptability in the spiritual journey.

The Leaven Metaphor

The leaven (or yeast) metaphor is employed by Jesus in various contexts in the New Testament. It's a powerful image that captures the pervasive and transformative nature of leaven when it's mixed with dough. Let's look at some of the ways Jesus uses this metaphor:

- Kingdom of Heaven: In one parable, Jesus likens the Kingdom of Heaven to leaven:

"He told them still another parable: 'The kingdom of heaven is like yeast that a woman took and mixed into about sixty pounds of flour until it worked all through the dough.'" - Matthew 13:33 (NIV)

In this context, the leaven represents the Kingdom of God, and the message is clear: just as a small amount of leaven can affect a large batch of dough, so the influence of the Kingdom of God starts small but eventually permeates and transforms the entire world. It's a metaphor for the subtle, yet profound, influence of God's reign.

- Beware of the Leaven of the Pharisees: In a different context, Jesus warns His disciples to "beware of the leaven of the Pharisees and Sadducees" (Matthew 16:6). After some confusion, the disciples understand that He wasn't speaking about literal bread but about the teachings and hypocrisy of these religious leaders. Here, the leaven metaphorically represents the corrupting influence of false teaching or hypocrisy. A little false teaching or a slight deviation from truth can spread and corrupt one's entire belief system or way of life.

- Leaven of the Pharisees and Herod: In Mark's Gospel, Jesus also warns about the "leaven of Herod" in addition to that of the Pharisees (Mark 8:15). While the Pharisees represented religious corruption, Herod represented political and moral corruption. In this broader context, the metaphor underscores the idea that one must be vigilant not just about religious influences but also about political and cultural influences that can subtly corrupt one's values and character.

In all these instances, the leaven metaphor underscores the idea of a small, often unnoticed influence that has the potential to bring about significant change, whether positive (as in the spread of God's Kingdom) or negative (as in the spread of hypocrisy or false teachings). The image serves as a reminder of the subtle yet powerful forces at work in our lives and the need for discernment and awareness.

The Mustard Seed Metaphor

The mustard seed metaphor is another of Jesus' parables, illustrating the nature of the Kingdom of Heaven. It's a story that emphasizes the contrast between humble beginnings and immense outcomes.
Here's the parable as recorded in the Gospel of Matthew:
"He put another parable before them, saying, 'The kingdom of heaven is like a grain of mustard seed that a man took and sowed in his field. It is the smallest of all seeds, but when it has grown it is larger than all the garden plants and becomes a tree, so that the birds of the air come and make nests in its branches.'" - Matthew 13:31-32 (ESV)
Let's break down the metaphor:
- Small Beginnings: The mustard seed is often cited in the biblical context as one of the smallest seeds. When Jesus speaks of the Kingdom of Heaven starting like a mustard seed, He's referencing the seemingly insignificant and humble beginnings of His ministry and the early Christian movement.
- Impressive Growth: Despite its small size, the mustard seed grows into a large plant, even described as a tree in this parable. This growth represents the expansive and encompassing nature of the Kingdom of God. From a small group of followers, the message of Jesus would grow to have a transformative impact on the world.
- Shelter and Nourishment: The fully grown mustard plant offers shelter to birds. This can be seen as an image of the Kingdom of Heaven providing refuge, nourishment, and peace to those who seek it. The birds may represent various nations or people groups, suggesting the universal nature of God's Kingdom that welcomes all.

The mustard seed metaphor encapsulates the essence of faith and the Kingdom of God: What begins as something tiny and seemingly inconsequential can, with time and nurturing, grow into something vast, influential, and nurturing for others. It underscores the message of hope and the transformative power of God's work in the world, reminding believers not to despise small beginnings and to recognize the potential of even the tiniest seeds of faith.

Splinter in your Brothers Eye Metaphor

The metaphor of the "splinter in your brother's eye and a log in your own" is a powerful teaching from Jesus about self-awareness, hypocrisy, and the human tendency to judge others harshly while overlooking our own faults.
Here's the passage from the Gospel of Matthew:
"Why do you see the speck that is in your brother's eye, but do not notice the log that is in your own eye? Or how can you say to your brother, 'Let me take the speck out of your eye,' when there is the log in your own eye? You hypocrite, first take the log out of your own eye, and then you will see clearly to take the speck out of your brother's eye." - Matthew 7:3-5 (ESV)
The metaphor can be broken down as follows:
- Splinter/Speck in Your Brother's Eye: This represents minor faults or mistakes we observe in others. It's something small, yet we tend to focus on it, magnify it, and sometimes even obsess over it, especially when we're in a judgmental mindset.
- Log/Beam in Your Own Eye: This represents our own significant faults or failings. The imagery is exaggerated to highlight the absurdity of the situation: how can we focus on someone else's minor fault when we have a glaringly obvious flaw ourselves? The log is obstructive, preventing clear vision and understanding.
- Act of Removing: The act of trying to remove the speck from someone else's eye while having a log in our own represents the hypocrisy of trying to correct or "help" others when we have not dealt with our own issues.

Jesus' teaching here underscores a few essential principles:
- Self-awareness and Self-reflection: Before judging or correcting others, we should examine ourselves, recognizing and addressing our own shortcomings.

- Empathy and Humility: We should approach others with understanding and compassion, realizing that everyone has flaws, including ourselves.
- Avoiding Hypocrisy: It's inconsistent and hypocritical to hold others to standards we ourselves do not meet. Genuine moral authority comes from integrity and consistency in our beliefs and actions.

The metaphor serves as a vivid reminder to be introspective and humble, recognizing our own imperfections before rushing to judge others.

A Camel through the Eye of a Needle Metaphor

The saying "it is easier for a camel to go through the eye of a needle than for a rich person to enter the kingdom of God" is one of Jesus' more vivid metaphors. It's found in the synoptic Gospels: Matthew 19:24, Mark 10:25, and Luke 18:25. This teaching was given in response to a rich young ruler who asked Jesus about eternal life but went away sorrowful when Jesus advised him to sell his possessions and give to the poor.
Here's a breakdown of the metaphor:

- Camel Through the Eye of a Needle: The camel was one of the largest animals familiar to Jesus' listeners in Palestine, and the eye of a needle, of course, is a very small opening. The imagery is intentionally hyperbolic, underscoring the sheer impossibility of the task.
- Rich People and the Kingdom of God: By saying it's difficult for the rich to enter the kingdom of God, Jesus isn't condemning wealth in itself. Instead, He's highlighting the spiritual dangers of wealth: it can lead to pride, self-sufficiency, greed, and a misplaced sense of security. Wealth can easily become an idol, displacing God as one's primary focus and trust. When the disciples heard this teaching, they were greatly astonished and asked, "Who then can be saved?" Jesus responded: "With man this is impossible, but with God all things are possible" (Matthew 19:26). This emphasizes that salvation is not about human effort but relies on God's grace.

A few important takeaways from this metaphor are:
- The Perils of Attachment: Wealth and material possessions can bind the heart, diverting one's attention from God and spiritual matters.
- Salvation is God's Work: While human effort falls short, salvation comes from God's grace and power.
- The Challenge of Priorities: Jesus is challenging His listeners to evaluate their priorities. For the rich young ruler, his wealth was a barrier to following Jesus wholeheartedly.

Throughout history, there have been various interpretations and attempts to soften the starkness of this metaphor, such as suggesting that "the eye of the needle" referred to a small gate in Jerusalem's wall. However, there's no solid historical evidence for this gate. The metaphor's power lies in its hyperbole, challenging listeners to reflect on the potential barriers to a genuine relationship with God.

Section II
Teaching Jesus

1. Jesus and God Teaching Jesus
2. Disciples of Jesus Teaching Jesus
3. Followers Teaching Jesus who Knew Him in His Human Life
4. Followers Teaching Jesus after His human Death

Jesus and God Teaching Jesus

Jesus Teaching Jesus

As the Son of God and the Savior of the world, Jesus taught about Himself and His mission throughout His life and ministry. Jesus's teachings emphasized the importance of faith in God and the need for repentance and forgiveness of sins.

In the New Testament, Jesus is described as performing miracles and signs to validate His message and demonstrate the power of God. He used parables and other storytelling techniques to convey spiritual truths and to illustrate the nature of God's kingdom. Jesus also engaged in dialogue with others, answering their questions and challenging their assumptions.
Jesus's teachings emphasized the need to love God and to love one's neighbor, and He demonstrated this love through His actions, including His healing of the sick and His interaction with social outcasts. Jesus also taught about the importance of obedience to God's will and the need to live a life of holiness and righteousness.
Ultimately, Jesus taught that He was the Son of God, sent to save humanity from sin and to offer eternal life to all who believe in Him. Through His life, teachings, death, and resurrection, Jesus provided a path to reconciliation with God and a way to experience true spiritual transformation.

Jesus did not teach about Himself as a separate entity, but rather

He taught about God, the Kingdom of God, and the fulfillment of the prophecies regarding the Messiah. He revealed His identity and purpose through His teachings, actions, and interactions with others.

1. Teaching about God: Jesus emphasized the concept of God as a loving Father. He taught about God's character, His desire for a relationship with humanity, and the need for repentance and forgiveness. Jesus frequently referred to God as "my Father" and invited others to see God in the same way.

2. Proclaiming the Kingdom of God: Jesus announced the arrival of the Kingdom of God and taught about its nature and significance. He described the Kingdom as a present reality and a future fulfillment, calling people to repentance and faith in God's reign. Jesus used parables, stories with spiritual lessons, to illustrate the principles and values of the Kingdom.

3. Demonstrating His Authority: Jesus performed miracles that revealed His divine authority and power. He healed the sick, cast out demons, raised the dead, and even demonstrated control over nature. Through these extraordinary acts, Jesus showed that He was not merely a teacher but also the Son of God with the authority to bring about transformation and salvation.

4. Fulfilling Prophecy: Jesus referred to Old Testament prophecies that pointed to the coming of the Messiah. He demonstrated how the Scriptures were fulfilled in Him, such as the prophecies about His birth in Bethlehem, His lineage from the house of David, His ministry, and His sacrificial death and resurrection.

5. Discourse with His Disciples: Jesus spent significant time teaching His disciples privately, explaining to them the deeper meaning of His teachings and preparing them to carry on His mission after His departure. He disclosed His impending suffering, death, and resurrection, as well as the significance of His sacrifice for the forgiveness of sins.

6. Personal Testimony: Jesus often spoke directly about Himself, asserting His unique relationship with God. He referred to Himself as the Son of God, the Son of Man, the Light of the World, the Bread of Life, the Good Shepherd, and the Way, the Truth, and the Life. These statements communicated His divine

nature and His role in salvation.

Overall, Jesus taught about Himself indirectly by focusing on God's kingdom, His relationship with God the Father, the fulfillment of prophecy, and the invitation to follow Him. His teachings and actions revealed His identity as the long-awaited Messiah and the Son of God.

God Teaching Jesus

As the divine Creator and ruler of the universe, God is believed by Christians to have communicated the message of Jesus Christ to humanity through a variety of means. According to Christian tradition, God's teachings about Jesus are primarily conveyed through the Bible, which is considered to be the inspired Word of God.

Throughout the Old and New Testaments of the Bible, God is described as revealing His plan for salvation and redemption through Jesus Christ. The prophecies in the Old Testament point to the coming of a Messiah who would be a Savior for all people, and the New Testament describes the fulfillment of these prophecies through the life, teachings, death, and resurrection of Jesus.

God's teachings about Jesus also come through the Holy Spirit, which is believed to be a guiding force that helps believers to understand and apply the message of the gospel. The Holy Spirit is also seen as a source of power and wisdom that enables believers to live according to God's will and to spread the message of Jesus to others.

Overall, God's teachings about Jesus emphasize the importance of faith, repentance, and obedience to God's will. The message of the gospel is one of love, grace, and redemption, and it is intended for all people, regardless of their background, status, or past actions.

According to Christian belief, God taught about Jesus through various means. Here are some of the key ways in which God communicated the message of Jesus:

    1. Prophecy: Throughout the Old Testament, God inspired

prophets to foretell the coming of the Messiah, who Christians believe is Jesus. These prophecies predicted specific details about Jesus' birth, life, ministry, death, and resurrection. They served as a way for God to reveal His plan and prepare people for the coming of Jesus.

2. Scriptures: The Bible, considered by Christians to be the inspired Word of God, contains the teachings and accounts of Jesus. The New Testament, in particular, provides information about Jesus' life, teachings, and significance. It includes the four Gospels (Matthew, Mark, Luke, and John), which document Jesus' life, ministry, miracles, and teachings. God communicated the message of Jesus through the writers of the biblical texts.

3. Miraculous events: God manifested His power through miracles performed by Jesus. These miracles, such as healing the sick, raising the dead, feeding multitudes, and turning water into wine, were not only acts of compassion but also served as evidence of Jesus' divinity and authority. They revealed God's presence and purpose in Jesus' mission.

4. Jesus' teachings: Jesus Himself was the primary teacher of His own message. Through His teachings, parables, and interactions with people, Jesus conveyed God's love, grace, and truth. He taught about the kingdom of God, moral principles, the nature of God, and the way to salvation. Jesus' teachings were grounded in His close relationship with God the Father, and He often referred to God's will and plan.

5. Personal revelation: God communicated with individuals directly or through visions and dreams. In the Bible, there are instances where God revealed Jesus' identity and purpose to individuals. For example, when Saul of Tarsus encountered Jesus on the road to Damascus, he experienced a personal revelation that transformed him into the apostle Paul, who played a significant role in spreading the message of Jesus.

6. The Holy Spirit: Christians believe that the Holy Spirit, the third person of the Trinity, plays a crucial role in revealing and teaching about Jesus. The Holy Spirit enlightens believers, brings understanding of Scripture, and helps individuals recognize Jesus as the Son of God and Savior. Through the indwelling of the Holy Spirit, believers can grow in knowledge and understanding of

Jesus' teachings.

It is important to note that these explanations are based on Christian belief and may not be universally accepted. Different religious traditions may have their own perspectives on how God taught about Jesus.

Who were the Disciples of Jesus?

The twelve disciples, also known as the twelve apostles, were the primary followers of Jesus Christ. Here is a list of the twelve disciples:

    1. Simon Peter (also called Simon or Cephas): He was a fisherman and one of the most prominent among the apostles. He later became a leader in the early Christian church.

    2. Andrew: The brother of Simon Peter, Andrew was also a fisherman and one of the first disciples called by Jesus.

    3. James, the son of Zebedee: Often referred to as James the Greater, he was a fisherman and the brother of John. James was part of Jesus' inner circle, along with Peter and his brother John.

    4. John, the son of Zebedee: The brother of James, John was also a fisherman and part of Jesus' inner circle. He is traditionally considered the author of the Gospel of John, the three Epistles of John, and the Book of Revelation.

    5. Philip: He came from the town of Bethsaida, the same town as Peter and Andrew, and played an active role in the early Christian church.

    6. Bartholomew (also known as Nathanael): He was introduced to Jesus by Philip and became one of the twelve disciples.

    7. Matthew (also known as Levi): He was a tax collector before becoming a disciple of Jesus. The Gospel of Matthew is traditionally attributed to him.

    8. Thomas (also called Didymus): Known as "Doubting Thomas" due to His initial disbelief in Jesus' resurrection,

he later affirmed His faith and became a devoted follower.

9. James, the son of Alphaeus: Often referred to as James the Less or James the Just, he was another one of the twelve disciples, but little else is known about him.

10. Thaddaeus (also known as Lebbaeus or Judas, son of James): He was one of the lesser-known disciples, and there is limited information about His life and ministry.

11. Simon the Zealot (also called Simon the Canaanite): He was a member of the Zealot party, a Jewish political group, before becoming a disciple of Jesus.

12. Judas Iscariot: He was the disciple who betrayed Jesus, leading to His arrest and crucifixion. After His betrayal, he was replaced by Matthias as one of the twelve apostles in the early Christian church.

These twelve disciples were chosen by Jesus to accompany him during His ministry, and they played a crucial role in the establishment and spread of Christianity after His death and resurrection.

Why did Jesus Choose the Disciples He Did?

Jesus chose His disciples from various backgrounds and walks of life, ultimately selecting them for a variety of reasons. Although the precise reasons for His choices are not explicitly stated in the Bible, we can infer several possible factors that contributed to His decision:

1. Divine guidance: Jesus was guided by the will of God in choosing His disciples. It is evident from the Scriptures that Jesus spent time in prayer before selecting His disciples (Luke 6:12-13), indicating that He sought divine guidance in making His decision.

2. Teachability and willingness to learn: Jesus chose individuals who demonstrated a willingness to learn from Him and be transformed by His teachings. The disciples were not necessarily the most educated or religiously knowledgeable people, but they were open to Jesus's message and willing to grow in their faith.

3. Commitment and loyalty: Jesus sought followers who were willing to commit to Him and His mission, even in the face of adversity. The disciples left their previous lives, occupations, and social ties behind to follow Jesus, showing their dedication and loyalty.

4. Diverse backgrounds: The disciples came from various social, economic, and occupational backgrounds, ranging from fishermen to tax collectors. This diversity may have been intentional, as it allowed Jesus's message to reach a wider audience and demonstrated that His teachings were relevant to people from all walks of life.

5. Potential for leadership and influence: Jesus chose individuals who had the potential to become leaders and influencers in the early Christian community. After His death and resurrection, the disciples played a crucial role in spreading the Gospel and establishing the foundations of the Church.

6. A reflection of God's grace: By choosing ordinary, flawed individuals as His disciples, Jesus demonstrated the transformative power of God's grace. The disciples were not perfect, and they made mistakes throughout their journey with Jesus, but they were transformed by their experiences and became effective witnesses for Christ.

Ultimately, Jesus chose His disciples based on their faith, commitment, and potential for growth and leadership. Their diverse backgrounds and imperfections demonstrated the universal nature of Jesus's message and the transformative power of God's grace.

Who was Jesus's Favorite Disciple?

While the New Testament does not explicitly state who Jesus's favorite disciple was, there are some instances in which certain disciples are singled out for special attention or interaction with Jesus. For example, Peter, James, and John are described as being present at several key moments in Jesus's ministry, such as the Transfiguration and the raising of Jairus's daughter from the dead.

However, it is important to note that the idea of a "favorite" disciple is not a concept found in the New Testament, and it is not appropriate to assign such a label to any one disciple. Each of the twelve apostles played a vital role in the spread of the gospel and the establishment of the early Church, and their contributions are recognized and celebrated by Christians around the world. Ultimately, Jesus loved all of His disciples equally and taught them to love one another as well.

Jesus's Disciples Teaching Jesus

Disciples Teaching Jesus

After Jesus's death, resurrection, and ascension into heaven, His disciples were tasked with spreading His teachings and sharing the Good News of the Gospel. Empowered by the Holy Spirit, the disciples began to teach about Jesus in various ways:

1. Preaching: The disciples preached in synagogues, public spaces, and private homes, sharing the message of Jesus's life, teachings, death, and resurrection. They proclaimed Jesus as the Messiah and urged people to repent and believe in Him for the forgiveness of their sins (Acts 2:14-41).

2. Personal testimony: The disciples shared their personal experiences with Jesus and the transformative impact He had on their lives. These testimonies provided powerful, relatable examples of how Jesus changed the lives of those who believed in Him (Acts 4:13, 20).

3. Performing miracles and healing: Empowered by the Holy Spirit, the disciples performed miracles and healings in Jesus's name, demonstrating His divine power and authority. These acts served as evidence of Jesus's divinity and provided opportunities to teach about Him (Acts 3:1-10, Acts 5:12-16).

4. Establishing and nurturing the early Church: The disciples played a crucial role in establishing and organizing the early Christian Church, which provided a supportive community for believers to learn about Jesus and grow in their faith. They

taught, guided, and provided pastoral care for the new converts (Acts 2:42-47, Acts 14:21-23).

5. Writing Scripture: Some disciples, such as Matthew, John, and Peter, wrote books or letters that became part of the New Testament. These writings preserve the teachings of Jesus and provide guidance for Christians throughout History (e.g., the Gospel of Matthew, the Gospel of John, and the letters of Peter).

6. Training new leaders: The disciples trained new leaders and missionaries, who in turn taught others about Jesus and expanded the reach of the Gospel. They passed on their knowledge and experience to the next generation of Christian leaders (Acts 13:1-3, Acts 14:23, 2 Timothy 2:2).

7. Engaging with different cultures: The disciples traveled to different regions and engaged with various cultural and religious groups, sharing the message of Jesus in ways that were relevant and understandable to these diverse audiences (Acts 8:26-40, Acts 17:16-34).

8. Modeling Jesus's teachings: The disciples lived out Jesus's teachings in their daily lives, exemplifying the virtues of love, forgiveness, and humility. Their actions served as a powerful witness to the transformative power of faith in Jesus (Acts 4:32-37).

By teaching Jesus through preaching, personal testimony, miracles, and community-building, the disciples played a crucial role in spreading the Gospel and laying the foundations of the Christian Church. Their efforts have had a lasting impact, inspiring countless generations of believers to follow in their footsteps and share the Good News of Jesus Christ.

Simon Peter Teaching Jesus

Simon Peter, one of Jesus' twelve apostles, played a significant role in teaching Jesus and spreading the Christian faith, especially after Jesus' crucifixion and resurrection. Here are some important ways in which Simon Peter taught about Jesus:

1. Preaching the Gospel: After Jesus' ascension, Peter emerged as a leader among the apostles and took an active role

in preaching about Jesus. In Acts 2, Peter delivers a sermon at Pentecost, explaining Jesus' life, death, and resurrection, and calling for people to repent and be baptized in Jesus' name. Throughout the Book of Acts, Peter continues to preach and teach about Jesus, emphasizing His role as the Messiah and the Savior.

2. Performing miracles: In the Book of Acts, Peter performs various miracles in the name of Jesus, demonstrating Jesus' power and divinity. These acts not only confirmed the apostles' authority but also served as evidence for Jesus' continued presence and activity through His followers.

3. Witnessing to Jesus' life and resurrection: As one of Jesus' closest disciples, Peter was a firsthand witness to Jesus' teachings, miracles, crucifixion, and resurrection. he shared these experiences with others, providing a direct testimony of Jesus' life and ministry.

4. Establishing the early church: Peter played a crucial role in establishing and guiding the early Christian church, helping to shape its theology, practices, and organization. His leadership helped to ensure that Jesus' teachings were preserved and passed down through the generations.

5. Providing pastoral care: In His two New Testament epistles, 1 Peter and 2 Peter, Simon Peter offers guidance, encouragement, and pastoral care to early Christians facing various challenges, including persecution and false teachings. He exhorts believers to remain steadfast in their faith and to follow Jesus' example of enduring suffering.

Overall, Simon Peter taught about Jesus through preaching, performing miracles, witnessing to Jesus' life and resurrection, leading the early church, and offering pastoral care to believers. As one of the most prominent apostles, Peter's teachings and actions had a lasting impact on the development of Christianity and continue to inform Christian beliefs and practices today.

Andrew Teaching Jesus

Andrew, the brother of Simon Peter, was one of the twelve apostles of Jesus. While the New Testament provides fewer details about Andrew's specific activities compared to some of the other apostles, there is still information about how he taught about Jesus:

1. Bringing others to Jesus: According to the Gospel of John, Andrew was a disciple of John the Baptist before he became a follower of Jesus. When John the Baptist pointed out Jesus as the "Lamb of God," Andrew followed Jesus and then brought His brother, Simon Peter, to meet Him as well (John 1:35-42). This act of introducing others to Jesus was a way in which Andrew taught about Jesus.

2. Participating in Jesus' ministry: As one of the twelve apostles, Andrew accompanied Jesus throughout His ministry, witnessing His teachings, miracles, and actions. This firsthand experience allowed Him to share what he had learned from Jesus with others.

3. Spreading the Gospel: After Jesus' resurrection and ascension, Andrew, like the other apostles, participated in spreading the Gospel and establishing the early Christian church. While the New Testament does not provide extensive details about Andrew's missionary activities, early Christian tradition suggests that he traveled to various regions, including present-day Greece, Turkey, and Ukraine, to preach about Jesus and convert people to Christianity.

4. Miracles and healings: Some apocryphal texts and early Christian traditions credit Andrew with performing miracles and healings in the name of Jesus, which would have served as a testimony to Jesus' power and divinity.

5. Martyrdom: According to tradition, Andrew was martyred for His faith, being crucified on an X-shaped cross, which is now known as St. Andrew's Cross. His willingness to die for His belief in Jesus and the Gospel message would have been a powerful testimony to His faith and the truth of Jesus' teachings. Although the New Testament provides less information about Andrew's specific teachings and actions compared to some other apostles, it is evident that he played an essential role in spreading Jesus' message, both during Jesus' ministry and after His resurrection and ascension.

James the Greater Teaching Jesus

James the Great, also known as James, the son of Zebedee, was one of the twelve apostles of Jesus. He was the brother of John, the author of the Gospel of John, and along with Peter and John, he was part of Jesus' inner circle. While the New Testament provides limited details about James the Great's specific teachings, it does offer some insights into His role in spreading Jesus' message:

    1. Close follower of Jesus: As one of Jesus' closest disciples, James witnessed Jesus' teachings, miracles, and actions firsthand. This experience allowed him to share what he had learned from Jesus with others.

    2. Participating in key events: James was present during several significant events in Jesus' ministry, such as the Transfiguration (Matthew 17:1-9, Mark 9:2-8, Luke 9:28-36) and Jesus' prayer in the Garden of Gethsemane before His arrest (Matthew 26:36-46, Mark 14:32-42). These experiences likely had a profound impact on James' understanding of Jesus and His teachings, which he could then share with others.

    3. Preaching the Gospel: After Jesus' resurrection and ascension, James, like the other apostles, participated in spreading the Gospel and establishing the early Christian church. While the New Testament does not provide extensive details about James the Great's missionary activities, he likely played a role in preaching about Jesus and converting people to Christianity.

    4. Martyrdom: According to the Book of Acts (12:1-2), James was the first apostle to be martyred for His faith. King Herod Agrippa I ordered His execution, which took place around AD 44. James' willingness to die for His belief in Jesus and the Gospel message would have been a powerful testimony to His faith and the truth of Jesus' teachings.

Though the New Testament provides limited details about the specific teachings and actions of James the Great, it is clear he played a crucial role in spreading Jesus' message, both during Jesus' ministry and after His resurrection and ascension.

His close relationship with Jesus, participation in key events, and eventual martyrdom all contributed to the growth and development of early Christianity.

John Teaching Jesus

The Gospel of John is the fourth of the four canonical gospels in the New Testament, which also include Matthew, Mark, and Luke. The authorship of the Gospel of John is traditionally attributed to John the Apostle, also known as John the Evangelist or John the Beloved Disciple. It is important to note, however, that the author's identity is still debated among scholars. Assuming that John is the author, we can discuss how he taught Jesus through His gospel.

The Gospel of John is distinct from the synoptic gospels (Matthew, Mark, and Luke) in terms of its structure, style, and content. It is characterized by its highly theological and spiritual nature, focusing on Jesus' divine nature and His relationship with God the Father. John presents Jesus as the eternal Word (Logos) of God, who became flesh to reveal the truth about God and bring salvation to humanity. Here are some key aspects of the Gospel of John teaching Jesus:

    1. The Prologue: John's gospel begins with a poetic prologue that presents Jesus as the eternal Word of God, who was with God in the beginning and through whom all things were created. This prologue emphasizes Jesus' divine nature and His unique relationship with God the Father.

    2. The "I am" sayings: The Gospel of John contains several "I am" sayings, in which Jesus makes profound declarations about His identity, such as "I am the bread of life," "I am the light of the world," "I am the good shepherd," and "I am the resurrection and the life." These sayings emphasize Jesus' divine nature and His role as the source of eternal life and salvation.

    3. Miraculous signs: John includes accounts of Jesus performing seven miraculous signs, such as turning water into wine, healing the sick, and raising Lazarus from the dead. These signs are intended to reveal Jesus' divine nature and authority,

and to evoke belief in Him as the Messiah and the Son of God.

    4. Discourses and dialogues: The Gospel of John contains several lengthy discourses and dialogues between Jesus and various individuals, such as His conversation with Nicodemus about being born again, His dialogue with the Samaritan woman at the well, and His farewell discourse with His disciples. These conversations delve into deep theological and spiritual matters, revealing Jesus' divine wisdom and His mission to bring eternal life to those who believe in Him.

    5. The Passion, Crucifixion, and Resurrection: John provides a detailed account of the events leading up to Jesus' arrest, crucifixion, and resurrection, emphasizing Jesus' voluntary sacrifice and His role as the Lamb of God who takes away the sins of the world. John's gospel also includes post-resurrection appearances, such as Jesus' encounter with Mary Magdalene and the doubting Thomas episode.

By presenting these events and teachings, the Gospel of John teaches Jesus and offers a unique perspective on His life, ministry, and divine nature. This gospel has been an essential resource for Christian teaching and belief for centuries, shaping our understanding of Jesus as the eternal Word of God who became flesh to reveal the truth about God and bring salvation to humanity.

Phillip Teaching Jesus

Philip was one of the twelve apostles of Jesus and is known for His missionary work in spreading the gospel. In the New Testament, he is credited with several important evangelistic efforts, including preaching to the people of Samaria and baptizing an Ethiopian eunuch.

According to the book of Acts in the New Testament, Philip was led by the Holy Spirit to approach the Ethiopian eunuch, who was reading the Book of Isaiah on a chariot. Philip asked the eunuch if he understood what he was reading, and the eunuch replied that he needed someone to guide him. Philip then used the passage to teach the eunuch Jesus and the gospel, which led to the eunuch's baptism and conversion.

In addition to His evangelistic efforts, Philip is also described in the New Testament as performing miraculous healings and exorcisms. These miracles were seen as a sign of the power of God and helped to validate the message of the gospel that he preached. Overall, Philip's teachings emphasized the importance of repentance, faith in Jesus Christ, and living a life in accordance with God's will.

Bartholomew Teaching Jesus

Bartholomew, also known as Nathanael, was one of the twelve apostles of Jesus Christ. While relatively little is known about Bartholomew's life and teachings, he is recognized as one of the early disciples who played a role in spreading the message of the gospel.

In the New Testament, Bartholomew is described as a close friend of Philip and is said to have been skeptical of Jesus at first. However, after Philip told him about Jesus and brought him to meet the Lord, Bartholomew became a devoted follower.

Like the other apostles, Bartholomew would have shared the message of the gospel and teachings of Jesus with others. The specific details of His teachings are not recorded in the Bible, but it is likely that His teachings emphasized the importance of repentance, faith in Jesus Christ, and living a life in accordance with God's will.

According to tradition, Bartholomew went on to preach the gospel in various places, including Armenia, India, and Mesopotamia. He is believed to have been martyred for His faith, possibly being flayed alive or beheaded. While the details of His life and teachings may be limited, Bartholomew is remembered as a faithful disciple who played a vital role in the spread of Christianity.

Matthew Teaching Jesus

There is no record of Matthew teaching Jesus in the Bible or in any other historical documents. Matthew, also known as Levi, was one of Jesus' twelve apostles. He was a tax collector before becoming a follower of Jesus.

As Jesus is regarded as the Messiah and the Son of God in Christianity, it is Jesus who taught, guided, and shared His teachings with His apostles, including Matthew. Jesus' teachings, along with the accounts of His life, death, and resurrection, form the basis of Christian belief and practice.

While the authorship of the Gospel of Matthew is traditionally attributed to the apostle Matthew, it is important to note that this attribution is debated among scholars. Assuming that Matthew is indeed the author of this gospel, we can say that he taught about Jesus through the written account of Jesus' life, teachings, and works found in the Gospel of Matthew.

The Gospel of Matthew is one of the four canonical gospels in the New Testament, alongside Mark, Luke, and John. It is particularly significant for its focus on Jesus' teachings and fulfillment of Old Testament prophecies, which Matthew presents as evidence that Jesus is the long-awaited Messiah. Some key aspects of the Gospel of Matthew that help to teach about Jesus include:

    1. The genealogy of Jesus: Matthew traces Jesus' lineage back to Abraham, emphasizing Jesus' connection to the Jewish people and the fulfillment of God's promises to them.

    2. The birth of Jesus: Matthew recounts the miraculous events surrounding Jesus' birth, including the visit of the Magi and the flight to Egypt, highlighting Jesus' divinity and role as the promised Messiah.

    3. The Sermon on the Mount: This is one of the most famous and important sections of the Gospel of Matthew, containing a collection of Jesus' teachings on various topics, such as the Beatitudes, the Lord's Prayer, and teachings about love, forgiveness, and living a righteous life.

    4. Parables: Matthew includes many of Jesus' parables, which are short stories or illustrations that convey moral or spiritual lessons. Some well-known parables in Matthew's Gospel are the Parable of the Sower, the Parable of the Weeds, and the

Parable of the Talents.

5. Miracles: Matthew recounts numerous miracles performed by Jesus, such as healing the sick, casting out demons, and raising the dead. These miracles demonstrate Jesus' divine authority and power.

6. The Passion, Crucifixion, and Resurrection: Matthew details the events leading up to Jesus' arrest, crucifixion, and resurrection, emphasizing the fulfillment of prophecies and Jesus' role as the Savior of humanity.

By recording and organizing these events and teachings, Matthew (or the author of the Gospel of Matthew) taught about Jesus to early Christians and provided a framework for understanding Jesus' life and ministry. This gospel has been central to Christian teaching and belief for over two millennia.

Thomas Teaching Jesus

Thomas, also known as "Doubting Thomas," was one of the twelve apostles of Jesus Christ. In the New Testament, he is known for His initial skepticism and doubt regarding the resurrection of Jesus, but he ultimately came to believe and became a faithful follower of Christ.

While the specific details of Thomas's teachings are not recorded in the Bible, he is recognized as an important evangelist who played a role in spreading the message of the gospel. According to tradition, Thomas went on to preach the gospel in various places, including Parthia, India, and Persia.

In the New Testament, Thomas is described as having a questioning and analytical mind, which may have influenced his teachings. He may have emphasized the importance of understanding and seeking the truth, as well as the need for faith in Jesus Christ as the Son of God and the Savior of the world. Thomas's story also highlights the importance of personal faith and the role of doubt and questioning in the process of coming to faith. His journey from skepticism to belief can serve as an example for others who may struggle with doubts and uncertainties about their faith. Overall, Thomas's teachings would have emphasized the transformative power of the gospel and the need to live a life in accordance with God's will.

James the Lesser Teaching Jesus

James the Lesser, also known as James the Just, was one of the twelve apostles of Jesus and a leader in the early Christian Church. He is often referred to as "the Lesser" to distinguish him from James the son of Zebedee.

While relatively little is known about James the Lesser's life and teachings, he is recognized as an important figure in the spread of the gospel and the development of the early Church. According to tradition, James was known for His strict adherence to Jewish law and His emphasis on righteous living.

In the New Testament, James is described as playing a leading role in the Jerusalem Church and as a prominent figure in the Council of Jerusalem, where he argued in favor of allowing Gentile converts to Christianity without requiring them to observe all aspects of Jewish law. His teachings would have emphasized the importance of faith in Jesus Christ as the Son of God, as well as the need for living a life of obedience to God's will.

According to tradition, James was eventually martyred for his faith, being stoned to death in Jerusalem. His teachings and leadership would have played a significant role in the development of the early Church and the spread of the gospel message.

Thaddeus teaching Jesus

Thaddeus, also known as Jude or Judas (not to be confused with Judas Iscariot), was one of the twelve apostles of Jesus Christ. While relatively little is known about his life and teachings, he is recognized as an important figure in the spread of the gospel message.

In the New Testament, Thaddeus is referred to by several different names, which has led to some confusion about his identity.

However, he is generally believed to be the same person as Jude, who is mentioned in the Gospels and who wrote the book of Jude in the New Testament.

Thaddeus's teachings would have emphasized the importance of faith in Jesus Christ as the Son of God and the Savior of the world. He would have shared the message of the gospel with others and encouraged them to turn from sin and follow Christ. Like the other apostles, Thaddeus would have also performed miracles and signs to validate his message and demonstrate the power of God.

According to tradition, Thaddeus went on to preach the gospel in various places, including Syria, Mesopotamia, and Persia. He is believed to have been martyred for his faith, possibly being beaten to death with a club or an axe. While the details of his life and teachings may be limited, Thaddeus is remembered as a faithful disciple who played a vital role in the spread of Christianity.

Simon the Zealot Teaching Jesus

Simon the Zealot, also known as Simon the Canaanite, was one of the twelve apostles of Jesus Christ. While relatively little is known about his life and teachings, he is recognized as an important figure in the spread of the gospel message.

Simon is often referred to as the "Zealot," which suggests that he may have been associated with a Jewish nationalist movement known as the Zealots, which sought to overthrow Roman rule in Palestine. While the details of Simon's political affiliations are not clear, his teachings would have emphasized the importance of faith in Jesus Christ as the true Savior, rather than political or military action.

Simon's teachings would have also emphasized the need for repentance, obedience to God's will, and living a life of service to others. Like the other apostles, Simon would have performed miracles and signs to validate his message and demonstrate the power of God.

According to tradition, Simon went on to preach the gospel in various places, including Egypt and Persia. He is believed to have been martyred for His faith, possibly being crucified or sawed in half. While the details of his life and teachings may be limited, Simon the Zealot is remembered as a faithful disciple who played a vital role in the spread of Christianity.

Judas Iscariot Teaching Jesus

Judas Iscariot was one of the twelve apostles of Jesus Christ, but he is best known for his role in the betrayal of Jesus, which led to Jesus' arrest, trial, and crucifixion. As a result of his actions, Judas is often viewed as a symbol of greed, treachery, and unfaithfulness.

While it is difficult to say how Judas would have taught Jesus, given the betrayal that he ultimately carried out, it is likely that his teachings would have emphasized the importance of repentance and the need for a sincere commitment to following Jesus. The New Testament does not provide many details about Judas's teachings or beliefs, as his actions overshadowed his ministry.

However, it is clear from the Bible that Judas's betrayal of Jesus was a significant departure from the teachings of the gospel. Jesus had taught His disciples to love one another, to put others before themselves, and to follow God's will above all else. Judas's decision to betray Jesus for thirty pieces of silver was a clear violation of these teachings and demonstrated a lack of faith and commitment to Jesus as the Son of God.

Overall, while Judas was one of the twelve apostles of Jesus, His ultimate betrayal of Christ stands in contrast to the teachings of the gospel and serves as a reminder of the dangers of greed, selfishness, and unfaithfulness, dangers of greed, selfishness, and unfaithfulness.

Followers Teaching Jesus
Who Knew Him During His Human Life

John the Baptist Teaching Jesus

John the Baptist did not teach Jesus in the sense of being Jesus's instructor or mentor. Instead, John the Baptist had a prophetic role in preparing the way for Jesus's ministry and proclaiming the coming of the Messiah. John the Baptist was Jesus's relative and a key figure in the New Testament who played a significant role in the beginning of Jesus's public ministry. Here's how John the Baptist's ministry connected with that of Jesus:

    1. Preaching repentance and the coming of the Messiah: John the Baptist preached in the wilderness, calling people to repent of their sins and be baptized as a sign of their repentance. He proclaimed that the Kingdom of God was near and that the Messiah was coming soon (Matthew 3:1-2, Luke 3:3-6).

    2. Baptizing Jesus: Although John initially hesitated to baptize Jesus (since Jesus had no sin to repent), he eventually agreed at Jesus's insistence. When Jesus was baptized by John in the Jordan River, the Holy Spirit descended upon Jesus, and a voice from heaven declared, "This is my beloved Son, with whom I am well pleased" (Matthew 3:13-17). This event marked the beginning of Jesus's public ministry.

    3. Testifying about Jesus: John the Baptist recognized Jesus as the Messiah and testified about Him to His own disciples and others, pointing them toward Jesus. John referred to Jesus as "the Lamb of God, who takes away the sin of the world" (John 1:29). When His disciples asked John about Jesus's growing popularity, he responded, "He must become greater; I must become less" (John 3:30), indicating that His own ministry was secondary to that of Jesus.

    4. Fulfilling Old Testament prophecy: John the Baptist's ministry fulfilled Old Testament prophecies about the coming of a forerunner who would prepare the way for the Messiah (Isaiah

40:3, Malachi 3:1). This connection further emphasized Jesus's role as the long-awaited Savior.

While John the Baptist did not teach Jesus in a traditional sense, his ministry played a vital role in preparing the way for Jesus's ministry and directing people's attention to the coming of the Messiah. Through his preaching, baptizing, and testimony, John the Baptist helped lay the groundwork for Jesus's teachings and the establishment of the Christian faith.

Mary, Jesus's Mother, Teaching Jesus

Mary, the mother of Jesus, played a significant role in the life and teachings of Jesus, and is recognized as an important figure in the Christian faith. While relatively little is known about Mary's specific teachings, she is revered by Christians as a model of faith, devotion, and obedience to God's will.

In the New Testament, Mary is described as having been visited by an angel, who informed her that she had been chosen by God to bear a son, Jesus, who would be the Savior of the world. Mary's response to This news, which was to accept it with humility and obedience, serves as an example of faith and trust in God's plan. Throughout Jesus's life and ministry, Mary supported Him and followed Him, even through His suffering and death on the cross. Mary's presence at the foot of the cross, as her son died for the sins of the world, is a powerful testament to her faith and her commitment to God's will.

While the details of Mary's teachings are not recorded in the Bible, her example of faith and devotion to Jesus serves as an inspiration to Christians around the world. Mary's story reminds believers of the importance of humility, obedience, and trust in God's plan, and of the transformative power of faith in Jesus Christ.

Mary Magdalene Teaching Jesus

Mary Magdalene is an important figure in the New Testament

and is recognized as a faithful follower of Jesus Christ. While relatively little is known about Mary's specific teachings, she is remembered as a witness to the resurrection of Jesus and as a model of faith and devotion.

In the New Testament, Mary Magdalene is described as having been present at several key moments in Jesus's ministry, including His crucifixion and burial, and His resurrection. Mary was the first person to witness the resurrected Jesus, and she played a significant role in spreading the news of His resurrection to others.

Mary's teachings would have emphasized the importance of faith in Jesus Christ as the Son of God and the Savior of the world. She would have shared the message of the gospel with others and encouraged them to turn from sin and follow Christ. Mary's example of faithful witness to the resurrection of Jesus is a powerful testament to the transformative power of the gospel message.

According to tradition, Mary Magdalene went on to preach the gospel in various places, including Rome and France. She is believed to have been a faithful disciple of Jesus Christ, and her example of devotion and service continues to inspire believers around the world today.

Nicodemus, a Jewish Pharisee, Teaching Jesus

Nicodemus is a figure in the New Testament who is recognized as a Pharisee, a member of the Jewish ruling council, and a secret follower of Jesus Christ. While relatively little is known about Nicodemus's specific teachings, he is remembered as a model of intellectual curiosity and as an example of someone who was open to the message of the gospel.

In the New Testament, Nicodemus is described as having come to Jesus at night to ask Him questions about His teachings. Jesus engaged Nicodemus in dialogue, explaining the importance of being born again in the Spirit and the nature of the kingdom of God. Nicodemus's willingness to seek out Jesus and to engage with Him in conversation demonstrates his openness to the message of the gospel.

According to tradition, Nicodemus went on to become a Christian and to spread the message of the gospel to others. While the details of his life and teachings may be limited, Nicodemus is remembered as an example of someone who was willing to ask questions and to seek out answers about the nature of God and the meaning of life.

He is described as a Pharisee and a member of the Jewish ruling council called the Sanhedrin. Nicodemus is most prominently featured in the Gospel of John, where he had a series of interactions with Jesus.

In the Gospel of John, Nicodemus first appears in chapter 3. He visits Jesus at night, expressing his recognition that Jesus is a teacher who has come from God. This is where Jesus famously tells Nicodemus, "Truly, truly, I say to you, unless one is born again, he cannot see the kingdom of God."

Nicodemus also appears later in the Gospel of John during discussions about the arrest and crucifixion of Jesus. In John 7:50-51, Nicodemus defends Jesus when the Pharisees accuse Him without a fair hearing, saying, "Does our law judge a man without first giving Him a hearing and learning what he does?" Finally, after Jesus' crucifixion, Nicodemus, along with another Pharisee named Joseph of Arimathea, helps prepare Jesus' body for burial by providing a mixture of myrrh and aloes and wrapping it in linen cloths according to Jewish burial customs (John 19:38-42).

Nicodemus is often cited as an example of someone who initially approached Jesus with curiosity and a desire to understand His teachings. His interactions with Jesus demonstrate a gradual spiritual transformation and a willingness to challenge the status quo within His own religious community.

Overall, Nicodemus's teachings would have emphasized the importance of intellectual curiosity and openness to the message of the gospel. He would have encouraged others to seek out answers to their questions about God and to be open to the transformative power of faith in Jesus Christ.

Followers Teaching Jesus after His Human Death

Mark Teaching Jesus

The Gospel of Mark is the second of the four canonical gospels in the New Testament, which also include Matthew, Luke, and John. Although the authorship of the Gospel of Mark is traditionally attributed to John Mark, a companion of the apostle Peter, it is important to remember that the author's identity is still debated among scholars. The Gospel of Mark is traditionally attributed to Mark the Evangelist (also known as John Mark), a companion of the Apostle Peter. This attribution comes from the writings of early Church fathers such as Papias, who wrote in the second century CE that Mark had been a translator for Peter and had written down His recollections of Jesus' life and teachings. However, the Gospel itself is anonymous as it doesn't explicitly name its author within the text. Many modern scholars question the traditional attribution, citing evidence that suggests the author may have been a Greek-speaking Christian, who was not a direct witness to the events described. While these scholars agree that the Gospel was likely written in the first century CE, they note that its author is ultimately unknown.
The precise identity of the author is therefore a matter of ongoing debate and depends on one's interpretation of the available Historical and textual evidence.

The disciple Mark, also known as John Mark, is mentioned several times in the New Testament. He is traditionally considered the author of the Gospel of Mark, one of the four canonical Gospels in the New Testament.
Mark is often identified with the "John, also called Mark" mentioned in the Acts of the Apostles (Acts 12:12, 25; Acts 13:5, 13; Acts 15:37-39). He is described as a companion of both Paul

and Barnabas in their missionary journeys, and later of Peter.
In Peter's first epistle, he refers to Mark as "my son" (1 Peter 5:13), which suggests a close spiritual relationship between the two. This connection, along with early Church tradition, has led to the belief that Mark's Gospel is based on Peter's teachings about Jesus.
So, in the New Testament, this disciple is known by the names "Mark" and "John Mark". Some scholars believe that "John" was His Jewish name, while "Mark" was His Roman name.

Did Mark meet Jesus?
According to tradition and accounts in the New Testament of the Bible, Mark was a follower of Jesus. Mark is believed to be the author of the Gospel of Mark, one of the four canonical Gospels. In the New Testament, Mark is mentioned in a few instances, but there is no direct mention of him meeting Jesus during Jesus' earthly ministry. However, Mark is often associated with Peter, one of the twelve apostles, and it is believed that Mark's Gospel is based on Peter's teachings and eyewitness accounts.
Early Christian tradition holds that Mark accompanied Peter as his interpreter and assistant, and he recorded Peter's firsthand accounts of Jesus' life, teachings, and miracles to compose the Gospel of Mark. This connection between Mark and Peter suggests a close association with Jesus and an indirect relationship with Jesus' ministry.
It's important to note that the specific details of Mark's relationship with Jesus are not extensively documented in the New Testament. However, Mark's Gospel is widely recognized as an important source of information about Jesus' life and ministry, providing valuable insights into the early Christian understanding of Jesus' teachings and actions.

Assuming John Mark is indeed the author, we can discuss how he taught about Jesus through his gospel. The Gospel of Mark is considered the earliest written gospel and is characterized by its succinct and fast-paced narrative. It presents Jesus as a powerful, authoritative figure who performs miraculous deeds and teaches with authority. Here are some key aspects of the Gospel of Mark that teach about Jesus:

1. The beginning of Jesus' ministry: Mark's gospel starts with the baptism of Jesus by John the Baptist, signaling the beginning of Jesus' public ministry. It emphasizes Jesus' divine origin and mission, as God's voice declares Jesus to be His beloved Son at His baptism.

2. Miracles and exorcisms: The Gospel of Mark contains numerous accounts of Jesus performing miracles, such as healing the sick, casting out demons, and calming storms. These accounts demonstrate Jesus' divine power and authority, confirming His status as the Son of God.

3. Parables: Mark includes several parables, which are short stories or illustrations that convey moral or spiritual lessons. Some well-known parables in Mark's Gospel are the Parable of the Sower and the Parable of the Mustard Seed.

4. Teachings on discipleship: Throughout His gospel, Mark highlights the importance of discipleship and following Jesus wholeheartedly. He includes stories and teachings that emphasize the cost of discipleship, self-sacrifice, and the need to put one's faith in Jesus.

5. The Passion, Crucifixion, and Resurrection: Mark narrates the events leading up to Jesus' arrest, crucifixion, and resurrection. Although the original ending of Mark's gospel may not have included detailed post-resurrection appearances, it emphasizes Jesus' victory over death and His role as the suffering servant who redeems humanity.

By presenting these events and teachings in a concise and action-oriented manner, the Gospel of Mark teaches about Jesus and offers insights into His life and ministry. The gospel has been an essential resource for Christian teaching and belief for centuries, shaping our understanding of Jesus as the Son of God and the Savior of the world.

Luke Teaching Jesus

The Gospel of Luke is the third of the four canonical gospels in the New Testament, which also include Matthew, Mark, and John. Luke is traditionally considered to be the author of this gospel, as well as the book of Acts, and is believed to have been a physician and a companion of the apostle Paul. It is important to note, however, that the author's identity is still debated among scholars. Assuming that Luke is the author, we can discuss how he taught about Jesus through His gospel.

While there is no direct mention in the New Testament of Luke meeting Jesus during Jesus' earthly ministry, Luke is considered to have been a companion and close associate of the apostle Paul. Luke is referred to in several of Paul's letters. In the letter to Philemon (Philemon 1:24), Paul mentions Luke as one of His fellow workers. In Colossians 4:14, Paul refers to Luke as the "beloved physician." These references indicate that Luke was intimately connected to Paul's ministry and traveled with him during His missionary journeys.

It is believed that Luke gathered information about Jesus' life and teachings through interviews and research, compiling them into the Gospel of Luke. Luke's Gospel includes unique accounts and perspectives on Jesus' ministry, including parables, miracles, and teachings that are not found in the other Gospels.

While there is no explicit mention of Luke meeting Jesus during His earthly ministry, Luke played an essential role in documenting and preserving the accounts of Jesus' life and spreading the message of Christianity through His Gospel and His partnership with the apostle Paul.

The Gospel of Luke is known for its emphasis on Jesus' compassion, His concern for the marginalized, and the universal scope of His message. Luke presents Jesus as the Savior for all people, regardless of their social status or background. Here are some key aspects of the Gospel of Luke that teach about Jesus:

    1. Infancy narratives: Luke provides a detailed account of the events surrounding Jesus' birth, including the annunciation to Mary, the visit of the shepherds, and Jesus' presentation in the temple. These stories emphasize Jesus' divinity and His role as the promised Messiah.

    2. Parables: The Gospel of Luke contains many of Jesus' parables, some of which are unique to This gospel. These parables are short stories or illustrations that convey moral or spiritual

lessons. Some well-known parables in Luke's Gospel are the Parable of the Good Samaritan, the Parable of the Prodigal Son, and the Parable of the Rich Man and Lazarus.

3. Teachings on social justice and compassion: Luke emphasizes Jesus' concern for the poor, the outcasts, and the marginalized throughout His gospel. He includes teachings and stories that highlight the importance of social justice, mercy, and compassion, such as the Beatitudes, the story of Zacchaeus, and Jesus' interactions with tax collectors and sinners.

4. The role of women: Luke's gospel gives special attention to the role of women in Jesus' ministry, mentioning several women by name and recounting their involvement in Jesus' life and work.

5. Miracles and healings: Like the other gospels, Luke contains numerous accounts of Jesus performing miracles and healings, demonstrating His divine power and authority.

6. The Passion, Crucifixion, and Resurrection: Luke narrates the events leading up to Jesus' arrest, crucifixion, and resurrection, emphasizing Jesus' role as the suffering servant who redeems humanity. Luke also includes detailed accounts of Jesus' post-resurrection appearances, such as the encounter with the disciples on the road to Emmaus.

By presenting these events and teachings, the Gospel of Luke teaches about Jesus and offers insights into His life, ministry, and the universal scope of His message. This gospel has been an essential resource for Christian teaching and belief for centuries, shaping our understanding of Jesus as a compassionate Savior who brings salvation to all people.

Paul Teaching Jesus

Paul, originally known as Saul, was a zealous Pharisee who initially persecuted Christians before experiencing a dramatic conversion on the road to Damascus (Acts 9:1-19). After His conversion, Paul became one of the most influential apostles and teachers of Christianity. Here are some of the ways Paul taught about Jesus:

1. Preaching and teaching: Paul traveled extensively throughout the Roman Empire, preaching and teaching in synagogues, public spaces, and private homes. He shared the message of Jesus's life, death, resurrection, and the salvation available to all who believed in Him (Acts 13:14-52, Acts 17:16-34).

2. Establishing and nurturing churches: During his missionary journeys, Paul established numerous churches in various cities, often returning to these communities to encourage and strengthen the believers. He provided guidance, instruction, and support to the growing Christian communities (Acts 14:21-23, Acts 15:36-41, Acts 18:23).

3. Writing letters: Paul wrote numerous letters (epistles) to various churches and individuals, addressing specific issues and providing theological insights, practical guidance, and encouragement. Many of these letters are part of the New Testament and continue to shape Christian thought and practice (e.g., Romans, Corinthians, Galatians, Ephesians, Philippians, Colossians, Thessalonians, and Philemon).

4. Discipleship and mentoring: Paul invested time in mentoring and training new Christian leaders, such as Timothy and Titus. He provided them with guidance, instruction, and encouragement, helping them become effective leaders and teachers in their own right (1 Timothy, 2 Timothy, Titus).

5. Engaging with diverse audiences: Paul was skilled at engaging with different cultural and religious groups, adapting his message and approach to make it relevant and understandable to his audience. As a Roman citizen and a former Pharisee, he was uniquely positioned to communicate the Gospel to both Jews and Gentiles (Acts 17:22-31, Acts 21:27-40).

6. Debating and reasoning: Paul frequently engaged in debates and reasoned with people from various backgrounds, using his knowledge of Scripture, philosophy, and local customs to present the Gospel message persuasively (Acts 17:2-4, Acts 19:8-10).

7. Personal testimony: Paul shared his own story of conversion and transformation, providing a powerful and relatable example of the life-changing impact of faith in Jesus (Acts 22:1-21, Acts 26:9-23, Galatians 1:11-24).

8. Modeling Christ-like behavior: Paul sought to live a life that reflected the teachings of Jesus, emphasizing virtues such as love, humility, and self-sacrifice. He encouraged others to follow his example as he followed Christ (1 Corinthians 11:1, Philippians 2:1-11).

Through his preaching, writing, mentoring, and personal example, Paul had a significant impact on the early Christian Church and continues to influence Christian thought and practice to this day. (see Section IV on Books of the New Testament)

Other People Teaching Jesus

Jesus Himself is considered the most important teacher in Christianity. However, if you are asking about the people who played significant roles in spreading His teachings and shaping early Christian doctrine, several key figures stand out:

1. The Apostles: Jesus' closest followers, also known as the Twelve Disciples, were instrumental in spreading His teachings after His death and resurrection. Among them, Peter, James, and John were particularly prominent. Peter, considered the first leader of the early Christian church, played a crucial role in establishing Christianity in Jerusalem. John is traditionally believed to be the author of the Gospel of John, three Epistles, and the Book of Revelation.

2. Paul the Apostle: Originally a persecutor of Christians, Paul underwent a dramatic conversion experience and became one of the most important early Christian missionaries and theologians. He is credited with writing a significant portion of the New Testament (13 of the 27 books) in the form of Epistles or letters, which addressed various theological and practical issues facing the early Christian communities. Paul's teachings were instrumental in shaping the doctrine of salvation by faith in Jesus Christ and in spreading Christianity among Gentiles.

3. Augustine of Hippo: Augustine was a prominent theologian and philosopher of the early Christian church. His works, particularly "Confessions" and "City of God," were influential in shaping Christian theology, particularly in

areas such as original sin, grace, and the nature of the church. Augustine's teachings continue to be studied and debated by theologians today.

4. Thomas Aquinas: A medieval philosopher and theologian, Thomas Aquinas sought to reconcile Christian teachings with the philosophy of Aristotle. His magnum opus, the "Summa Theologica," represents an extensive synthesis of Christian theology and philosophy. Aquinas' work laid the foundation for much of Roman Catholic theology and contributed significantly to the development of Christian thought.

5. Martin Luther: A 16th-century German monk and theologian, Martin Luther was a key figure in the Protestant Reformation. His critique of certain practices within the Catholic Church, along with His emphasis on salvation by faith alone and the authority of the Bible, led to a major schism in Western Christianity and the emergence of Protestant denominations. Luther's teachings have had a lasting impact on the course of Christian History.

These are just a few of the many important teachers in the history of Christianity. Each of these figures has made significant contributions to the understanding, interpretation, and spread of Jesus' teachings, shaping Christian theology and practice in various ways throughout History.

Section III
How We Teach Jesus Today

1. Teaching Jesus Today - Sermons, Bible Study Groups, etc.
2. Teaching Jesus through Media and Technology
3. Teaching Jesus in Movies, TV, Music, Art and Poetry
4. Teaching Jesus in Personal Evangelism and Prayer

Teaching Jesus Today

People are teaching Jesus today through various methods, aiming to spread His teachings and share the message of the Gospel with others. Some common ways people are teaching Jesus include:

1. Church sermons: Pastors, priests, and other religious leaders deliver sermons in churches and places of worship, explaining and interpreting the life and teachings of Jesus, as well as their relevance to contemporary life.

2. Bible study groups: Many churches and communities organize Bible study groups where people gather to study the Scriptures together, discuss their meanings, and learn more about Jesus and His teachings.

3. Chris tian education: Christian schools, Sunday schools, and religious education programs teach children and adults about Jesus, His life, and His teachings through a structured curriculum.

4. Theological institutions: Seminaries and theological colleges offer higher education and training for those pursuing careers in ministry, theology, or religious education. These institutions provide in-depth study of the Bible and the life of Jesus.

5. Christian literature: Books, articles, and commentaries on the Bible and the life of Jesus help people learn more about Him and His teachings. These works can range from scholarly examinations to more accessible materials for general audiences.

6. Media and technology: Films, documentaries, podcasts, and online resources provide diverse platforms for teaching about Jesus. Digital platforms, such as social media and websites, allow

for the sharing of Christian content and discussions about Jesus's life and teachings.

7. Personal evangelism: Individual Christians share their faith with others through personal conversations, testimonies, and acts of kindness, following Jesus's command to "go and make disciples of all nations" (Matthew 28:19).

8. Art and music: Christian artists and musicians express the life and teachings of Jesus through various art forms, such as paintings, sculptures, hymns, and contemporary Christian music.

9. Retreats, conferences, and workshops: Special events and gatherings focused on Christian spirituality and teaching provide opportunities for people to deepen their understanding of Jesus and His message.

By utilizing these various methods, people continue to teach about Jesus and share His message of love, forgiveness, and salvation with others, both within the Christian community and beyond.

Teaching Jesus in Church Sermons

Church sermons can vary depending on the specific denomination, tradition, and style of the church. However, here are some common elements and approaches that are often used when teaching in church sermons:

1. Scripture Reading: Sermons typically begin with the reading of a passage from the Bible. This sets the foundation for the teaching and provides the biblical basis for the message.

2. Exposition of Scripture: The sermon usually involves an in-depth explanation and interpretation of the selected biblical passage. The preacher may explore the historical context, literary style, and original meaning of the text to help the congregation understand its intended message.

3. Application: The preacher then seeks to apply the teachings of the Scripture to the lives of the congregation. This involves making relevant connections between the biblical message and the challenges, joys, and circumstances faced

by the listeners. The aim is to provide practical guidance, encouragement, and inspiration for daily Christian living.

4. Illustrations and Examples: Sermons often incorporate real-life illustrations, stories, or examples to help illustrate and reinforce the main points. These illustrations can help make the teaching more relatable and memorable for the listeners.

5. Personal Reflection and Testimony: Preachers may share their personal experiences, insights, or testimonies related to the sermon topic. This adds a personal touch and helps establish a connection with the congregation.

6. Worship and Prayer: Sermons are often situated within a worship service, which may include singing hymns or contemporary worship songs. Prayers may be offered before, during, or after the sermon, seeking God's guidance, wisdom, and transformation in response to the teaching.

7. Invitation and Response: Some sermons include an invitation for the congregation to respond to the message. This could involve an altar call for prayer, an opportunity for confession or rededication, or a call to action in serving others or sharing the gospel.

8. Conclusion: Sermons typically end with a summarizing statement or a call to remember and apply the teachings of the sermon in the upcoming week.

It's important to note that sermon styles and approaches can vary greatly. Some sermons may be more lecture-style, focusing on teaching and exegesis, while others may be more interactive or emphasize emotional engagement. The goal is to effectively communicate the Word of God, provide spiritual nourishment, and facilitate growth and transformation in the lives of the listeners.

Teaching Jesus in Bible Study Groups

Teaching Bible study groups involves facilitating a small group setting where participants can delve deeper into the study and application of the Bible. Here are some general steps and considerations for effectively teaching Bible study groups:

1. Preparation:
- Select a specific passage, book, or topic from the Bible for study.
- Study the selected material yourself, using commentaries, study guides, or other resources to gain a deeper understanding.
- Prepare discussion questions and key points to guide the study and facilitate group interaction.

2. Create a Welcoming Environment:
- Set up a comfortable and inviting space for the Bible study group.
- Begin the session with a time of fellowship and building relationships among participants.
- Create an atmosphere of respect, openness, and inclusivity where everyone feels comfortable sharing their thoughts and questions.

3. Introduction and Context:
 Begin the Bible study session with a brief introduction, providing background information about the selected passage, book, or topic.
- Share any relevant historical, cultural, or theological context that can help participants understand the text better.

4. Reading and Study:
- Read the selected Bible passage aloud, allowing participants to follow along in their own Bibles.
- Encourage participants to ask questions, share their initial observations, and discuss their understanding of the text.
- Guide the study by highlighting key themes, significant details, and relevant cross-references.

5. Facilitate Discussion:
- Ask thought-provoking questions to stimulate discussion and engage participants. Encourage everyone to share their insights, interpretations, and personal applications of the Scripture.
- Actively listen to participants' contributions and ensure that different perspectives are respected and valued.

- Provide clarifications or explanations when needed, but also allow room for participants to explore and discover answers together.

6. Application and Reflection:
- Help participants bridge the gap between the ancient text and their everyday lives by discussing practical applications.
- Encourage participants to reflect on how the Scripture passage or topic can impact their attitudes, beliefs, relationships, and actions.
- Facilitate a discussion on how the Bible study can be lived out in practical ways within the group and individually.

7. Prayer and Closing:
- Conclude the Bible study session with a time of prayer, allowing participants to share their prayer requests and intercede for one another.
- Summarize the main insights and takeaways from the study.
- Provide any necessary follow-up resources, readings, or assignments for participants to deepen their understanding or continue personal study.

Remember that teaching Bible study groups involves both guiding the discussion and facilitating meaningful interaction among participants. It is essential to create a supportive environment where participants can grow spiritually, learn from one another, and apply the teachings of the Bible to their lives.

Some Common Bible Study Programs Today

There are several popular Bible study programs and resources used by individuals and churches around the world. Please keep in mind that new programs may have emerged since then. Here are some common Bible study programs that were widely used at the time:

1. YouVersion Bible App: Developed by Life.Church, the YouVersion Bible App is a free application offering various

Bible translations, reading plans, devotionals, and multimedia resources. It's available on multiple platforms and has a large user base.

2. Logos Bible Software: Created by Faithlife, Logos Bible Software provides a comprehensive digital library of Bibles, commentaries, theological resources, and study tools. It caters to scholars, pastors, and anyone interested in in-depth Bible study.

3. Bible Study Fellowship (BSF): BSF is an international interdenominational Bible study program with structured study materials and classes held in various locations. It offers in-depth Bible study and encourages group discussions.

4. Precept Ministries International: Precept Ministries focuses on inductive Bible study methods. They provide study guides and resources to help individuals and groups dig into the Bible verse by verse.

5. The Bible Project: While not a traditional study program, The Bible Project offers free animated videos, podcasts, and other resources to help people understand the overarching themes and messages of each book of the Bible.

6. Community Bible Study (CBS): CBS is another interdenominational Bible study program that offers comprehensive study courses and materials for both individuals and groups.

7. She Reads Truth and He Reads Truth: These are separate Bible study programs designed for women (She Reads Truth) and men (He Reads Truth). They provide devotionals, study plans, and resources for understanding the Bible.

8. InSight Bible Study: This program focuses on inductive Bible study methods, with tools and guides to aid in personal or group study.

9. Bible Study Tools Online: Websites like BibleStudyTools.com and BibleGateway.com offer a wide range of Bible translations, commentaries, concordances, and study resources for free.

Please note that the popularity and availability of these programs may vary depending on your location and language preferences.

Teaching Jesus in Christian Education

Teaching Jesus in Christian education is central to sharing the message of the Gospel and helping individuals understand and grow in their faith. Here are some key considerations for effectively teaching about Jesus:

1. Study the Life and Teachings of Jesus:
   - Immerse yourself in the Gospels to gain a deep understanding of Jesus' life, teachings, ministry, and interactions with people.
   - Familiarize yourself with the key events, parables, miracles, and teachings of Jesus recorded in the New Testament.

2. Emphasize Jesus' Identity:
   - Teaching Jesus as the Son of God, the Messiah, and the Savior of humanity.
   - Explain the significance of Jesus' divinity and humanity, emphasizing His unique role in God's plan for salvation.

3. Present Jesus' Message:
   - Highlight the core teachings of Jesus, such as love, forgiveness, humility, compassion, and the Kingdom of God.
   - Examine His ethical and moral teachings, addressing topics such as mercy, justice, serving others, and living a life pleasing to God.

4. Explore Jesus' Miracles and Signs:
   - Discuss the miracles and signs performed by Jesus, such as healings, exorcisms, nature miracles, and the raising of the dead.
   - Explain the purpose and significance of these miracles in revealing Jesus' power, compassion, and authority as the Son of God.

5. Teach about Jesus' Death and Resurrection:
   - Explain the significance of Jesus' sacrificial death on the cross, emphasizing His atoning work and the forgiveness of sins through His shed blood.
   - Discuss the transformative power of Jesus' resurrection,

highlighting its victory over sin, death, and the hope it brings to believers.

6. Connect Jesus to Old Testament Prophecies:
- Show how Jesus fulfilled numerous prophecies from the Old Testament, demonstrating His messianic identity and the continuity between the Old and New Testaments.
- Discuss specific prophecies related to Jesus' birth, ministry, death, and resurrection.

7. Encourage Personal Relationship with Jesus:
- Teach about the importance of personal faith in Jesus Christ and the need for repentance, acceptance, and surrender to Him as Lord and Savior.
- Encourage participants to develop a personal relationship with Jesus through prayer, studying the Word, and following His teachings.

8. Emphasize Jesus' Role as the Model and Example:
- Showcase Jesus as the ultimate example of faith, obedience, humility, and love.
- Encourage participants to imitate Jesus' character and actions in their own lives, reflecting His love and grace to others.

9. Foster Worship and Devotion:
- Include opportunities for worship, prayer, and reflection that focus on Jesus, His attributes, and His work in the lives of believers.
- Encourage participants to deepen their personal worship and devotion to Jesus.

Remember, teaching Jesus in Christian education is not just about conveying information but also fostering a personal encounter and transformational experience with Him. It is essential to approach the teaching with reverence, love, and a genuine desire to draw people closer to Jesus Christ.

Well Know Examples of Christian Education Today

As of my last update in September 2021, there were several well-known examples of Christian education institutions and programs around the world. Please note that the status and prominence of these institutions may have evolved since then. Here are some widely recognized examples:

1 Liberty University: Located in Lynchburg, Virginia, USA, Liberty University is one of the largest and most well-known Christian universities in the world. It offers a wide range of undergraduate and graduate programs with a Christian perspective.

2. Biola University: Based in La Mirada, California, USA, Biola University is a private Christian university offering various undergraduate and graduate degrees with a strong emphasis on biblical integration.

3. Wheaton College: Located in Wheaton, Illinois, USA, Wheaton College is a prominent Christian liberal arts college with a strong commitment to the integration of faith and learning.

4. Gordon College: Situated in Wenham, Massachusetts, USA, Gordon College is another reputable Christian liberal arts college that emphasizes Christian faith and values in its academic programs.

5. Oral Roberts University: Based in Tulsa, Oklahoma, USA, Oral Roberts University is a Christian university known for its emphasis on spiritual life and education.

6. Regent University: Located in Virginia Beach, Virginia, USA, Regent University is a Christian institution offering a wide range of graduate and undergraduate programs with a focus on faith-based education.

7. Loyola Marymount University: Located in Los Angeles, California, USA, Loyola Marymount University is a Catholic institution that combines academic excellence with a strong Jesuit tradition.

8. Saint John's University and College of Saint Benedict: These two institutions, located in Minnesota, USA, are renowned for their Benedictine heritage and commitment to Catholic education.

9. King's College London (Department of Theology and Religious Studies): While not a Christian institution, King's College London houses a distinguished Department of Theology and Religious Studies with a reputation for its scholarly approach

to Christianity and other religions.

10. Trinity Evangelical Divinity School (TEDS): TEDS is a prominent seminary located in Deerfield, Illinois, USA, and is affiliated with Trinity International University.

These are just a few examples of Christian education institutions that were well-known at the time of my last update. Many other Christian universities, colleges, seminaries, and schools exist worldwide, offering various educational programs and degrees with a Christian perspective. Always verify the current status and reputation of any educational institution before making decisions related to your education.

Well Know Examples of Christian Education in K-12 Today

There were several well-known Christian K-12 education institutions and programs around the world. Please keep in mind that the status and prominence of these institutions may have evolved since then, and there may be other notable schools that have emerged. Here are some widely recognized examples:

1. Lutheran Schools: Lutheran K-12 schools, affiliated with various Lutheran denominations, are well-known for providing Christian education with a Lutheran perspective.

2. Catholic Schools: Catholic K-12 schools, run by the Roman Catholic Church and various Catholic religious orders, are widespread and highly regarded for their emphasis on Catholic teachings and values.

3. Christian Schools Association: Many countries have Christian school associations that oversee and support a network of Christian K-12 schools. Examples include the Association of Christian Schools International (ACSI) and Christian Schools Australia (CSA).

4. Adventist Schools: Seventh-day Adventist K-12 schools are known for their emphasis on the teachings of the Seventh-day Adventist Church.

5. Calvinist or Reformed Schools: Some Christian K-12 schools align with Calvinist or Reformed theological traditions and integrate these perspectives into their curriculum and

teachings.

6. Classical Christian Schools: These schools emphasize a classical education model infused with Christian principles and teachings.

7. Christian Montessori Schools: Christian Montessori schools combine the Montessori educational approach with Christian values and teachings.

8. Christian Homeschooling Programs: Homeschooling families often use Christian homeschooling curricula and resources that align with their faith.

9. Christian International Schools: In some countries, there are international schools that cater to expatriate families and offer a Christian education with a global perspective.

It's important to note that the availability and popularity of these schools may vary depending on the country and region. Additionally, the specific focus and denomination of each Christian K-12 school can differ, even within the same broader category. If you are interested in finding a Christian K-12 school for yourself or your children, research local options, consider visiting the schools, and assess how well they align with your educational and spiritual values.

Teaching Jesus in Theological Institutions

In theological institutions, teaching Jesus takes on a more in-depth and scholarly approach, focusing on theological and doctrinal aspects. Here are some key considerations for teaching about Jesus in theological institutions:

1. Christology:
- Explore the theological study of Christology, which examines the nature, person, and work of Jesus Christ.
- Discuss different theological perspectives on the divinity and humanity of Jesus, such as the hypostatic union and the Incarnation.

2. Biblical Studies:
- Engage in detailed exegesis and analysis of the New Testament texts that describe the life, teachings, and

ministry of Jesus.
- Discuss Historical and cultural contexts, literary genres, and the critical study of the Gospels to deepen understanding.

3. Theological Frameworks:
- Present various theological frameworks, such as soteriology (study of salvation), atonement theories, and the Kingdom of God, to help students grasp the significance of Jesus' work in salvation History.

4. Historical and Cultural Context:
- Provide Historical and cultural background information to better understand the socio-political, religious, and philosophical context in which Jesus lived and ministered.

5. Church History:
- Examine the development of Christology and the understanding of Jesus in the early church and throughout church History.
- Explore the theological debates, ecumenical councils, and major Christological controversies, such as the Arian controversy and the Chalcedonian Definition.

6. Comparative Religions:
- Engage in comparative studies to understand how Jesus is perceived and understood in other religious traditions.
- Examine the uniqueness of Jesus' claims and the Christian understanding of His role in comparison to other religious figures.

7. Theological Reflection and Integration:
- Encourage students to reflect on the implications of Jesus' teachings and work for contemporary theology, ethics, and social issues.
- Explore how Jesus' life and teachings inform Christian responses to justice, peace, poverty, and other pressing societal concerns.

8. Practical Implications:
- Help students bridge theological understanding with practical ministry and leadership applications.
- Discuss how the knowledge of Jesus and Christology

shapes pastoral care, preaching, worship, and discipleship in ministry contexts.

9. Research and Scholarship:
- Encourage students to engage in academic research, write papers, and contribute to the ongoing scholarly discourse on Jesus and Christology.
- Support students in developing critical thinking, research skills, and the ability to engage with diverse theological perspectives.

Teaching about Jesus in theological institutions involves a combination of biblical scholarship, theological reflection, historical analysis, and critical thinking. It aims to equip students with a deep understanding of Jesus' significance within Christian theology and to inspire them to integrate This knowledge into their personal faith, ministry, and scholarly pursuits.

Examples of Theological Institutions Today

There are several well-known theological institutions around the world that offer high-quality education and training in theology and related disciplines. These institutions are recognized for their academic excellence, historical significance, and contributions to theological scholarship. Please note that the status and prominence of these institutions may have evolved and there may be other notable institutions that have emerged. Here are some widely recognized theological institutions:

1. Harvard Divinity School: Located in Cambridge, Massachusetts, USA, Harvard Divinity School is one of the oldest and most prestigious theological schools in the world, offering a wide range of programs and disciplines within theology and religious studies.

2. Yale Divinity School: Situated in New Haven, Connecticut, USA, Yale Divinity School is known for its rigorous academic programs and diverse theological perspectives.

3. Princeton Theological Seminary: Located in Princeton, New Jersey, USA, Princeton Theological Seminary is one of the oldest seminaries in the United States, with a strong focus on

Reformed theology.

 4. University of Oxford (Faculty of Theology and Religion): Oxford University in the United Kingdom has a distinguished Faculty of Theology and Religion with a long history of theological scholarship.

 5. University of Cambridge (Faculty of Divinity): Cambridge University, also in the United Kingdom, has a Faculty of Divinity known for its academic excellence in theology and religious studies.

 6. University of Notre Dame (Department of Theology): Located in Indiana, USA, the University of Notre Dame is well-known for its Catholic theological studies and ecumenical approach.

 7. Duke Divinity School: Situated in Durham, North Carolina, USA, Duke Divinity School is a leading institution offering diverse theological programs.

 8. Vatican's Pontifical Universities: The Vatican oversees several pontifical universities in Rome, Italy, which provide advanced studies in theology and related fields. Some notable ones include the Pontifical Gregorian University and the Pontifical Urbaniana University.

 9. Fuller Theological Seminary: With campuses in California and online programs, Fuller Theological Seminary is renowned for its interdenominational approach and emphasis on practical theology.

 10. Emory University (Candler School of Theology): Located in Atlanta, Georgia, USA, Emory University's Candler School of Theology offers a diverse and inclusive theological education.

These institutions represent just a few examples of well-known theological schools. Many other reputable seminaries, divinity schools, and faculties of theology exist worldwide, each contributing to the exploration and study of theological matters. When considering theological education, it's essential to research the specific programs, faculty, and denominational affiliations to find the best fit for one's academic and spiritual needs.

Teaching Jesus through Christian Literature

Teaching Jesus in Christian literature involves exploring the portrayal and significance of Jesus in various forms of written works, including books, novels, poetry, and other forms of literary expression. Here are some key considerations for teaching about Jesus in Christian literature:

1. Selection of Literary Works:
- Choose literary works that explicitly or implicitly address themes related to Jesus, His life, teachings, or the impact of His ministry.
- Include a variety of genres and authors to provide a diverse range of perspectives and styles.

2. Analysis of Characterization:
- Examine how Jesus is portrayed as a character in the literature. Analyze the author's portrayal of His personality, actions, and relationships with other characters.
- Discuss how the literary depiction of Jesus aligns with biblical accounts and Christian theological understanding.

3. Exploration of Themes:
- Identify and discuss recurring themes related to Jesus, such as love, sacrifice, redemption, forgiveness, and the Kingdom of God.
- Analyze how these themes are developed, explored, or challenged within the literary works.

4. Symbolism and Allegory:
- Explore the use of symbolism, allegory, and metaphor in literary works to convey deeper spiritual or theological truths about Jesus.
- Discuss how Jesus is represented symbolically or metaphorically and the implications of these representations.

5. Engagement with Context:
- Examine the historical, cultural, and social context in which the literary works were written.
- Discuss how the author's cultural and religious

background influences their portrayal of Jesus and the message they convey.

6. Literary Analysis:
- Utilize literary analysis techniques to examine the narrative structure, plot, character development, and other elements of the literature.
- Consider the literary devices and techniques employed by the authors to convey their understanding of Jesus and His significance.

7. Integration of Theology:
- Discuss how the literary works engage with theological concepts, doctrines, or biblical narratives related to Jesus.
- Explore how the literature contributes to theological reflection, understanding, and dialogue.

8. Reader Response and Reflection:
- Encourage readers to reflect on their personal response to the literature and its portrayal of Jesus.
- Discuss how the literature impacts readers' understanding of Jesus, their faith, and their relationship with Him.

9. Application and Implications:
- Explore how the themes, symbolism, and characterizations in the literature can inform and inspire the readers' Christian life and discipleship.
- Encourage readers to consider how the literary works can deepen their understanding of Jesus and impact their relationship with Him.

Teaching Jesus in Christian literature offers an opportunity to engage with artistic and imaginative expressions of faith. It encourages readers to explore diverse perspectives, deepen their understanding of Jesus, and reflect on their own spiritual journey. The focus is on integrating literary analysis, theological reflection, and personal response to inspire a deeper appreciation for Jesus' significance in Christian literature.

Examples of Christian Literature

There are several well-known examples of Christian literature that have had a significant impact on the Christian faith and have been widely read and celebrated. Here are some of the most notable examples:

1. The Bible: The Bible is the foundational text of the Christian faith and is divided into the Old Testament and the New Testament. It contains a collection of sacred scriptures, including historical accounts, poetry, prophecy, teachings, and letters, all of which are considered sacred and authoritative by Christians worldwide.

2. Pilgrim's Progress by John Bunyan: Published in 1678, Pilgrim's Progress is an allegorical novel that depicts the journey of a Christian pilgrim named Christian, who travels from the City of Destruction to the Celestial City. It has been widely read and translated into numerous languages, making it one of the most popular Christian books of all time.

3. Mere Christianity by C.S. Lewis: Mere Christianity, published in 1952, is a book by C.S. Lewis that presents a systematic defense and explanation of the Christian faith. It addresses core Christian beliefs and explores moral and theological concepts, making it a widely read and influential work in Christian apologetics.

4. The Divine Comedy by Dante Alighieri: The Divine Comedy, written by Dante Alighieri in the 14th century, is an epic poem divided into three parts: Inferno, Purgatorio, and Paradiso. It follows Dante's journey through Hell, Purgatory, and Heaven, exploring themes of sin, redemption, and divine love.

5. The Imitation of Christ by Thomas à Kempis: Published in the 15th century, The Imitation of Christ is a devotional book that offers practical guidance on Christian spirituality and the pursuit of a deeper relationship with God. It emphasizes the imitation of Christ's life and teachings as a means of spiritual growth.

6. Confessions by Augustine of Hippo: Confessions, written by Augustine of Hippo in the 4th century, is an autobiographical work that recounts Augustine's spiritual journey, struggles, and conversion to Christianity. It addresses themes of sin, grace, and the search for truth, making it one of the

most influential works in Christian literature.

      7. The Chronicles of Narnia by C.S. Lewis: The Chronicles of Narnia is a series of seven fantasy novels by C.S. Lewis. Although primarily seen as children's literature, the series incorporates Christian allegory and explores theological themes, including redemption, sacrifice, and the nature of God.

      8. The Hiding Place by Corrie ten Boom: The Hiding Place is an autobiographical book by Corrie ten Boom, published in 1971. It tells the story of ten Boom's experiences during the Holocaust and her family's efforts to hide Jews from the Nazis. The book reflects her Christian faith and the power of forgiveness and love in the face of adversity.

These are just a few examples of Christian literature that have left a lasting impact on readers and contributed to the spiritual and intellectual growth of individuals throughout history.

Teaching Jesus Through Media and Technology

Teaching Jesus in the realm of media and technology provides opportunities to reach a wide audience and engage with individuals through various digital platforms. Here are some ways people teach about Jesus in media and technology:
      1. Online Sermons and Preaching:
    • Utilize video streaming platforms or websites to deliver sermons and teachings about Jesus to a global audience.
    • Present engaging and dynamic sermons that incorporate multimedia elements, such as visuals, graphics, and video clips, to enhance the message.
      2. Podcasts and Audio Content:
    • Create and distribute podcasts or audio recordings that focus on teaching about Jesus, His life, teachings, and the significance of His work.
    • Engage listeners through interviews, discussions, and narrative storytelling to convey the message effectively.
      3. Christian Video Channels and Websites:
    • Develop Christian video channels or websites that offer

a variety of video content related to Jesus, including teachings, interviews, documentaries, and testimonies.
• Curate and produce high-quality videos that present Jesus in a compelling and accessible manner.

4. Mobile Apps and Devotionals:
• Design mobile applications and devotionals that provide users with daily teachings, meditations, and reflections on Jesus and His teachings.
• Incorporate multimedia elements, such as videos, audio recordings, and interactive features, to enhance the learning experience.

5. Social Media and Online Communities:
• Leverage social media platforms to share short teachings, Bible verses, and inspirational content related to Jesus.
• Foster online communities and discussion forums where individuals can connect, ask questions, and engage in meaningful conversations about Jesus and their faith.

6. Online Courses and Webinars:
• Develop online courses and webinars that focus on specific aspects of Jesus' life, teachings, or theological concepts related to Him.
• Utilize interactive features, such as quizzes, discussion boards, and live Q&A sessions, to enhance engagement and promote deeper understanding.

7. Visual Media and Films:
• Produce Christian films or documentaries that explore Jesus' life, teachings, and the impact of His ministry.
• Utilize visual storytelling techniques to engage viewers emotionally and intellectually.

8. Online Study Resources and E-books:
• Create and share digital study resources, e-books, and study guides that delve into Jesus' life, teachings, and theological concepts.
• Provide online resources that allow individuals to deepen their understanding of Jesus at their own pace.

9. Virtual Reality (VR) and Augmented Reality (AR):
• Utilize emerging technologies such as VR and AR to

create immersive experiences that bring biblical stories and teachings about Jesus to life.
- Develop virtual tours or interactive experiences that allow users to explore significant biblical locations related to Jesus.

When teaching Jesus in media and technology, it is important to ensure that the content remains faithful to biblical teachings and aligns with sound Christian theology. The goal is to utilize digital platforms and media tools to effectively communicate the message of Jesus and make His teachings accessible to individuals in an engaging and transformative way.

Movies Teaching Jesus

Many movies have been created over the years teaching Jesus and share His life, teachings, and impact on humanity. These films often depict key events from Jesus's life, drawing from the Gospels and Historical research. They aim to inspire, educate, and entertain viewers while presenting the message of Christianity. Some notable movies about Jesus include:

 1. The King of Kings (1927): Directed by Cecil B. DeMille, this silent film is one of the earliest cinematic depictions of Jesus's life, focusing on His last weeks, crucifixion, and resurrection.

 2. The Gospel According to St. Matthew (1964): Directed by Pier Paolo Pasolini, This Italian film presents the life of Jesus as told in the Gospel of Matthew. The movie is known for its naturalistic style and unique artistic approach.

 3. The Greatest Story Ever Told (1965): Directed by George Stevens, this epic film chronicles the life of Jesus from His birth to His resurrection. With an all-star cast, the movie was a significant production of its time.

 4. Jesus Christ Superstar (1973): Directed by Norman Jewison, this film is an adaptation of the popular rock opera by Andrew Lloyd Webber and Tim Rice. It presents the story of Jesus's last week in a modern and musical context, exploring the relationships between Jesus, Judas, and Mary Magdalene.

5. Jesus of Nazareth (1977): Directed by Franco Zeffirelli, This Italian-British miniseries provides a detailed portrayal of Jesus's life, from His birth to His resurrection. The series features an impressive international cast and is known for its historical accuracy and attention to detail.

6. The Last Temptation of Christ (1988): Directed by Martin Scorsese and based on the novel by Nikos Kazantzakis, this film explores the human side of Jesus, focusing on His internal struggles and temptations. The movie sparked controversy for its unconventional portrayal of Jesus but is considered a thought-provoking work of art.

7. The Passion of the Christ (2004): Directed by Mel Gibson, this film portrays the final 12 hours of Jesus's life, emphasizing His suffering and crucifixion. The movie is known for its graphic violence, emotional intensity, and the use of Aramaic, Latin, and Hebrew languages.

8. Son of God (2014): Produced by Roma Downey and Mark Burnett, this film is an adaptation of the miniseries "The Bible" and presents a more traditional portrayal of Jesus's life, teachings, crucifixion, and resurrection.

These movies and others have helped to share the story of Jesus with millions of people worldwide. While they differ in style, approach, and interpretation, their goal is teaching Jesus and inspire faith and reflection on His life and message.

TV Shows Teaching Jesus

While there aren't many mainstream TV shows entirely dedicated to teaching Jesus, there have been some notable TV programs that feature Jesus or explore Christian themes. Here are a few examples:

1. "The Chosen" (2019-present):
   - "The Chosen" is a multi-season TV series that portrays the life of Jesus Christ and His interactions with His disciples and other characters from the Gospels. It aims to provide a n authentic and intimate portrayal of Jesus and His ministry.

2. "The Bible" (2013):
• "The Bible" is a miniseries that presents various biblical stories and characters, including Jesus, in a dramatic and visually captivating format. It covers both the Old and New Testaments, with episodes dedicated to the life, death, and resurrection of Jesus.

3. "A.D. The Bible Continues" (2015):
• "A.D. The Bible Continues" is a follow-up series to "The Bible," focusing on the events following Jesus' crucifixion and resurrection. It depicts the early days of the Christian movement and the challenges faced by the disciples as they spread the teachings of Jesus.

4. "The Gospel of John" (2003):
• "The Gospel of John" is a film adaptation of the biblical Gospel of John. It presents a word-for-word retelling of the Gospel narrative, highlighting Jesus' ministry, teachings, miracles, and the ultimate sacrifice on the cross.

5. "VeggieTales" (1993-2015):
• While not specifically centered on Jesus, "VeggieTales" is a beloved children's animated series that incorporates Christian values, biblical stories, and moral lessons. Episodes often include references to Jesus and His teachings in an accessible and entertaining manner.

6. "Jesus of Nazareth" (1977):
• "Jesus of Nazareth" is a miniseries that offers a detailed and comprehensive portrayal of the life of Jesus Christ, covering His birth, ministry, crucifixion, and resurrection. It features a star-studded cast and has been highly regarded for its accurate and reverent portrayal of Jesus.

These TV shows provide opportunities to explore Jesus' life, teachings, and the biblical narratives in a visual and engaging format. While not exhaustive, they offer a starting point for those seeking TV programs that touch upon Jesus and Christian themes.

How Does the TV Show The Chosen Teach Jesus?

"The Chosen" is a television drama series created, directed, and co-written by Dallas Jenkins. It portrays the life of Jesus Christ through the eyes of those who encountered Him, including His disciples and other people He interacted with during His ministry. The show presents a unique perspective on Jesus's life and teachings by focusing on the lives of His followers and their personal experiences with Him. Here's how "The Chosen" teaches Jesus:

1. Humanizing Jesus and His followers: The show brings Jesus, His disciples, and other biblical figures to life by portraying them as relatable, multi-dimensional characters with their own struggles, hopes, and dreams. This helps viewers connect with Jesus and His teachings on a more personal level.

2. Exploring Jesus's teachings: "The Chosen" delves into Jesus's teachings by presenting various scenes where Jesus shares parables, preaches to the crowds, and engages in conversations with His disciples and others. This allows viewers to see the context in which these teachings were given and how they impacted the lives of those who heard them.

3. Depicting Jesus's miracles: The show includes several episodes that depict Jesus performing miracles, such as healing the sick, casting out demons, and raising the dead. These miracles highlight Jesus's divine nature and emphasize His compassion and love for humanity.

4. Portraying Jesus's relationships: "The Chosen" emphasizes the relationships Jesus formed with His disciples and others during His ministry. These relationships reveal Jesus's character and how His interactions with others transformed their lives.

5. Focusing on personal transformation: The show highlights the transformative power of encountering Jesus and how it changed the lives of those who followed Him. By presenting the individual stories of His followers, "The Chosen" allows viewers to witness the impact of Jesus's teachings and the profound changes they brought about in the lives of those who encountered Him.

6. Encouraging deeper exploration: "The Chosen" inspires viewers to engage more deeply with the Bible and Jesus's teachings. By presenting a fresh perspective on familiar biblical stories, the show invites viewers to explore the Gospels and other biblical texts for themselves.

While "The Chosen" is a creative interpretation of the Gospel accounts and not a strict retelling of the biblical narrative, it serves as a valuable resource for teaching Jesus and fostering a deeper understanding of His life, ministry, and impact on those who encountered Him.

Social Media Teaching Jesus

Social media has become a powerful tool for sharing information, connecting people, and spreading messages, including messages about faith and spirituality. While the specific ways in which social media is used to teach Jesus may vary, there are several common methods that are employed.

One way that social media is used to teach Jesus is through the sharing of Bible verses, devotional readings, and other forms of spiritual content. Social media platforms provide a platform for individuals and organizations to share inspirational messages and to connect with others who are interested in learning more about the Christian faith.

Another way that social media is used to teach Jesus is through the sharing of personal testimonies and stories of faith. Social media users can share their own experiences of encountering God's love and grace and can use their stories to inspire and encourage others who may be struggling with their own faith journeys.

Social media is also used to promote events, such as church services, conferences, and retreats, that provide opportunities for people to learn more about Jesus and to connect with other believers. These events can be promoted through social media platforms, allowing individuals and organizations to reach a wider audience and to invite others to join them in their faith journey.

There are many ways that people use social media teaching Jesus. Here are a few examples:

1. Sharing Bible verses and devotional readings: Many people use social media to share Bible verses and devotional readings with their followers. This can include posting a daily Bible verse, sharing a devotional thought, or posting a prayer or meditation.

2. Sharing personal testimonies: People can use social media to share their own stories of how they have encountered Jesus and how their lives have been transformed by their faith. This can include sharing photos, videos, or written posts that detail their experiences.

3. Promoting events: Social media is a powerful tool for promoting events that teach Jesus, such as church services, retreats, conferences, and more. By sharing information about these events on social media, people can reach a wider audience and invite others to participate.

4. Connecting with others: Social media provides a way for people to connect with others who are interested in learning more about Jesus. This can include joining online communities, participating in online discussions, and following individuals and organizations that share messages about faith and spirituality.

5. Sharing inspirational content: People can use social media to share inspirational content, such as uplifting quotes, encouraging messages, and stories of hope and healing. By sharing positive messages, people can help to spread hope and positivity in their social media networks.

Overall, social media provides a powerful tool for teaching Jesus, and it allows people to connect with others in new and meaningful ways. By using social media to share messages of faith and spirituality, people can help to spread the message of the gospel and inspire others to learn more about Jesus.

Popular Social Media Teaching Jesus

It is difficult to determine which social media platform that teaches Jesus is the most popular, as this may vary depending on factors such as region, language, and target audience. However, some of the most popular social media platforms for sharing messages about faith and spirituality include:

1. Facebook: With over 2.8 billion monthly active users, Facebook is one of the largest social media platforms in the world. Many churches, religious organizations, and individuals use Facebook to share Bible verses, devotional readings, and inspirational messages with their followers.

2. Instagram: Instagram is a photo and video sharing platform that is popular among younger users. Many individuals and organizations use Instagram to share images and messages that promote faith and spirituality.

3. Twitter: Twitter is a micro-blogging platform that allows users to share short messages (called "tweets") with their followers. Many religious leaders and organizations use Twitter to share quotes from the Bible, inspirational messages, and updates on events and activities.

4. YouTube: YouTube is a video-sharing platform that is popular among users of all ages. Many churches and religious organizations use YouTube to share video sermons, worship music, and other forms of spiritual content.

Overall, while the specific social media platform that is the most popular for teaching Jesus may vary, these platforms provide powerful tools for sharing messages of faith and connecting with others who are seeking to learn more about the Christian faith.

Teaching Jesus through Personal Evangelism

Teaching Jesus in personal evangelism involves sharing the message of the Gospel and the person of Jesus Christ on a one-on-one basis. Here are some key considerations for teaching Jesus in personal evangelism:

1. Build Relationships:
- Focus on building genuine relationships with individuals, demonstrating care, respect, and compassion.
- Take time to listen to their stories, concerns, and questions, creating a safe and trusting environment.

2. Share Your Personal Testimony:
- Share your own personal experiences of encountering Jesus and how your life has been transformed by faith in Him.
- Emphasize the impact Jesus has had on your life, highlighting specific changes or blessings you have experienced.

3. Communicate the Gospel Message:
- Clearly articulate the core message of the Gospel, including the need for salvation, the reality of sin, the work of Jesus on the cross, and the call to repentance and faith.
- Explain that Jesus is the only way to a restored relationship with God and eternal life.

4. Use Scripture:
- Share relevant Bible passages that highlight Jesus' life, teachings, and redemptive work. Use verses that convey God's love, grace, and the significance of Jesus' sacrifice.
- Engage in a dialogue around these passages, allowing the individual to interact and ask questions.

5. Address Questions and Objections:
- Be prepared to address common questions, doubts, and objections individuals may have about Jesus, Christianity, or faith in general.
- Respond with patience, humility, and a willingness to listen. Provide thoughtful answers or direct them to resources that can address their concerns.

6. Emphasize Jesus' Love and Forgiveness:
- Highlight Jesus' unconditional love, grace, and His offer of forgiveness to all who come to Him in repentance and faith.
- Illustrate how Jesus' love and forgiveness can bring hope, healing, and a transformed life.

7. Pray with and for Others:
- Offer to pray with individuals, asking God to reveal Himself, grant understanding, and touch their hearts.
- Pray for their specific needs, concerns, or struggles, demonstrating the power of prayer and God's care for them.

8. Encourage Further Exploration:
- Recommend reading materials, Bible studies, or resources that provide more in-depth teachings about Jesus and the Christian faith.
- Invite them to attend church services, small group gatherings, or other Christian events where they can continue to learn about Jesus and experience Christian community.

9. Walk Alongside Them:
- Offer ongoing support, encouragement, and discipleship to those who show interest in learning more about Jesus.
- Be available to answer questions, provide guidance, and walk alongside them as they explore their faith journey.

Remember, personal evangelism is about sharing the love and truth of Jesus in a respectful and caring manner. It is important to be sensitive to the individual's unique circumstances, journey, and spiritual receptiveness. Allow the Holy Spirit to guide your interactions, relying on prayer and dependence on God to work in the hearts of those you engage with.

Teaching Jesus in Art and Music

Teaching Jesus through art and music provides a creative and expressive avenue to convey His message, life, and teachings. Here are some ways people teach about Jesus in art and music:

1. Visual Art:
- Create and showcase paintings, sculptures, or other visual art forms that depict scenes from Jesus' life, parables, miracles, or His crucifixion and resurrection.
- Use symbols and imagery associated with Jesus, such as the cross, the lamb, or the crown of thorns, to convey

His significance and message.
- Encourage viewers to reflect on the artwork and its representation of Jesus, sparking contemplation and discussion.

2. Sacred Music and Hymns:
- Compose and perform sacred music and hymns that focus on Jesus, His attributes, and His redemptive work.
- Incorporate biblical themes, passages, and teachings about Jesus into the lyrics and melodies of the music.
- Utilize various musical styles and genres to engage a diverse audience and evoke different emotions.

3. Liturgical Dance and Drama:
- Choreograph liturgical dance performances that depict stories or concepts related to Jesus, such as His birth, ministry, or sacrifice.
- Develop dramatic presentations or skits that convey Jesus' teachings, parables, or significant events from His life.
- Use movement, gestures, and expressions to enhance the portrayal of Jesus' character and message.

4. Christian Films and Visual Media:
- Produce and screen films, documentaries, or short videos that explore Jesus' life, teachings, and impact on individuals and society.
- Utilize cinematography, storytelling techniques, and visual effects to engage viewers and convey the significance of Jesus' life and message.

5. Performance Arts and Theater:
- Stage theatrical performances or dramatic productions that bring to life stories, parables, or teachings from Jesus' ministry.
- Engage actors, performers, and artists to portray Jesus and other biblical characters, creating a visual and immersive experience for the audience.
- Use live performances to evoke emotions, captivate attention, and communicate the transformative power of Jesus' message.

6. Christian Literature and Poetry:

- Write and publish Christian literature and poetry that explores the person and teachings of Jesus.
- Incorporate poetic elements, metaphors, and vivid imagery to capture the essence of Jesus' character and His impact on humanity.
- Invite readers to contemplate the words and themes presented, fostering a deeper understanding of Jesus' significance.

7. Exhibitions and Art Installations:
- Curate exhibitions or art installations that focus on Jesus, His life, teachings, or the Christian narrative.
- Collaborate with artists to create thought-provoking installations that engage the audience visually, emotionally, and intellectually.
- Provide opportunities for viewers to reflect on the art, its symbolism, and its connection to Jesus' message.

When teaching Jesus through art and music, it is essential to ensure that the content remains faithful to biblical teachings and aligns with sound Christian theology. The goal is to utilize the power of artistic expression to engage hearts and minds, inviting individuals to encounter and reflect upon the life, teachings, and significance of Jesus Christ.

Artists Teaching Jesus

Artists have played a significant role in teaching Jesus throughout history by creating visual representations and expressions of His life, teachings, and impact on humanity. Various art forms, such as painting, sculpture, mosaic, stained glass, and frescoes, have been used to convey the message of Christianity and inspire faith in people across different cultures and time periods. Some ways in which artists have taught Jesus over time include:

    1. Depicting key events: Artists have portrayed significant moments from Jesus's life, such as the Nativity, the Last Supper, the Crucifixion, and the Resurrection. These works have helped to visually narrate the story of Jesus and make the events of His life more accessible to people of all ages and backgrounds.

2. Creating iconic images: Certain iconic images of Jesus, such as the Sacred Heart or the Divine Mercy, have been popularized through artistic depictions. These images often serve as reminders of Jesus's love, compassion, and sacrifice and become focal points for prayer and meditation.

3. Illustrating parables and teachings: Artists have also visually represented the parables and teachings of Jesus, making it easier for people to understand and remember the lessons He shared. For example, paintings of the Good Samaritan, the Prodigal Son, or the Sermon on the Mount provide visual interpretations of Jesus's teachings.

4. Highlighting Jesus's humanity and divinity: Artworks have depicted Jesus in various ways, sometimes emphasizing His humanity by portraying Him as a suffering and compassionate figure, and other times highlighting His divinity through the use of symbols, such as halos or radiant light. These contrasting portrayals help to convey the dual nature of Jesus as both fully human and fully divine.

5. Using cultural and historical context: Artists have often depicted Jesus within the context of their own cultures and historical periods, making the story of Jesus more relatable and relevant to their audiences. This approach has allowed the message of Jesus to transcend geographical and cultural boundaries, reaching people of diverse backgrounds.

6. Inspiring personal reflection and devotion: Artworks featuring Jesus can elicit strong emotional responses and inspire personal reflection, prayer, and devotion. They can serve as a means to deepen one's faith and connect with Jesus on a more intimate level.

7. Encouraging contemplation and meditation: Christian art, particularly in the context of religious spaces like churches and monasteries, has been used to encourage contemplation and meditation on the life and teachings of Jesus. These artworks often invite viewers to enter into a deeper spiritual experience and grow in their understanding of Jesus.

Throughout history, artists have used their talents to teach Jesus in visually compelling and inspiring ways, helping to spread the Christian message and deepen people's faith and understanding of His life and teachings.

Art Teaching Jesus

Numerous works of art depicting Jesus have been created throughout History, but some stand out as particularly well-known and influential. These artworks have captured the essence of Jesus's life and teachings and have become iconic representations within Christian art. Some of the most known pieces of art that teach about Jesus include:

1. The Last Supper by Leonardo da Vinci (1495-1498): This iconic mural, located in Milan, Italy, depicts Jesus's final meal with His disciples before His crucifixion. The painting captures the moment when Jesus reveals that one of the disciples will betray Him.

2. The Sistine Chapel Ceiling by Michelangelo (1508-1512): The ceiling of the Sistine Chapel in Vatican City features numerous frescoes by Michelangelo, with a central composition illustrating scenes from the Old Testament. The frescoes also include several depictions of Jesus, such as in the scene of the Last Judgment.

3. The Crucifixion by Fra Angelico (c. 1420): This early Renaissance fresco, located in the San Marco Convent in Florence, Italy, portrays the Crucifixion of Jesus, with the Virgin Mary, St. John the Evangelist, and other figures present. The artwork is a powerful representation of Jesus's suffering and sacrifice.

4. The Isenheim Altarpiece by Matthias Grünewald (c. 1512-1516): This multi-paneled altarpiece, housed in the Unterlinden Museum in Colmar, France, features a central depiction of the Crucifixion, with a particularly graphic portrayal of Jesus's suffering. The altarpiece also includes scenes of the Annunciation, Nativity, and Resurrection.

5. Christ Pantocrator by an unknown artist (c. 6th century): This famous Byzantine mosaic, located in the Hagia Sophia in Istanbul, Turkey, presents Jesus as the ruler of the universe, with a stern gaze and an authoritative pose. The Christ Pantocrator image has become a symbol of Jesus's divine authority and

power.

6. The Pieta by Michelangelo (1498-1499): This marble sculpture, housed in St. Peter's Basilica in Vatican City, depicts the Virgin Mary holding the lifeless body of Jesus after His crucifixion. The artwork is renowned for its emotional intensity and technical mastery, capturing both the sorrow of Jesus's death and the hope of His resurrection.

7. The Ghent Altarpiece (Adoration of the Mystic Lamb) by Jan van Eyck (c. 1432): This large, multi-paneled altarpiece, located in St. Bavo's Cathedral in Ghent, Belgium, includes several scenes depicting Jesus, such as the central image of the Lamb of God, symbolizing Jesus's sacrifice.

These artworks and others have played a crucial role in shaping the visual language of Christian art and teaching about Jesus's life, teachings, and impact on humanity. They continue to inspire viewers and deepen their understanding and appreciation of Jesus and the Christian faith.

Musicians Teaching Jesus

Music has been an essential medium for teaching Jesus and expressing Christian faith throughout history. Various genres, styles, and traditions of music have been used to convey the message of Jesus, His life, teachings, and impact on humanity. Some of the key types of music that teach Jesus include:

1. Hymns: Traditional Christian hymns have been sung in churches and worship gatherings for centuries, often telling stories of Jesus's life, His love, and His sacrifice. Classic hymns such as "Amazing Grace," "How Great Thou Art," and "What a Friend We Have in Jesus" have been passed down through generations.

2. Gospel Music: Gospel music is a genre that emerged from African-American Christian communities in the United States, featuring powerful vocals, harmonies, and lyrics that celebrate Jesus and the Christian faith. Gospel songs often highlight Jesus's role as Savior and Redeemer, such as "Oh Happy Day" and "He's Got the Whole World in His Hands."

3. Contemporary Christian Music (CCM): CCM is a modern genre of Christian music that encompasses various styles, including pop, rock, folk, and worship music. CCM songs often focus on Jesus's teachings, the Christian walk, and personal relationships with Jesus. Some popular CCM artists include Chris Tomlin, Casting Crowns, and Hillsong United.

4. Worship Music: Worship music is specifically designed for use in Christian worship gatherings, aiming to lead congregations in praising and connecting with Jesus. These songs often emphasize Jesus's divinity, love, and saving work on the cross. Examples of popular worship songs include "10,000 Reasons (Bless the Lord)" by Matt Redman and "Reckless Love" by Cory Asbury.

5. Christian Rock: Christian rock is a genre that incorporates elements of rock music into songs with Christian themes and messages, often focusing on Jesus's teachings and impact on believers' lives. Notable Christian rock bands include Switchfoot, Skillet, and Relient K.

6. Christian Hip Hop/Rap: Christian hip hop and rap music use the stylistic elements of hip hop and rap to communicate Christian themes and teachings about Jesus. Artists like Lecrae, Andy Mineo, and NF have gained popularity in this genre, reaching both Christian and secular audiences.

7. Classical Music: Many classical composers have created sacred music inspired by Jesus and Christian themes, such as Johann Sebastian Bach's "St. Matthew Passion," Handel's "Messiah," and Beethoven's "Missa Solemnis."

8. Christmas Carols: Christmas carols are songs that celebrate the birth of Jesus and are traditionally sung during the Christmas season. Examples include "O Come, All Ye Faithful," "Hark! The Herald Angels Sing," and "Silent Night."

These various types of music that teach Jesus cater to diverse musical tastes and preferences while conveying the core message of Christianity. Music has a unique ability to inspire, teach, and connect people with Jesus, making it a powerful medium for sharing the Christian faith.

Music Teaching Jesus

It is difficult to definitively pinpoint the most popular Jesus music of all time, as tastes and preferences vary across different cultures, generations, and Christian traditions. However, some songs have gained widespread recognition and enduring popularity within the Christian community. A few examples of these include:

1. "Amazing Grace": Written by John Newton in 1779, This hymn is one of the most well-known and beloved Christian songs. Its powerful lyrics express the theme of redemption and God's grace through Jesus Christ.

2. "How Great Thou Art": This hymn, based on a Swedish poem and set to a traditional Swedish melody, has been translated into many languages and is widely sung in Christian worship services. Its lyrics praise God and reflect on the awe-inspiring nature of His creation, as well as Jesus's sacrificial death.

3. "Hallelujah Chorus" from Handel's "Messiah": The "Hallelujah Chorus" is a renowned piece from George Frideric Handel's oratorio, "Messiah." This choral work, often performed during the Christmas and Easter seasons, celebrates the life, death, and resurrection of Jesus Christ.

4. "What a Friend We Have in Jesus": Written by Joseph M. Scriven in 1855, This hymn highlights the comfort and solace found in a personal relationship with Jesus. It has become a classic in Christian hymnody.

5. "10,000 Reasons (Bless the Lord)": Released in 2011 by Matt Redman, this contemporary worship song has gained immense popularity in recent years. Its lyrics express gratitude and praise to God for His love, faithfulness, and grace through Jesus Christ.

While these songs represent some of the most popular Jesus music of all time, the Christian music landscape is vast and diverse, with countless songs and compositions that have touched the hearts of believers around the world.

Writers and Books Teaching Jesus

Numerous books have been written teaching Jesus throughout history, exploring various aspects of His life, teachings, and the impact of His ministry. Some of the most famous and influential books teaching Jesus include:

1. The Gospels: The four Gospels—Matthew, Mark, Luke, and John—are the primary accounts of Jesus' life and teachings. They are part of the New Testament and form the foundation for understanding Jesus in Christian tradition.

2. "The Life and Times of Jesus the Messiah" by Alfred Edersheim (1883): This classic work provides a detailed account of Jesus' life within the context of first-century Judaism, offering insights into His teachings, customs, and the Historical setting in which He lived.

3. "Jesus and the Victory of God" by N.T. Wright (1996): This scholarly work is part of a larger series by N.T. Wright, a renowned New Testament scholar. The book examines Jesus' life and teachings within their Historical context, focusing on His mission to inaugurate the kingdom of God and His role as the Messiah.

4. "The Historical Jesus: The Life of a Mediterranean Jewish Peasant" by John Dominic Crossan (1991): Crossan, a prominent biblical scholar, presents a historical portrait of Jesus, reconstructing His life based on cultural, social, and political contexts of the time.

5. "Jesus Through the Centuries: His Place in the History of Culture" by Jaroslav Pelikan (1985): This influential book examines how Jesus has been understood and portrayed throughout History, exploring His impact on culture, art, literature, and theology across various periods and societies.

6. "The Quest of the Historical Jesus" by Albert Schweitzer (1906): This groundbreaking work evaluates previous scholarship on the historical Jesus and calls for a renewed focus on the apocalyptic message of Jesus in its original context.

7. "Zealot: The Life and Times of Jesus of Nazareth" by Reza Aslan (2013): In This popular book, Aslan presents Jesus as a Jewish revolutionary figure who sought to challenge the religious and political establishment of His time.

These are just a few examples of the many books written about Jesus. Some focus on historical research, while others examine theological aspects of His life and teachings. The variety of perspectives and interpretations reflects the ongoing fascination and importance of Jesus in religious and cultural discourse.

Poets and Poems Teaching Jesus

Many poets throughout history have been inspired by Jesus and have written poems that reflect on His life, teachings, and spiritual significance. Here are a few famous poems about Jesus:
   1. "The Divine Comedy" by Dante Alighieri (1308-1320): Although not exclusively about Jesus, this epic poem is an allegorical journey through Hell, Purgatory, and Heaven, with Jesus playing a central role in the salvation of the poem's protagonist. The poem ultimately leads to a vision of God, including Jesus and the Holy Spirit, in the Empyrean Heaven.
   2. "The Dream of the Rood" (circa 8th-10th century): This Old English poem recounts a vision of the crucifixion from the perspective of the cross itself. The poem presents Jesus as a heroic figure who willingly sacrifices Himself for humanity's salvation.
   3. "Paradise Lost" by John Milton (1667): This epic poem tells the story of the Fall of Man and the expulsion from the Garden of Eden, with Jesus appearing as a central figure in the poem's narrative. Jesus is portrayed as the Son of God who will ultimately bring redemption to humanity.
   4. "The Wound in the Water" by W. H. Auden (1940): This poem is a reflection on the life and teachings of Jesus, focusing on themes of suffering, redemption, and the transformative power of love.
   5. "The Hound of Heaven" by Francis Thompson (1893): In This narrative poem, the speaker is pursued by the "Hound of Heaven," which symbolizes the relentless love of Jesus. The poem explores themes of spiritual longing, divine grace, and the human soul's journey towards God.
   6. "Christ's Nativity" by Henry Vaughan (1650): This poem celebrates the birth of Jesus and the divine light He brings into

the world, with vivid imagery and a sense of awe and wonder.

7. "The Second Coming" by William Butler Yeats (1919): Though not explicitly about Jesus, this poem reflects on the apocalyptic imagery of the Second Coming of Christ and the profound changes it will bring to the world.

These poems represent just a small sample of the vast body of poetry inspired by Jesus. Poets from various cultural and religious backgrounds have been drawn to His life and teachings, expressing their thoughts and emotions in diverse ways.

Teaching Jesus in Retreats, Conferences, and Workshops

Teaching Jesus in retreats, conferences, and workshops provides opportunities for focused and immersive learning experiences. Here are some ways people teach about Jesus in these settings:

1. Theme Development:
- Establish a central theme or focus for the retreat, conference, or workshop that specifically highlights Jesus and His teachings.
- Ensure that all sessions, activities, and discussions align with the theme, reinforcing the message and facilitating a cohesive learning experience.

2. Expository Teaching:
- Utilize expository teaching methods to explore specific passages or teachings of Jesus in-depth.
- Present clear explanations of the biblical text, providing historical and cultural context to aid understanding.

3. Interactive Discussions and Small Groups:
- Foster interactive discussions where participants can explore Jesus' teachings, ask questions, and share insights.
- Facilitate small group sessions where participants can engage in deeper conversations, personal reflection, and application of Jesus' teachings.

4. Personal Reflection and Prayer:
- Provide designated time for personal reflection and prayer, allowing participants to connect with Jesus individually and seek His guidance.

- Offer guided reflection exercises or prayer stations that focus on specific aspects of Jesus' life, teachings, or character.

5. Testimonies and Life Stories:
- Incorporate personal testimonies and life stories that highlight how individuals have encountered Jesus and experienced transformation through their relationship with Him.
- Encourage speakers or participants to share their personal experiences of encountering Jesus in their lives.

6. Worship and Devotional Times:
- Include worship sessions that center around Jesus, His attributes, and His redemptive work.
- Incorporate devotional times where participants can engage in guided prayer, scripture reading, and meditations focused on Jesus.

7. Creative Expressions:
- Encourage participants to express their understanding of Jesus through creative outlets, such as art, music, or writing.
- Provide opportunities for participants to share their creative expressions and discuss how it deepens their understanding of Jesus.

8. Practical Application:
- Help participants connect Jesus' teachings to their everyday lives and provide practical guidance for living out His principles.
- Offer workshops or breakout sessions that explore how Jesus' teachings can be applied in various areas of life, such as relationships, work, and personal growth.

9. Fellowship and Community Building:
- Facilitate opportunities for participants to connect with one another, fostering a sense of community and support.
- Provide structured activities or free time for participants to engage in meaningful conversations and build relationships centered around Jesus.

10. Follow-up Resources:
- Offer resources, such as books, study guides, or online

materials, to help participants continue their study and reflection on Jesus beyond the retreat, conference, or workshop.
- Provide information about local church communities, Bible studies, or ongoing discipleship programs where participants can further explore Jesus' teachings.

When teaching Jesus in retreats, conferences, and workshops, it is important to create an atmosphere of authenticity, openness, and spiritual growth. By providing a well-rounded and engaging experience, participants can deepen their understanding of Jesus, be inspired in their faith journey, and be equipped to live out His teachings in their lives.

Using Prayer to Teach Jesus

Prayer can be used to guide someone in understanding Jesus, or to share the teachings of Jesus, here are a few ways This might happen:
- Praying the Lord's Prayer: Jesus Himself gave the disciples an example of how to pray in what is often referred to as the "Lord's Prayer" or the "Our Father" (Matthew 6:9-13, Luke 11:2-4). By praying this prayer, and reflecting on its words, people can understand more about the values and teachings of Jesus.
- Praying for Understanding: Christians often pray for God to open their minds and hearts to better understand the teachings of Jesus. For example, the apostle Paul prays in Ephesians 1:17-18 that the Ephesian believers may receive "a spirit of wisdom and of revelation in the knowledge of Him."
- Praying with Scripture: Some people practice lectio divina, a method of prayer that involves reading a Bible passage (often from the Gospels, which contain the teachings of Jesus), meditating on it, praying about it, and then contemplating its meaning for their lives.
- Intercessory Prayer: When Christians pray for others to come to know Jesus, or to grow in their understanding of His teachings, they are using prayer as a form of teaching or evangelism.

- Teaching about Prayer: By teaching others how to pray, and how Jesus prayed and taught His disciples to pray, people can also teach about the nature of Jesus, His relationship with God the Father, and the kind of humble, trusting attitude His followers are encouraged to adopt.

Remember, in Christian belief, prayer isn't just about asking for things, but about developing a closer relationship with God. Through prayer, people can come to better know and understand Jesus and His teachings.

Suggestions for a Style of Storytelling for Teaching Jesus

Storytelling can be a powerful way to teach Jesus and bring His teachings to life. Here are a few styles of storytelling that you might consider using:

1. Narrative: This style of storytelling involves telling the story of Jesus' life, teachings, and miracles in a straightforward, chronological manner. This can help students understand the context and events of Jesus' life, and the impact of His teachings.

2. Parable: This style of storytelling involves using short, memorable stories to illustrate Jesus' teachings. This can help students understand complex concepts in a simple and relatable way and can also make the teachings more memorable.

3. Character-Driven: This style of storytelling involves focusing on the characters in the stories of Jesus' life, and exploring their motivations, thoughts, and feelings. This can help students understand the human elements of the stories and can also make the teachings more relatable.

4. Interactive: This style of storytelling involves engaging students in the story, either through role-playing, discussion, or other interactive activities. This can help students internalize the teachings and understand them on a deeper level.

Regardless of the style you choose, it's important to approach the stories of Jesus' life and teachings with sensitivity and respect for the beliefs of others.

Section IV
The Bible Teaching Jesus

1. Versions of the Bible since the Time of Christ
2. Testaments Teaching Jesus - Old and New
3. Books and their Authors of Old and New Testaments
4. Apostles and Nicene Creeds

Where does the Bible Get its Name?

The word "Bible" comes from the Latin word "biblia," which itself is derived from the Greek word "biblia," (βιβλία) meaning "books" or "scrolls." The Bible is a collection of sacred texts or scriptures that are considered holy by Christians and Jews. It is composed of multiple books written over a period of many centuries by various authors. The Bible is divided into two main sections: the Old Testament, which contains religious texts and Historical accounts predating the birth of Jesus Christ, and the New Testament, which focuses on the life, teachings, death, and resurrection of Jesus Christ.

The Various Versions of the Bible since the Time of Christ

Since the time of Christ, there have been several versions and translations of the Bible into different languages. Here are some notable versions throughout history:

    1. Septuagint (3rd century BCE): The Septuagint is a Greek translation of the Hebrew Bible (Old Testament) and was widely used in the Greek-speaking Jewish community and early Christian church.

    2. Latin Vulgate (4th century CE): The Latin Vulgate, translated by Jerome, became the standard Latin translation of the Bible in Western Christianity during the Middle Ages.

    3. Wycliffe's Bible (14th century): The first complete

English translation of the Bible was done by John Wycliffe and His associates. It was translated from the Latin Vulgate.

4. Gutenberg Bible (15th century): The Gutenberg Bible, printed by Johannes Gutenberg, was the first major book printed using movable type. It was printed in Latin and played a significant role in the spread of the Bible during the Reformation.

5. King James Version (17th century): The King James Version (KJV), also known as the Authorized Version, is one of the most widely read and influential English translations. It was commissioned by King James I of England and was completed in 1611.

6. Revised Version (19th century): The Revised Version, published in the late 19th century, was an update of the KJV. It aimed to provide a more accurate and contemporary English translation based on older manuscripts.

7. New International Version (20th century): The New International Version (NIV) is a popular and widely used English translation that was first published in 1978. It seeks to strike a balance between accuracy and readability.

8. New American Standard Bible (20th century): The New American Standard Bible (NASB) is known for its literal and precise translation style. It was first published in 1971 and has undergone revisions since then.

These are just a few examples, and there are many other translations and versions of the Bible in various languages. Each translation has its own translation philosophy, aiming to balance faithfulness to the original texts with readability for contemporary readers.

The Bible Teaching Jesus

The Bible teaches Jesus in both the Old Testament and the New Testament, though the New Testament provides more detailed accounts of His life, teachings, and significance. Here are some key ways in which the Bible teaches about Jesus:

1. Old Testament Prophecies: The Old Testament contains numerous prophecies that foretell the coming of a Messiah, who

Christians believe is Jesus Christ. These prophecies describe details about His birth, lineage, ministry, and the redemptive work He would accomplish. For example, Isaiah 7:14 prophesies that a virgin will conceive and give birth to a son, and Isaiah 53 foretells the suffering and sacrificial death of the Messiah.

2. Types and Shadows: The Old Testament contains various people, events, and rituals that foreshadow or symbolize aspects of Jesus' life, ministry, and salvation. These include characters like Moses, David, and the sacrificial system, which point to Jesus as the ultimate deliverer, king, and sacrificial Lamb.

3. Gospel Accounts: The four Gospels—Matthew, Mark, Luke, and John—provide detailed narratives of Jesus' life, teachings, miracles, death, and resurrection. They present Jesus as the fulfillment of Old Testament prophecies, the Son of God, and the Savior of humanity. The Gospels highlight His teachings on love, forgiveness, repentance, and the coming kingdom of God.

4. Epistles and Letters: The New Testament epistles, written by apostles and early Christian leaders, expound on the significance of Jesus' life, death, and resurrection. They address theological and practical aspects of the Christian faith, emphasizing the redemptive work of Jesus, His role as the mediator between God and humanity, and the implications of His teachings for believers' lives.

5. Revelation: The book of Revelation provides a prophetic vision of the future and depicts Jesus as the exalted Lord who will ultimately triumph over evil and establish His eternal kingdom. It reveals His authority, power, and sovereignty.

Throughout the Bible, it teaches Jesus by highlighting His divine nature, His sacrificial death as atonement for sin, His resurrection, and the call for people to have faith in Him as the way to salvation and eternal life. The Bible presents Jesus as the central figure in God's plan of redemption, offering forgiveness, reconciliation, and the hope of eternal life to all who believe in Him.

Essential Differences between the Old and New Testament

The Old Testament and the New Testament are the two main parts of the Christian Bible, and there are several essential differences between them:

1. Time period and context: The Old Testament covers a much longer time period than the New Testament, beginning with the creation of the world and ending a few centuries before the birth of Jesus. The New Testament focuses on a much shorter time span, roughly encompassing the life of Jesus and the first century of the Christian church.

2. Language: The Old Testament was primarily written in Hebrew, with a few portions written in Aramaic. The New Testament was written in Koine Greek, the common language of the eastern Mediterranean region at the time.

3. Cont ent and structure: The Old Testament consists of a diverse collection of texts, including history, law, poetry, wisdom literature, and prophecy. It is divided into three main sections: the Torah (or Pentateuch), the Prophets, and the Writings. The New Testament, on the other hand, is more focused on the life, teachings, and ministry of Jesus Christ and the early Christian church. It includes the four Gospels, the Acts of the Apostles, the Epistles (letters), and the Book of Revelation.

4. Covenant and relationship with God: The Old Testament primarily deals with the covenant between God and the nation of Israel, emphasizing the importance of obedience to God's laws and the consequences of disobedience. The New Testament introduces a new covenant, established by Jesus Christ, which emphasizes salvation through faith in Jesus and the importance of love, forgiveness, and grace.

5. Focus on Jesus: While the Old Testament contains prophecies and expectations about a coming Messiah, the New Testament centers on Jesus as the fulfillment of those prophecies. The New Testament presents Jesus as the Son of God, the Messiah, and the savior of humanity, whose life, death, and resurrection provide salvation for all who believe in Him.

These differences reflect the distinct Historical, cultural, and theological contexts in which the Old and New Testaments were written. While they have different emphases and contents, both Testaments are considered sacred scripture in Christianity and are believed to be inspired by God, together forming a unified narrative of God's relationship with humanity.

The Old Testament Teaching Jesus

The Old Testament contains various prophecies, types, and foreshadowing that are seen as pointing towards the coming of Jesus Christ in the New Testament. Here are a few ways in which the Old Testament teaches Jesus:

1. Messianic Prophecies: The Old Testament contains numerous prophecies that foretell the coming of a Messiah, a chosen deliverer sent by God. These prophecies describe specific details about the Messiah's birth, life, ministry, death, and resurrection. Some well-known Messianic prophecies include Isaiah 53, which foretells the suffering and sacrifice of the Messiah, and Micah 5:2, which predicts that the Messiah will be born in Bethlehem.

2. Typology: The Old Testament contains various people, events, and institutions that are seen as types or prefigurations of Jesus. For example, Adam is seen as a type of Christ because, through Adam's disobedience, sin entered the world, while through Christ's obedience, salvation was brought. Similarly, the story of Moses leading the Israelites out of slavery in Egypt is seen as a type of Jesus as the ultimate deliverer who sets humanity free from the bondage of sin.

3. Sacrificial System: The Old Testament sacrificial system, particularly the offering of animal sacrifices for the atonement of sins, foreshadows Jesus' ultimate sacrifice on the cross. The blood of the sacrificial animals symbolized the shedding of blood for the forgiveness of sins. Christians see Jesus as the ultimate sacrificial Lamb of God who takes away the sins of the world.

4. Wisdom Literature: The wisdom literature in the Old

Testament, such as Proverbs and Ecclesiastes, contains teachings that align with Jesus' teachings in the New Testament. These teachings emphasize righteousness, humility, the fear of God, and the pursuit of wisdom, which are central themes in Jesus' teachings.

5. Covenant Promises: Throughout the Old Testament, God makes various covenants and promises with His people, such as the Abrahamic Covenant and the Davidic Covenant. These covenants contain promises of a future descendant who will bring blessings, salvation, and eternal rule. Christians see these covenant promises fulfilled in Jesus Christ.

It's important to note that the Old Testament teachings about Jesus are understood in light of the New Testament revelation. Christians interpret and understand the Old Testament in connection with the person and work of Jesus Christ as revealed in the New Testament.

Books of the Old Testament

The Old Testament, also known as the Hebrew Bible, is divided into several sections and contains 39 individual books. These books are organized into different genres, including Historical narratives, wisdom literature, prophetic writings, and poetic works. Here is a list of the books in the Old Testament:

1. Pentateuch (Torah):
- Genesis
- Exodus
- Leviticus
- Numbers
- Deuteronomy

2. Historical Books:
- Joshua
- Judges
- Ruth
- 1 Samuel
- 2 Samuel
- 1 Kings

- 2 Kings
- 1 Chronicles
- 2 Chronicles
- Ezra
- Nehemiah
- Esther

3. Wisdom and Poetry:
- Job
- Psalms
- Proverbs
- Ecclesiastes
- Song of Solomon (Song of Songs)

4. Major Prophets:
- Isaiah
- Jeremiah
- Lamentations
- Ezekiel
- Daniel

5. Minor Prophets:
- Hosea
- Joel
- Amos
- Obadiah
- Jonah
- Micah
- Nahum
- Habakkuk
- Zephaniah
- Haggai
- Zechariah
- Malachi

It's worth noting that the ordering of these books may vary slightly among different religious traditions or versions of the Bible. For example, the Catholic and Orthodox canons include additional books known as the deuterocanonical books, which are not found in the Protestant Old Testament.

Who Wrote the Books of the Old Testament?

The books of the Old Testament were written by multiple authors over a long period of time. Traditional Jewish and Christian beliefs attribute the authorship of these books to various individuals, including prophets, kings, and other figures. For example, the first five books of the Old Testament, known as the Pentateuch or the Torah, are traditionally attributed to Moses. These books are Genesis, Exodus, Leviticus, Numbers, and Deuteronomy. However, modern biblical scholarship suggests that the Pentateuch is likely a compilation of texts from different sources, known as the Documentary Hypothesis, rather than being solely authored by Moses.

Other books of the Old Testament were written by different authors. Some examples include:

- The Book of Psalms, which is a collection of songs and poems, was composed by various authors, including King David.
- The Prophetic books, such as Isaiah, Jeremiah, and Ezekiel, were written by the respective prophets whose names they bear.
- The Historical books, such as Joshua, Judges, Samuel, and Kings, were likely written by multiple authors and editors.

It is important to note that the authorship of many Old Testament books is a subject of scholarly debate, and definitive authorship attributions may not always be possible due to the nature of ancient textual traditions and the complexities of compiling and editing these works over time.

Who Decided the Order of the Books in the Old Testament?

The order of the books in the Old Testament was not determined by a single individual or authority. Instead, it evolved over time through a combination of factors, including historical, cultural, and religious considerations.

The Jewish tradition, specifically the Masoretic Text, which is the authoritative Hebrew text of the Jewish Bible, arranges the books of the Old Testament in a specific order. The exact process and timeframe for the establishment of This order are not entirely clear, but it likely developed gradually within Jewish communities over several centuries.

The arrangement of the Old Testament books in the Christian Bible is influenced by the Septuagint, a Greek translation of the Hebrew Scriptures. The Septuagint was widely used in the early Christian Church, and its order of books influenced the organization of the Old Testament in Christian Bibles.

It's important to note that there are slight variations in the order of the Old Testament books among different Jewish and Christian traditions. For example, the Catholic and Orthodox traditions include additional books, known as the Deuterocanonical books or the Apocrypha, which are not found in the Jewish or Protestant canons.

In summary, the specific order of the books in the Old Testament developed over time through the collective practices and decisions of Jewish and Christian communities, influenced by various factors and traditions.

The New Testament Teaching Jesus

The New Testament is centered on Jesus Christ and provides detailed accounts of His life, teachings, death, and resurrection. It presents Jesus as the promised Messiah, the Son of God, and the Savior of humanity. Here are some key ways in which the New Testament teaches Jesus:

    1. The Gospels: The four Gospels—Matthew, Mark, Luke, and John—are the primary sources for information about Jesus' life and ministry. They provide firsthand accounts of His teachings, miracles, interactions with people, and the events leading up to His crucifixion and resurrection. The Gospels present Jesus as the fulfillment of Old Testament prophecies, the embodiment of God's love and grace, and the ultimate sacrifice for the forgiveness of sins.

    2. Epistles and Letters: The New Testament epistles, written

by apostles and early Christian leaders, further expound on the person and work of Jesus. They address various theological, practical, and ethical aspects of the Christian faith, emphasizing the significance of Jesus' death and resurrection, His role as the mediator between God and humanity, and the implications of His teachings for believers' lives.

3. Acts of the Apostles: The book of Acts chronicles the early days of the Christian Church and highlights the ministry and mission of the apostles. It portrays Jesus' disciples proclaiming His teachings, performing miracles, and spreading the message of salvation in His name. Acts demonstrates the continuing presence and work of Jesus through the Holy Spirit in the lives of believers.

4. Revelation: The book of Revelation, often considered prophetic literature, provides a vision of the future and the ultimate triumph of Jesus Christ. It depicts Jesus as the exalted and victorious Lord who will judge the world, establish His kingdom, and bring about the renewal of all creation.

Overall, the New Testament presents Jesus as the central figure in God's redemptive plan for humanity. It highlights His teachings on love, forgiveness, compassion, and righteousness, emphasizing the importance of faith in Him as the means of salvation and eternal life. The New Testament teaching Jesus shapes the core beliefs and practices of Christianity, providing a foundation for understanding the nature of God's grace and the call to follow Christ.

Books of the New Testament

The New Testament consists of 27 individual books, which are primarily focused on the life, teachings, death, and resurrection of Jesus Christ, as well as the early development of the Christian faith. Here is a list of the books in the New Testament:

1. The Gospels:
- Matthew
- Mark
- Luke

- John
2. Historical Book:
- Acts (or Acts of the Apostles)
3. Pauline Epistles (Letters written by the Apostle Paul):
- Romans
- 1 Corinthians
- 2 Corinthians
- Galatians
- Ephesians
- Philippians
- Colossians
- 1 Thessalonians
- 2 Thessalonians
- 1 Timothy
- 2 Timothy
- Titus
- Philemon
4. General Epistles (Letters written by other apostles mand early Christian leaders):
- Hebrews (authorship is debated)
- James
- 1 Peter
- 2 Peter
- 1 John
- 2 John
- 3 John
- Jude
5. Apocalyptic Book:
- Revelation (or the Book of Revelation)

The New Testament books were written in the first century AD by various authors, including apostles, disciples, and other early Christian leaders. They provide a record of the life and teachings of Jesus, the establishment of the early Christian community, and theological instruction for believers.

Who Wrote the Books of the New Testament?

The New Testament books were written by various authors, including apostles, disciples, and other early Christian leaders. Here is a list of the traditionally attributed authors for each book:

1. The Gospels:
- Matthew: Traditionally attributed to apostle - Matthew
- Mark: Traditionally attributed to John Mark, a companion of the apostle Peter.
- Luke: Traditionally attributed to Luke, a companion of the apostle Paul.
- John: Traditionally attributed to the apostle John, the son of Zebedee.

2. Historical Book:
- Acts: Traditionally attributed to Luke, the same author of the Gospel of Luke.

3. Pauline Epistles (Letters written by the Apostle Paul):
- Romans
- 1 Corinthians
- 2 Corinthians
- Galatians
- Ephesians
- Philippians
- Colossians
- 1 Thessalonians
- 2 Thessalonians
- 1 Timothy
- 2 Timothy
- Titus
- Philemon

4. General Epistles (Letters written by other apostles and early Christian leaders):
- Hebrews: The authorship of Hebrews is uncertain, and there are various theories regarding the author's identity.
- James: Traditionally attributed to James, the brother of Jesus.
- 1 Peter: Traditionally attributed to the apostle Peter.
- 2 Peter: Traditionally attributed to the apostle Peter.
- 1 John: Traditionally attributed to the apostle John.

- 2 John: Traditionally attributed to the apostle John.
- 3 John: Traditionally attributed to the apostle John.
- Jude: Traditionally attributed to Jude, possibly a brother of James and Jesus.

5. Apocalyptic Book:
- Revelation: Traditionally attributed to the apostle John.

It's important to note that there is some scholarly debate and discussion about the authorship of certain New Testament books, particularly Hebrews and some of the general epistles. The traditional attributions are based on early Christian tradition and historical sources.

How did They Decide the Order of the Books of the New Testament?

The order of the books in the New Testament was not decided at once but evolved gradually over time as the early Christian church collected, copied, and circulated these texts. Several factors influenced the arrangement of the New Testament books, which eventually solidified into the order commonly found in modern Bibles:

1. Genre: The New Testament books can be categorized into four main genres: the Gospels, the Acts of the Apostles, the Epistles (letters), and the book of Revelation. The order generally reflects This grouping, with the Gospels appearing first, followed by Acts, the Epistles, and finally, Revelation.

2. Chronology: While the exact chronology of the New Testament writings is difficult to determine, the arrangement of some books roughly follows the order in which they were believed to have been written. For example, the letters of Paul are often placed in the order of their assumed composition, with earlier letters like Romans and Corinthians appearing before later letters like Timothy and Titus.

3. Importance: The prominence and significance of certain books played a role in their placement within the New Testament. For example, the Gospel of Matthew is traditionally placed first

among the Gospels because it was considered the most important and comprehensive Gospel by many early Christians. Similarly, the book of Romans is placed first among Paul's letters due to its theological depth and significance.

4. Authorship: The arrangement of some New Testament books is influenced by their attributed authorship. For example, the Gospel of John and the three Epistles of John are grouped together, and the letters of Peter and James are placed near each other, reflecting the connection between these texts and their respective authors.

5. Canonical acceptance: The process of canonization, or the formal acceptance of texts as part of the sacred Christian scripture, also influenced the arrangement of the New Testament books. As various texts were debated, accepted, or rejected by different Christian communities, the order of the books sometimes changed to reflect their canonical status.

It is important to note that the order of the books in the New Testament was not fixed by a single authoritative decision or council. Instead, it developed gradually as the early Christian communities copied, shared, and debated these texts. The order found in most modern Bibles reflects centuries of tradition and the evolving understanding of the significance and interrelationships of these sacred writings.

Who Decided the Order of the Books in the King James Version of the New Testament?

The order of the books in the King James Version (KJV) of the New Testament follows the same order as the majority of the preceding English Bible translations and the Latin Vulgate, the primary Bible used in Western Christianity for over a thousand years. The KJV did not introduce a new order for the New Testament books; it simply adopted the established order that had been widely accepted by the time of its translation in 1611. The King James Version was commissioned by King James I of England and was produced by a committee of around 50 scholars from various universities, including Oxford, Cambridge, and

Westminster. These scholars relied on earlier translations and source texts, such as the Textus Receptus for the New Testament, to create an updated and accurate English translation of the Bible. In doing so, they maintained the order of the books as they found it in those earlier translations and texts.

Thus, the order of the books in the KJV New Testament was not decided by the translators themselves but rather inherited from earlier Bible translations and the manuscript tradition that had developed in the centuries before the KJV was produced. This order reflects a combination of factors, such as genre, chronology, importance, and authorship, as well as the evolving tradition and acceptance of these texts within the Christian community.

The Apostles' Creed

The Apostles' Creed is an early statement of Christian belief, a creed or "symbol." It is widely used by a number of Christian denominations for both liturgical and catechetical purposes, most visibly by liturgical Churches of Western tradition, including the Roman Catholic Church, Lutheranism and Anglicanism. It is called the Apostles' Creed because of its early origin – it was believed to have been composed by the apostles themselves, although this has been questioned by modern scholarship.
Here is the text of the Apostles' Creed:

"I believe in God, the Father almighty,
creator of heaven and earth.
I believe in Jesus Christ, his only Son, our Lord,
who was conceived by the Holy Spirit,
born of the Virgin Mary,
suffered under Pontius Pilate,
was crucified, died, and was buried;
he descended to the dead.
On the third day he rose again;
he ascended into heaven,
he is seated at the right hand of the Father,
and he will come to judge the living and the dead.

I believe in the Holy Spirit,
the holy catholic Church,
the communion of saints,
the forgiveness of sins,
the resurrection of the body,
and the life everlasting. Amen."

The term "catholic" in the Apostles' Creed is used in the sense of "universal" – indicating all Christians regardless of denominational affiliation.
This creed is recited in the Western Church during the daily office and at the Eucharist, and in the Eastern Church during daily prayers. It is also used in personal devotion and during the rites of Christian initiation.

The Nicene Creed

The Nicene Creed is a statement of the orthodox faith of the early Christian church, in opposition to certain heresies, particularly Arianism. These heresies, which disturbed the church during the fourth century, concerned the doctrine of the trinity and the person of Christ. Both the Greek (Eastern) and the Latin (Western) church held this creed in honor, though with one important difference. The Western church insisted on the inclusion of the phrase "and the Son" (known as the filioque clause) in the article on the procession of the Holy Spirit; this phrase still is repudiated by the Eastern church.
The Nicene Creed as traditionally used in Christian liturgy is as follows:

"We believe in one God,
the Father almighty,
maker of heaven and earth,
of all things visible and invisible.
And in one Lord Jesus Christ,
the only Son of God,
begotten from the Father before all ages,

God from God,
Light from Light,
true God from true God,
begotten, not made;
of the same essence as the Father.
Through him all things were made.
For us and for our salvation
he came down from heaven;
he became incarnate by the Holy Spirit and the virgin Mary,
and was made human.
He was crucified for us under Pontius Pilate;
he suffered and was buried.
The third day he rose again, according to the Scriptures.
He ascended to heaven
and is seated at the right hand of the Father.
He will come again with glory
to judge the living and the dead.
His kingdom will never end.
And we believe in the Holy Spirit,
the Lord, the giver of life.
He proceeds from the Father [and the Son],
and with the Father and the Son is worshiped and glorified.
He spoke through the prophets.
We believe in one holy catholic and apostolic Church.
We affirm one baptism for the forgiveness of sins.
We look forward to the resurrection of the dead,
and to life in the world to come. Amen."

The phrase in brackets ("and the Son") is included in the Western tradition of the creed, but not in the Eastern tradition. This creed played an essential role in defining Christian doctrine and establishing consensus around core Christian beliefs across different traditions and practices.

Differences and Similarities between the Apostles and Nicene Creed

The Nicene Creed and the Apostles' Creed are both important

statements of Christian faith that have been used for centuries in the Church. Here are some similarities and differences between the two:

Similarities:

1. Trinitarian structure: Both the Nicene Creed and the Apostles' Creed affirm belief in the triune God, Father, Son, and Holy Spirit.

2. Key Christian doctrines: Both creeds affirm the core Christian beliefs such as the incarnation, the resurrection of Christ, the coming judgment, and the life of the world to come.

3. Use in liturgy: Both creeds have been used historically in Christian worship and liturgy, and they continue to be used in many Christian traditions today.

Differences:

4. Origins and historical context: The Apostles' Creed is an older and simpler statement of faith, traditionally believed to have been composed by the apostles themselves (though this is not historically verifiable). It originated in the Western Church and is most commonly used in Western Christian traditions. The Nicene Creed was composed during the Council of Nicea in AD 325 in response to Arianism, a heresy that denied the divinity of Christ. It is used by both Western and Eastern Christian traditions, although there are minor differences in wording between the two (notably the filioque clause).

5. Detail and complexity: The Nicene Creed is more detailed and complex than the Apostles' Creed. It includes more developed language about the nature of God the Father, the person and work of Jesus Christ, and the role of the Holy Spirit. It specifically emphasizes the full divinity of Jesus Christ ("God from God, Light from Light, true God from true God").

6. Language about the Church: The Nicene Creed includes the phrase "one, holy, catholic and apostolic Church," which the Apostles' Creed does not. Both creeds mention the forgiveness of sins and the resurrection of the body, but only the Nicene Creed speaks of the "life of the world to come."

These are some of the main similarities and differences, but both creeds serve to unite Christians around the world in shared faith and belief.

Section V
How Other Religions Teach about Jesus

1. Judaism
2. Islam
3. Baha'i Faith
4. Hinduism
5. Buddhism
6. Church of Jesus Christ and and Latter-Day Saints

How do Other Religions Teach About Jesus?

The figure of Jesus Christ is interpreted differently across various religions. Here are a few examples:

   • Judaism: In traditional Judaism, Jesus is not considered divine or messianic. The Messiah, as expected by Jews, is yet to come and will be an earthly figure who will gather Jews back into the Land of Israel, rebuild the Holy Temple in Jerusalem, and bring peace to the world. Some Jewish sects, like Messianic Jews, do believe in Jesus as the Messiah but they are generally not recognized as part of mainstream Judaism.

   • Islam: In Islam, Jesus (known as Isa) is considered one of God's important prophets, a messenger of monotheism, and the Messiah. However, Islam rejects the divinity of Jesus, viewing such a belief as incompatible with its strict monotheism. Muslims also believe that Jesus was not crucified but was raised to heaven by God.

   • Baha'i Faith: In the Baha'i faith, Jesus is considered a Manifestation of God, and His teachings are seen as part of a progressive revelation from God, which includes the teachings of other religious leaders like Moses, Muhammad, Buddha, Krishna, and the Baha'i faith's own founder, Bahá'u'lláh.

   • Hinduism: As Hinduism is a diverse tradition with a variety of beliefs, views about Jesus can vary widely. Some

Hindus might regard Jesus as a spiritual teacher or even a saint, and His teachings on love and charity might be appreciated. Some may consider Him a god or an avatar, akin to Hindu gods and divine figures, but This is not a widespread belief in Hinduism.

- Buddhism: Similarly, in Buddhism, there isn't a unified view of Jesus. Some Buddhists might see Jesus as a bodhisattva, a being who compassionately refrains from entering nirvana in order to save others, or as a wise and enlightened teacher. But these views are more common in areas where Buddhism and Christianity have had a significant interaction.

Remember, interpretations can vary widely even within each of these religions, given the diversity and complexity of religious belief.

Judaism

Judaism is one of the oldest monotheistic religions and was founded over 3500 years ago in the Middle East. It holds several key beliefs and practices:

- Monotheism: Jews believe in a single, all-knowing, all-powerful God. This belief in one God is the foundational principle of Judaism.
- The Torah: The Torah is the most important religious text in Judaism. It consists of five books (Genesis, Exodus, Leviticus, Numbers, Deuteronomy), which narrate the History of the universe from the creation to the death of Moses. It also contains the 613 commandments, or Mitzvot, which Jews are obligated to follow.
- Covenant: There's a belief in the covenant, or agreement, between God and the Jewish people. This covenant is marked by following God's laws as outlined in the Torah and it forms the basis for the Jews' enduring relationship with God.
- Messiah: In Jewish eschatology, there is a belief in the coming of the Messiah, a future Jewish king from the Davidic line, who will rule the Jewish people during the Messianic Age.
- Afterlife: Judaism has varied beliefs about the afterlife,

with views ranging from the resurrection of the dead to an immortal soul. However, there is less emphasis on the afterlife and more on moral and ethical actions in this life.
- Sabbath: Observing the Sabbath (Shabbat, from Friday evening to Saturday evening) as a day of rest is one of the key commandments. The Sabbath is seen as a gift from God and is a day of rest, prayer, and family.
- Holidays and Festivals: There are several important holidays and festivals in Judaism, including Rosh Hashanah (the Jewish New Year), Yom Kippur (Day of Atonement), Sukkot, Hanukkah, Passover, and Shavuot.
- Kosher: Dietary laws known as Kashrut dictate what is permissible to eat and how it must be prepared. Foods that are acceptable are known as Kosher.
- Prayer: Prayer in Judaism can take multiple forms and it is a means of connecting with God. The prayer service is often conducted in a synagogue and led by a rabbi.
- Life cycle rituals: There are several important life cycle rituals, including circumcision (Brit Milah) for newborn boys, Bar and Bat Mitzvahs for teenagers, marriage, and mourning rituals. In addition to these basic beliefs and practices, Judaism has different branches including Orthodox, Conservative, Reform, and Reconstructionist Judaism, each with its own interpretation of Jewish law and tradition.

How does Judaism Teach about Jesus?

Judaism's perspective on Jesus is fundamentally different from that of Christianity. In Christianity, Jesus is viewed as the Son of God and the Messiah (Christ), whose life, death, and resurrection offer salvation to humanity.
However, in Judaism, Jesus is not seen as divine or as the Messiah. Traditional Jewish teachings do not recognize the New Testament as sacred scripture and therefore do not contain direct teachings about Jesus. When historical records, such as those from Jewish Historians of the era like Josephus, or the Babylonian Talmud, mention Jesus, they generally view Him as a teacher or

rabbi, and sometimes as a false prophet, but not as the Messiah or divine.

The reason for this lies in the differing interpretations and expectations of the Messiah. In Judaism, the Messiah is anticipated to be a human leader, from the Davidic line, who will rebuild the Temple in Jerusalem, gather all Jews back to the Land of Israel, bring world peace by ending all wars, and unite humanity in the worship of the Jewish God. Jesus, having not fulfilled these requirements, is not considered the Messiah in Jewish belief.

Moreover, the concept of God as a Trinity, which is central to many Christian denominations, is considered by Judaism to be a form of polytheism and thus incompatible with Jewish monotheism.

In modern times, while the majority of Jewish thought still does not consider Jesus as the Messiah or divine, there is a wider range of views about Jesus the Historical figure. Some Jewish scholars and individuals take interest in studying Jesus as a Jewish historical figure, recognizing Him as a teacher or rabbi in the context of first-century Judaism, while still not accepting Him as Messiah or divine.

It's important to note that the above are general tendencies within Judaism, and individual beliefs may vary.

Islam

Islam is one of the major monotheistic religions in the world and was founded in the 7th century CE in Arabia by the Prophet Muhammad. Here are some of the key beliefs and practices in Islam:

- Monotheism: Islam teaches that there is only one God, known in Arabic as Allah, who is all-powerful, all-knowing, and merciful. The concept of monotheism in Islam is referred to as Tawhid.
- Quran: The Quran is the holy book of Islam. Muslims believe it to be the literal word of God as revealed to Prophet Muhammad through the Angel Gabriel.

- Prophets: Islam recognizes a long line of prophets (including Adam, Noah, Abraham, Moses, and Jesus) with Muhammad being the last and final prophet. These prophets are highly respected, but only as servants and messengers of God.
- Five Pillars: The Five Pillars of Islam form the framework of a Muslim's life. They are the Shahada (faith), Salat (prayer), Zakat (charity), Sawm (fasting during Ramadan), and Hajj (pilgrimage to Mecca).
- Life After Death: Islam teaches the belief in life after death. Muslims believe in resurrection, final judgment, and heaven (Jannah) and hell (Jahannam).
- Halal and Haram: Muslims follow dietary laws known as Halal (permitted) and Haram (forbidden). For example, pork and alcohol are considered Haram.
- Sharia: Sharia is the moral and religious law of Islam. It covers a wide range of topics, including crime, politics, and economics, as well as personal matters such as sexual intercourse, hygiene, diet, prayer, and fasting.
- Jihad: The term Jihad means "struggle" or "striving". It has both an internal aspect (striving against one's own sinful tendencies) and an external aspect (striving to make society more in line with God's commandments).
- Community (Ummah): The global Muslim community, or Ummah, is an important aspect of Islamic faith and identity. Muslims around the world see themselves as part of this broader community of belief.

It's important to note that just like any other religion, interpretations and practices of Islam can vary widely among different cultures, communities, and individuals. There are two major sects in Islam: Sunni and Shia, each with its own interpretation of Islamic law and tradition.

How does Islam Teach about Jesus?

In Islam, Jesus (known as 'Isa) (عيسى in Arabic) is highly revered and considered one of God's greatest and most respected messengers. However, the Islamic understanding of Jesus is different from the Christian understanding in several key respects:

- Jesus as a Prophet: Muslims believe that Jesus was a prophet of God and that he performed miracles such as healing the blind and the sick and bringing the dead back to life. These miracles were performed by the will of God, not by Jesus's own power.
- Jesus as Messiah: In Islam, Jesus is also referred to as the Messiah (Al-Masih (الَمسيح in Arabic). However, the term Messiah in Islam does not imply divinity as it does in Christianity. Instead, it acknowledges Jesus' special status and role as a prophet and messenger of God.
- Virgin Birth: Islam affirms the Christian belief in the virgin birth of Jesus. The Quran teaches that Jesus was born miraculously to the Virgin Mary (Maryam)("مَيرم" in Arabic) without a human father by the will of God.
- No Divinity or Sonship: Unlike Christianity, Islam does not consider Jesus to be divine or the son of God. The Quran emphasizes the monotheistic nature of God and states that attributing a son to God is a misinterpretation. According to Islamic belief, God is singular and without partners or children.
- Crucifixion and Resurrection: One of the most significant differences between Islamic and Christian teachings regarding Jesus concerns His death. The Quran states that Jesus was not crucified but was raised to heaven by God. Many Muslims believe that Jesus was not killed but was made to appear so to His enemies. Muslims believe that Jesus will return to Earth before the Day of Judgment.
- Second Coming: Muslims believe in the second coming of Jesus. They believe that near the end of times, Jesus will return to Earth, defeat the Antichrist (known as Dajjal)("الدّجّال" in Arabic), and establish peace and justice on Earth.

These teachings come from the Quran, the central religious text of Islam, which Muslims believe is a revelation from God, and from the Hadith, which are collections of the sayings, actions, and approvals of the Prophet Muhammad regarding daily life, including His interpretations and elaborations of Quranic verses.

Bahá'í Faith

The Bahá'í Faith is a monotheistic religion that emerged in the 19th century in Persia, in what is now Iran. It was founded by Bahá'u'lláh, who is considered by Bahá'ís to be the latest prophet, or "Manifestation of God," in a line of prophets that includes Abraham, Moses, Buddha, Zoroaster, Christ, Muhammad, and others. Here are some key beliefs and principles of the Bahá'í Faith:

- Oneness of God: Bahá'ís believe there is one God who is the source of all creation. God is transcendent and unknowable, but he has made Himself known to humanity through a series of divine messengers, or Manifestations of God.
- Oneness of Religion: Bahá'ís believe that all the world's major religions come from the same source, God, and are essentially different stages in the spiritual development of humanity. This principle is often referred to as "progressive revelation," the idea that religious truth is not absolute but relative, God's will is progressively revealed over time as humanity matures.
- Oneness of Humanity: The Bahá'í Faith emphasizes the unity of humanity transcending race, class, creed, and nation. Bahá'ís strive for global justice and peace through the establishment of equality and the elimination of prejudice.
- Equality of Men and Women: The Bahá'í Faith teaches that men and women are equal in the sight of God and should be accorded the same rights, privileges, and opportunities.
- Independent Investigation of Truth: Bahá'ís are encouraged to seek the truth for themselves, rather than relying on the opinions of others.
- Elimination of Prejudices: The Bahá'í Faith teaches the elimination of all forms of prejudice, whether based on race, religion, nationality, or social background.
- Universal Education: The Bahá'í Faith places great emphasis on education, advocating for universal education and literacy.

- Harmony of Religion and Science: Baháʼís view religion and science as complementary systems of knowledge that must work together to advance humanity.

The Baháʼí community is governed by elected bodies at the local, national, and international levels, known respectively as Local Spiritual Assemblies, National Spiritual Assemblies, and the Universal House of Justice, which is the highest governing body located in Haifa, Israel. The Baháʼí Faith does not have clergy. Baháʼís engage in regular devotional practices, such as daily prayer and an annual period of fasting and observe various holy days throughout the year. They also engage in individual and collective efforts to improve their communities and the world.

How does Baháʼí Faith teach about Jesus?

The Baháʼí Faith recognizes Jesus as a Manifestation of God, or a divine prophet. This means that, in Baháʼí belief, Jesus is one of a series of prophets or teachers who have appeared throughout human history, each of whom has revealed aspects of God's will and teachings suited to the time and place of their appearance. These prophets, also called Manifestations of God, include figures like Abraham, Moses, Buddha, Krishna, Zoroaster, Muhammad, and others, culminating in Baháʼuʼlláh, the founder of the Baháʼí Faith. Baháʼís believe that Baháʼuʼlláh's revelation fulfills many prophecies found in the world's major religions, including those of Jesus' return in Christianity.

In Baháʼí teachings, Jesus is recognized as having made a profound impact on the world, as a teacher of great wisdom, as a revealer of God's word, and as a manifestation of God's attributes. Jesus' teachings, as recorded in the New Testament, are considered an important part of God's ongoing revelation to humanity.

However, the Baháʼí view of Jesus differs from traditional Christian doctrine in several key respects. For example, Baháʼís do not view Jesus as God incarnate or as a part of a Trinity. Rather, Jesus is seen as a mirror reflecting God's qualities and attributes, a divine educator who helps humanity understand and draw closer to God.

Bahá'ís also believe in the crucifixion and resurrection of Jesus, but they interpret these events in a somewhat different light than traditional Christianity. The crucifixion is seen as a physical event, but the resurrection is generally understood in a spiritual sense, as the influence and teachings of Jesus continuing to inspire and guide people after His death, rather than a physical rising from the dead.

Finally, it's important to note that the Bahá'í Faith promotes the principle of the independent investigation of truth. This means that Bahá'ís are encouraged to study and reflect upon the scriptures of all religions, including the teachings of Jesus in the Bible, in their efforts to understand truth and to develop their spiritual understanding.

Hinduism

Hinduism, one of the world's oldest religions, originated in the Indian subcontinent and boasts a diverse system of beliefs and practices. While Hinduism encompasses a wide variety of beliefs due to its decentralized nature, here are some key concepts and practices that are common in Hindu thought:

- Dharma: Dharma refers to moral duty or righteousness. It varies based on one's age, caste, gender, profession, and occupation. Following one's dharma is a moral responsibility that needs to be fulfilled for a balanced and orderly life.
- Karma: The law of Karma states that every action has consequences. Good actions lead to positive outcomes, while bad actions lead to negative ones. Karma influences life circumstances in this life and determines the nature of future rebirths.
- Samsara: Samsara is the cycle of birth, death, and rebirth. The ultimate goal of Hindu spiritual practice is to escape This cycle.
- Moksha: Moksha or liberation is the release from the cycle of Samsara. It is achieved through realization of one's deepest self (Atman) and its unity with the ultimate reality (Brahman).

- Atman: This is the individual soul or self, which is considered eternal and divine.
- Brahman: Brahman is the ultimate reality or supreme cosmic power in Hinduism. It is formless, infinite, and eternal.
- Devas/Devis: Hindus worship a multitude of gods and goddesses (devas and devis), which are considered manifestations of Brahman. Some of the most widely worshipped deities include Brahma, Vishnu, Shiva, Lakshmi, Durga, and Saraswati.
- Yoga and Meditation: These are important spiritual practices in Hinduism aimed at achieving self-realization and union with the divine.
- Vedas and Upanishads: These are the sacred scriptures of Hinduism. The Vedas contain hymns, incantations, and rituals, while the Upanishads contain philosophical discussions about Brahman, Atman, and Moksha.
- Rituals and Festivals: Rituals in temples and homes, pilgrimages to holy sites, and numerous festivals form an integral part of Hindu practice.
- AHimsa: This is the principle of non-violence and respect for all living things. It's an important principle for many Hindus.
- Four Stages of Life: Hindu dharma recognizes four stages of life (ashramas): student life (Brahmacharya), householder life (Grihastha), hermit life (Vanaprastha), and ascetic life (Sannyasa).

It's important to note that these beliefs and practices may vary significantly among different communities and individuals due to the diverse nature of Hinduism. There are numerous philosophical schools and cultural traditions within Hinduism, including but not limited to, Vaishnavism, Shaivism, Shaktism, and Smartism.

How does Hinduism Teach about Jesus?

Hinduism does not traditionally include teachings about Jesus, as it predates Christianity by many centuries. The scriptures of

Hinduism, including the Vedas, Upanishads, Bhagavad Gita, Ramayana, and Mahabharata, were composed before the birth of Jesus and hence do not mention Him.

However, with the interaction of Hindu and Christian cultures, particularly in India, various views on Jesus have developed within Hindu thought. The way Jesus is understood in these contexts often reflects the plurality and diversity of Hindu perspectives.

For some Hindus, Jesus is seen as a holy man, a wise teacher, or even a 'satguru' (a spiritual teacher of the highest order). His teachings, particularly those on love, compassion, and selflessness, are highly respected.

Some of the philosophies and teachings of Jesus, such as the Sermon on the Mount, have been interpreted by certain Hindu thinkers, like Mahatma Gandhi, as aligning with the core Hindu philosophy of non-violence (AHimsa) and selfless action (Karma Yoga).

There are also certain Hindu movements and figures who interpret Jesus as an avatar (a divine incarnation) much like Krishna, Rama, or other divine figures in Hindu mythology. However, this perspective is not universally accepted within Hinduism, and traditional Hindu scriptures do not present Jesus as an avatar.

It's important to note that while these interpretations exist, they represent attempts to understand Jesus within a Hindu framework and do not necessarily align with Christian beliefs about Jesus. For example, the Christian belief in Jesus as the unique Son of God who grants salvation, the concept of original sin, and the belief in Jesus' death and resurrection as an atoning sacrifice for humanity's sins, are generally not congruent with Hindu beliefs.

In summary, while Hinduism does not traditionally teach about Jesus, various perspectives exist due to intercultural exchange and the inherently pluralistic nature of Hindu thought. These range from seeing Jesus as a spiritual teacher to viewing Him as a divine figure.

Buddhism

Buddhism is a major world religion founded by Siddhartha Gautama, who became known as the Buddha, or "enlightened one", in the 5th to 4th century BCE in ancient India. Buddhism has various forms, but all traditions share fundamental beliefs and practices:

- The Four Noble Truths: These are the truths that the Buddha came to understand during His enlightenment. They are: the truth of suffering (Dukkha), the truth of the cause of suffering (Samudaya, often identified as craving or attachment), the truth of the end of suffering (Nirodha), and the truth of the path leading to the end of suffering (Magga, identified as the Noble Eightfold Path).
- The Noble Eightfold Path: This path is the practical guideline to ethical and mental development with the goal of freeing individuals from attachments and delusions, ultimately leading to understanding. The path consists of Right Understanding, Right Thought, Right Speech, Right Action, Right Livelihood, Right Effort, Right Mindfulness, and Right Concentration.
- Karma: Karma refers to the law of cause and effect. Actions have consequences that can affect a person in this life and the next. Positive actions contribute to happiness and enlightenment, while negative actions lead to suffering.
- Samsara and Rebirth: Buddhists believe in a cycle of death and rebirth, called samsara. The conditions of one's current life are thought to be a result of the actions of previous lifetimes. The ultimate goal of Buddhism is to escape this cycle by achieving Nirvana.
- Nirvana: Nirvana is the ultimate goal of Buddhist practice. It represents liberation from the cycle of rebirth and the extinguishing of all attachments and desires, leading to ultimate peace and enlightenment.
- The Three Je wels: These are the three central Buddhist ideals that followers of Buddhism take refuge in: the Buddha (the

enlightened one), the Dharma (the teachings), and the Sangha (the community of practitioners).
- The Five Precepts: These are basic ethical guidelines for the followers of Buddhism: refrain from killing living things, refrain from stealing, refrain from sexual misconduct, refrain from lying, and refrain from taking intoxicants.
- Meditation and Mindfulness: These are central practices in Buddhism aimed at developing insight, clarity, and tranquility.
- Anatman: Unlike many religions, Buddhism does not teach the existence of a permanent self or soul. The concept of anatman, or no-self, suggests that the self is constantly changing and is composed of five aggregates: form, sensation, perception, mental formations, and consciousness.

Buddhism has many diverse branches and schools, including Theravada, Mahayana (which includes Zen and Pure Land Buddhism), and Vajrayana (Tibetan Buddhism), each with their own interpretations and practices. However, all uphold the core principles of the Four Noble Truths, the Noble Eightfold Path, and the aim of achieving enlightenment.

How does Buddhism Teach about Jesus?

Buddhism, as a religious tradition, predates Christianity by several centuries and originated in a different geographical and cultural context. Consequently, the Historical Buddha and the original Buddhist texts do not mention Jesus. Similarly, Jesus and the authors of the New Testament do not mention Buddhism. However, as Buddhism spread and developed over the centuries, and particularly in the modern era, Buddhists have come into contact with Christianity and have formed various perspectives on Jesus.

For many Buddhists, Jesus is seen as a spiritual teacher who espoused values of compassion, love, and morality, much like the Buddha. His teachings on love, forgiveness, and non-judgment may resonate with Buddhist teachings on compassion, loving-kindness, and non-harming.

Some Buddhists may view Jesus as a bodhisattva. In Mahayana Buddhism, a bodhisattva is a being who seeks enlightenment not only for themselves but also to help all sentient beings achieve liberation from suffering. The acts of self-sacrifice and compassion that Jesus is portrayed as demonstrating could be interpreted as bodhisattva-like qualities.

The Dalai Lama, a prominent Buddhist leader, has expressed respect for Jesus as a spiritual leader and has encouraged interfaith dialogue to find common ground between different religious traditions.

It's important to note that while these interpretations exist, they are attempts to understand Jesus within a Buddhist framework, and they do not align with orthodox Christian beliefs about Jesus. For example, the Christian understanding of Jesus as the unique incarnation of God who provides salvation to humanity is not easily reconcilable with core Buddhist concepts like anatta (non-self) and the goal of achieving nirvana.

In summary, while Buddhism does not have formal teachings on Jesus, various perspectives exist due to interfaith dialogue and the inherently pluralistic nature of Buddhist thought. These range from seeing Jesus as a spiritual teacher to viewing Him as a bodhisattva-like figure.

The Church of Jesus Christ of Latter-Day Saints

The Church of Jesus Christ of Latter-Day Saints, often informally known as the LDS Church or Mormon Church, is a Christian denomination that emerged in the United States in the early 19th century. The church was founded by Joseph Smith, whom members regard as a prophet. Here are some key beliefs and practices of the faith:

- The Book of Mormon: In addition to the Bible, Latter-Day Saints regard the Book of Mormon as scripture. Joseph Smith stated that he translated the Book of Mormon from golden plates that he discovered in New York, guided by the angel Moroni. The book is understood as another testament of Jesus Christ and tells the story of ancient peoples in the Americas.

- Continuing Revelation: Latter-Day Saints believe that God continues to communicate with humanity. Joseph Smith and each of His successors as president of the church is regarded as a prophet who can receive revelation from God for the entire church. Individuals are also encouraged to seek personal revelation for their own lives.
- Restoration: The LDS Church teaches that the original Church as organized by Jesus Christ was lost and that the church is a restoration of the original church, with the fullness of the gospel.
- Priesthood: The church has a lay priesthood in which worthy male members can be ordained, starting in their early teens. The priesthood is used to perform ordinances like baptism and the sacrament (communion).
- Temples and Ordinances: The LDS Church has temples around the world where special ordinances are performed, like eternal marriages and baptisms for the dead. These ordinances are seen as essential and are often performed by proxy for those who have died.
- Plan of Salvation: Latter-Day Saints believe in a plan of salvation that includes pre-mortal life, mortal life, and life after death. This includes a belief in a heavenly Father, His son Jesus Christ, and the Holy Ghost as three separate beings.
- Health Code (Word of Wisdom): The LDS Church has a health code known as the Word of Wisdom, which prohibits the consumption of alcohol, tobacco, coffee, and tea.
- Missionary Work: Missionary work is a significant focus of the LDS Church. Young men, young women, and retired couples serve missions around the world to share their beliefs and provide humanitarian service.

It's important to note that not all individuals or groups who identify as "Latter-Day Saints" or "Mormon" are part of the Church of Jesus Christ of Latter-Day Saints. There are various offshoots and splinter groups that emerged particularly after the death of Joseph Smith, each with their own beliefs and practices.

The LDS Church based in Salt Lake City, Utah, is by far the largest of these groups.

How does the Church of Jesus Christ of Latter-Day Saints Teach about Jesus?

The Church of Jesus Christ of Latter-Day Saints (LDS Church) has a unique perspective on Jesus Christ compared to other Christian denominations. While they hold many beliefs in common with mainstream Christianity, there are also significant differences.

- Jesus as the Son of God and the Messiah: similar to other Christian denominations, the LDS Church believes that Jesus Christ is the Son of God and the Savior of the world. They believe that Jesus was born to the Virgin Mary, performed miracles, suffered and died on the cross, and was resurrected on the third day.
- Jesus in the Americas: A distinctive belief of the LDS Church, as stated in the Book of Mormon, is that after His resurrection, Jesus visited the Americas and preached to the ancient inhabitants there, establishing His church among them.
- Jesus' Role in the Godhead: Latter-Day Saints believe in the Godhead as three distinct beings who are one in purpose: God the Father, Jesus Christ, and the Holy Ghost. This differs from traditional Christian Trinitarianism, which sees the Father, Son, and Holy Spirit as three persons in one substance. In LDS theology, Jesus is literally the Son of God the Father, not merely a spiritual or metaphorical son.
- Jesus and the Plan of Salvation: Jesus plays a central role in the LDS Church's teachings about the Plan of Salvation (also known as the Plan of Happiness). They believe that because of Jesus' atonement, all people will be resurrected, and those who accept the gospel of Jesus Christ and follow His commandments can receive eternal life.
- Jesus and the Restoration: Latter-Day Saints believe that Jesus Christ restored His true church in the latter days through the prophet Joseph Smith. This restoration included the re-

establishment of the priesthood authority that Jesus had given to His apostles in the New Testament.

• Continuing Revelation from Jesus: LDS Church believes that Jesus continues to guide the church today through revelation to the church's president, whom members regard as a prophet. These teachings are derived from multiple sources of scripture, including the Bible, the Book of Mormon, the Doctrine and Covenants, and the Pearl of Great Price, as well as teachings of modern-day prophets and apostles.

Glossary

Amen

The word "Amen" is a declaration of affirmation found in both the Hebrew Bible and the New Testament. Originating from the Hebrew word ""אָמֵן"" ('āmēn), it is closely related to the Hebrew verbs "aman," "emunah," and "emun," which generally involve trust, reliability, or faithfulness. In Greek, it is transliterated as "ἀμήν" (amēn) and serves a similar function in liturgical and biblical texts.
Usage and Meaning:
* Affirmation or Agreement: "Amen" is often used to indicate agreement, acceptance, or acknowledgment of something said previously, much like saying "so be it," "truly," or "indeed."
* End of Prayers: In Christian, Jewish, and Islamic traditions, "Amen" is commonly used to conclude prayers, hymns, or blessings, signaling the end of an interaction with the divine and affirming the content of the prayer.
* Ritualistic Usage: In religious contexts, it's a ritualistic way to affirm a congregation's participation and agreement with a reading, prayer, or hymn.
* Cultural Usage: In more modern, secular contexts, "Amen" can be used to strongly agree with a statement or sentiment expressed by someone else.
* In Legal Contexts: Historically, the term has also been used in formal oaths and covenants, both religious and legal.
Interpretations:
* Judaism: In Jewish tradition, saying "Amen" expresses agreement with a blessing and participation in the act of blessing. It is a central part of synagogue services and rituals.
* Christianity: Christians inherited the term from Jewish tradition and similarly use it to conclude prayers and hymns. The Lord's Prayer in the Christian New Testament ends with "Amen," and it appears frequently throughout the biblical text.

- Islam: In Islamic tradition, a similar term "Amin" is used. It is the Arabic form of "Amen" and is used to conclude prayers and blessings.

In summary, "Amen" is a versatile term with deep historical and religious roots. It serves as a form of affirmation or agreement in both religious and secular contexts.

Aramaic

Aramaic is a Semitic language closely related to Hebrew, and it was widely spoken in the Middle East from the 6th century BC until the 7th century AD. In the context of the Bible, it plays a significant role in both the Old and New Testaments.

In the Old Testament, portions of the books of Daniel (Daniel 2:4b through 7:28) and Ezra (Ezra 4:8-6:18 and 7:12-26) were written in Aramaic, reflecting the fact that Aramaic had become the common language of the Near East during the Babylonian Exile.

In the New Testament, while the main text was written in Greek, Aramaic words and phrases are preserved in the text, especially in the Gospels. These usually represent direct words or sayings of Jesus, who likely spoke Aramaic as His primary language. Examples of Aramaic in the New Testament include the phrase "Talitha cumi" (ܛܠܝܬܐ ܩܘܡܝ) (Mark 5:41), which means "Little girl, I say to you, arise," and "Eloi, Eloi, lema sabachthani?" (ܐܠܗܝ ܐܠܗܝ ܠܡܢܐ ܫܒܩܬܢܝ)(Mark 15:34), which means "My God, my God, why have you forsaken me?"

Thus, the use of Aramaic in the Bible reflects the Historical and cultural contexts in which the biblical texts were composed. Studying these texts in their original languages can provide deeper insights into their meanings. However, accurate translations are also widely available for those who don't read these languages

Baptise

The term "baptise" comes from the Greek word

"baptizo,"(βαπτίζω) which means to "immerse" or "submerge." In a religious context, baptism is a ritual that symbolizes purification or regeneration and admission to the Christian faith. The exact practice can vary among different Christian denominations, but it usually involves water, either through immersion, pouring, or sprinkling, and it is done in the name of the Father, Son, and Holy Spirit.

In many Christian traditions, baptism is considered a sacrament, an outward sign of an inward spiritual grace. It is often seen as a means of initiation into the Christian community, the Church, and is viewed as necessary for salvation in certain denominations.

The act of baptism is not only limited to Christianity. Variations of purifying rituals involving water can be found in various religions around the world, often symbolizing spiritual cleansing or rebirth.

Please note that the interpretations and significance of baptism can vary widely among different Christian traditions and other religions.

Being on the Road to Damascus

"Being on the road to Damascus" is a reference to the conversion of Saul of Tarsus (who later became known as Paul the Apostle) as described in the New Testament book of Acts, chapter 9. In the biblical narrative, Saul was a zealous persecutor of the early Christian community. While he was traveling on the road to Damascus to arrest followers of Jesus, he is said to have been suddenly surrounded by a bright light from heaven. He heard the voice of Jesus asking, "Saul, Saul, why do you persecute me?" Struck blind, Saul continued to Damascus, where His sight was restored by a disciple named Ananias. After this encounter, Saul became a follower of Jesus and changed His name to Paul. He went on to be one of the most influential figures in early Christianity, authoring many of the letters in the New Testament. In modern usage, "being on the road to Damascus" or having a "Damascus road experience" often refers to a sudden or radical conversion or change of belief, especially one that involves a dramatic and fundamental change from one extreme to another. It signifies a transformative moment of insight or revelation that leads to a complete shift in perspective or life direction.

Bible

The word "Bible" comes from the Latin "biblia," which is derived from the Greek "ta biblia" (τα βιβλία). These terms mean "the books" or "little books." The usage of "Bible" as a singular term came about because it represents a collection of religious texts or scriptures that are considered sacred and authoritative by various religious groups.
In Christian contexts, the Bible is composed of two main sections:
    • The Old Testament, which consists of religious texts shared with Judaism, including books of law (the Torah), History, wisdom literature, and the prophets.
    • The New Testament, which contains writings specific to Christianity, including the Gospels (accounts of Jesus Christ's life and teachings), the Acts of the Apostles, the Epistles (letters), and the Book of Revelation.
In a more general sense, the term "bible" can also be used to refer to any book or work that is considered authoritative or definitive on a particular subject.

Canaan

"Canaan" in the Bible refers to an ancient region in the Near East, which corresponds approximately to present-day Israel, Palestine, Lebanon, and parts of Jordan, Syria, and northeastern Egypt.
Here are key points to understand the biblical usage of "Canaan":
    • Land of Promise: In the biblical narrative, Canaan is the land God promised to give to Abraham and His descendants (Genesis 12:1-7; 17:8). The term "Promised Land" often refers to Canaan because of this divine promise.
    • Historical Inhabitants: The Canaanites were the

inhabitants of Canaan. They were often in conflict with the Israelites, and the Bible frequently presents the Canaanites as engaging in practices and worship that were contrary to the laws and worship of the God of Israel (Deuteronomy 18:9-12).
    • Conquest by Israelites: After the Exodus from Egypt, the Israelites, under the leadership of Joshua, entered and conquered Canaan, dividing the land among the Twelve Tribes of Israel (the Book of Joshua). The Canaanite culture and presence, however, persisted in the land.
    • Historical Significance: The Canaanite culture had significant influence on the surrounding region. Canaan was a crossroads of the ancient Near East and was influenced by many of the key civilizations of the time, including the Egyptians, Hittites, Assyrians, and Babylonians.
It's important to note that the Historical and archaeological record of Canaan and the Canaanites is complex and sometimes controversial, and interpretations can vary among biblical scholars, Historians, and archaeologists.

Christian

The term "Christian" comes from the Greek word "christianos," (Χριστιανός) which means "follower of Christ." It is used to den ote someone who follows the teachings of Jesus Christ and accepts Him as their savior. The term was first used in the city of Antioch in the first century A.D. as recorded in the New Testament of the Bible in Acts 11:26.
Christianity as a religion is centered around the life, teachings, death, and resurrection of Jesus Christ, whom Christians believe to be the Son of God and the Messiah prophesied in the Old Testament. Christianity teaches the doctrine of salvation, asserting that through faith in Jesus Christ, individuals can receive forgiveness for their sins and obtain eternal life.
The beliefs and practices within Christianity can vary widely, with numerous denominations and traditions, including but not limited to Roman Catholicism, Eastern Orthodoxy, and various branches of Protestantism. Despite this diversity, the belief in

Jesus Christ as Lord and Savior is the unifying factor among Christians.

Compassion

Compassion is a fundamental concept in the Bible, central to the character of God and the ethical instructions for believers. Compassion, as a term, refers to a deep empathy for the suffering of others and a desire to alleviate that suffering.

In the Old Testament, the Hebrew word often translated as compassion is "rachamim"(רחמים), derived from the word "rehem" which means "womb." This suggests the kind of deep, nurturing love and concern a mother has for her child. God is frequently described as being compassionate. For example, in the book of Exodus, God describes Himself to Moses: "The Lord, the Lord, a God merciful and gracious, slow to anger, and abounding in steadfast love and faithfulness" (Exodus 34:6).

In the New Testament, the Greek word for compassion is "splagchnizomai" (σπλαγχνίζομαι,)which suggests a feeling from deep within, a kind of visceral reaction to the suffering of others. Jesus, in particular, is often described as being moved by compassion in the Gospels. He feels compassion for the crowds who are like "sheep without a shepherd" (Mark 6:34), for the lepers who seek healing (Mark 1:41), and for the bereaved (Luke 7:13).

Believers, too, are called to show compassion. In the parable of the Good Samaritan (Luke 10:25-37), Jesus uses the example of the Samaritan man, who shows compassion for the injured man on the road, to teach about the importance of loving one's neighbor and showing mercy.

In essence, compassion in the Bible refers not only to feelings of empathy and concern but also to actions of kindness, mercy, and care. It is a characteristic of God and a quality that believers are called to emulate in their dealings with others.

Covenant

In the Bible, a covenant is a solemn agreement or contract between God and His people. It is a binding relationship that outlines the terms and conditions of the agreement, often accompanied by promises and obligations from both parties involved. Covenants are significant in the biblical narrative as they establish God's relationship with humanity, reveal His character and purposes, and provide a framework for understanding His redemptive plan.
Throughout the Bible, several covenants are mentioned, each serving a specific purpose in God's overall plan. Here are some notable covenants found in the Bible:

- The Noahic Covenant: This covenant is established in the book of Genesis after the great flood. God promises never to destroy the earth by a flood again and sets the rainbow as a sign of this covenant.
- The Abrahamic Covenant: God establishes this covenant with Abraham in Genesis 12. He promises to make Abraham a great nation, bless him and his descendants, and give them the land of Canaan as an everlasting possession.
- The Mosaic Covenant: Also known as the Law or Old Covenant, this covenant is given to Moses on Mount Sinai. It includes the Ten Commandments and the laws and regulations that the Israelites were to follow. It served as a guideline for their worship, moral conduct, and social interactions.
- The Davidic Covenant: God establishes this covenant with King David in 2 Samuel 7. He promises that David's descendants will establish an everlasting kingdom, and the Messiah, Jesus Christ, will come from the lineage of David.
- The New Covenant: Foretold by the prophets, the New Covenant is fulfilled in Jesus Christ. It is an agreement between God and humanity, where Jesus' sacrifice on the cross provides forgiveness of sins and establishes a personal relationship with

God. It is characterized by grace, faith, and the indwelling of the Holy Spirit.
These covenants illustrate God's faithfulness, His desire for a relationship with His people, and His plan for redemption. They form a crucial framework for understanding the biblical narrative and the unfolding of God's purpose throughout history.

Crucifixion

Crucifixion is an ancient method of execution in which the condemned person is tied or nailed to a large wooden beam and left to hang, often for several days, until eventual death from exhaustion and asphyxiation. The term comes from the Latin "crucifixio," which translates to "fixing to a cross," derived from "crux" (cross) and "figere" (to fasten or fix).
In the context of Christianity, the Crucifixion usually refers to the execution of Jesus Christ by Roman authorities around 30-33 A.D., an event central to Christian beliefs. According to the New Testament, Jesus was arrested, tried, and sentenced by Pontius Pilate to be scourged and finally executed on a cross. Christians believe that Jesus's death and subsequent resurrection three days later is a pivotal event in human History, providing redemption and salvation for those who accept and follow Him.
"Crucifixion" is often misspelled as "crucifiction." The correct spelling is "crucifixion."

Disciple

The term "disciple" in the Bible is derived from the Greek word "mathētēs," (μαθητής) which means a learner or follower. In a general sense, it can refer to anyone who follows the teaching of another.
However, in the context of the New Testament, "disciple" usually refers specifically to the followers of Jesus Christ. The term is most often used to refer to the 12 Apostles, whom Jesus

personally chose to follow Him closely and learn from His teachings. These 12 disciples, sometimes also referred to as the "Twelve," include Peter, James (son of Zebedee), John, Andrew, Philip, Bartholomew, Matthew, Thomas, James (son of Alphaeus), Thaddaeus, Simon the Zealot, and Judas Iscariot, who was later replaced by Matthias.

The term "disciple" is also used more broadly in the New Testament to refer to all who followed Jesus, accepted His teachings, and committed themselves to His mission. For instance, in the book of Acts, disciples are those who believe in Jesus and spread His message.

Being a disciple in the Biblical sense implies not just accepting and believing certain doctrines, but also living in accordance with Jesus's teachings and seeking to emulate His life and character. It is a call to a lifestyle of learning from and following Jesus. This includes embracing His teachings, adopting His ethical and moral standards, and participating in the mission of spreading the Gospel.

Eucharist

The Last Supper is called the Eucharist because it was during this meal that Jesus instituted the sacrament of the Eucharist, which is also known as Holy Communion, the Lord's Supper, or the Mass in various Christian denominations.

The word "Eucharist" comes from the Greek word "eucharistia," which means thanksgiving. During the Last Supper, Jesus took bread and wine, blessed them, and distributed them to his disciples, saying, "This is my body, which is given for you. Do this in remembrance of me...This cup that is poured out for you is the new covenant in my blood" (Luke 22:19-20). By doing so, Jesus instituted the Eucharist as a way for his followers to remember and participate in his sacrifice for the forgiveness of sins.

In the Eucharist, the bread and wine are believed to become the body and blood of Christ, and through this sacrament, Christians believe that they are united with Christ and with one another. The

Eucharist is central to the liturgy and worship of many Christian denominations and is seen as a way to receive grace and spiritual nourishment.

Forgiveness

Forgiveness in the Bible refers to the act of pardoning an offender and renouncing anger, resentment, or the desire for retaliation. It is a central concept in Christianity and a key attribute of God. In the Old Testament, God's forgiveness of human sin is a recurring theme, reflecting His mercy and loving-kindness. For instance, in Psalm 103:12, it says, "As far as the east is from the west, so far has He removed our transgressions from us." This underscores the completeness of God's forgiveness.
In the New Testament, the concept of forgiveness is central to the teachings of Jesus. In the Lord's Prayer, Jesus teaches His followers to ask for God's forgiveness and to forgive others: "Forgive us our debts, as we also have forgiven our debtors" (Matthew 6:12). Jesus emphasizes the importance of forgiveness in various parables, like the Parable of the Unforgiving Servant (Matthew 18:21-35).
Furthermore, in Christian belief, the death and resurrection of Jesus Christ provide the ultimate act of divine forgiveness. Christians believe that Jesus' sacrifice offers forgiveness of sins for all who believe in Him (Ephesians 1:7).
It's important to note that forgiveness in the Bible doesn't mean ignoring or excusing wrongdoing. Rather, it involves a conscious decision to release feelings of resentment or vengeance toward a person who has harmed you, regardless of whether they deserve your forgiveness.
Forgiveness also doesn't necessarily mean reconciliation or returning to the same relationship dynamic. It's possible to forgive someone without restoring a relationship to its previous state, particularly in cases of abuse or ongoing harm.
In summary, forgiveness in the Bible reflects God's mercy towards humanity and is a model for human behavior. It's both a divine gift and a human responsibility.

Galilee

Galilee is a region in modern-day northern Israel, known for its lush landscapes, featuring hills, valleys, and the freshwater Sea of Galilee (also called Lake Kinneret or Lake Tiberias). In ancient times, Galilee was divided into two main parts: Lower and Upper Galilee. The area was agriculturally rich and known for its fishery. During the time of Jesus, Galilee was part of the Roman Empire, and its population was a mix of Jews and Gentiles. Major cities included Tiberias, Sepphoris, and Capernaum.

Cultural and Religious Landscape

The cultural and religious landscape of Galilee was diverse. Although the region was predominantly Jewish, the influence of neighboring regions and the Roman Empire created a more cosmopolitan environment than in Judea to the south. This influenced local practices, trade, and interaction among different communities.

Jesus and Galilee

Jesus of Nazareth was born in Bethlehem, but he grew up in Nazareth, a small town in Galilee. Much of Jesus' ministry took place in this region. The Gospels report that he performed many miracles here, such as the feeding of the 5,000 near the Sea of Galilee, walking on water, and various healings and exorcisms. He also delivered key teachings, like the Sermon on the Mount, which is thought to have taken place in Galilee.

Significance of Galilee in Jesus' Ministry

- **Home and Family:** Nazareth, where Jesus grew up, is in Galilee. His family, including Mary and Joseph, were Galileans.
- **Initial Public Ministry:** After his baptism by John the Baptist and his temptation in the desert, Jesus began his public ministry in Galilee. He initially settled in Capernaum, a town near the Sea of Galilee, which served as a sort of "home base" for his ministry.
- **Disciples:** Most of Jesus' disciples were Galileans. Notably, Peter, Andrew, James, and John were fishermen from the Sea of Galilee.
- **Teaching and Preaching:** Galilee was the setting for

much of Jesus' teaching. Many of the parables and sermons that constitute the core of Christian ethical teachings were delivered here.
- Miracles: Many of the miracles attributed to Jesus in the New Testament occurred in Galilee, often around the Sea of Galilee.
- Jewish Context: Jesus was engaging with a largely Jewish audience in Galilee, and much of his teaching can be understood as a dialogue with or expansion of Jewish law, tradition, and Messianic expectations.
- Outreach to Gentiles: The region's mixed population also gave Jesus the opportunity to engage with non-Jews (Gentiles), and some of his miracles and teachings are explicitly directed at or involve Gentiles.
- Final Journey to Jerusalem: Although Galilee was the main focus of his ministry, Jesus eventually left for Judea and Jerusalem in the south, where he was crucified.

Conclusion

Galilee was not just a backdrop but a significant context that influenced and shaped Jesus' ministry. The region's cultural diversity, combined with its religious and socio-political landscape, played a role in how Jesus' message was received and would later be spread to other parts of the world.

Gentile

The term "Gentile" in the Bible refers to anyone who is not a part of the Jewish people. It comes from the Latin term "gentilis," meaning "of or belonging to the same people or nation," but in the context of the Bible, it's used to differentiate between the Jewish people and all other nations.
In the Old Testament, the Hebrew word typically translated as "Gentile" is "goy,"(גוֹי) which simply means "nation." It can be used to refer to any nation, including Israel itself, but it often refers to nations other than Israel.
In the New Testament, the Greek word typically translated as "Gentile" is "ethnos,"(ἔθνος) which can mean "nation,"

"people," or "Gentiles." It's usually used to refer to non-Jewish people.

The distinction between Jews and Gentiles becomes a significant theme in the New Testament, particularly in the letters of the Apostle Paul. In the early Christian Church, a major point of contention was whether Gentile converts to Christianity needed to observe Jewish customs and laws. In letters to various churches, Paul argues that faith in Jesus Christ is sufficient for salvation and that Gentile Christians are not obligated to follow Jewish customs and laws (Galatians 2:15-16; Romans 3:28-30). Thus, in the biblical context, a "Gentile" is essentially anyone who is not Jewish. This term represents the universal scope of the Christian gospel, emphasizing that salvation through Jesus Christ is available to all people, regardless of their ethnic or religious background.

Gentle

The term "gentle" in the Bible often refers to a quality of character that is kind, considerate, humble, and compassionate, without harshness or violence. It is listed as one of the fruits of the Spirit in Galatians 5:22-23 and is presented as a desirable trait for Christians to cultivate.

Here are some key biblical passages where the concept of gentleness is mentioned:
- Matthew 5:5: In the Sermon on the Mount, Jesus says, "Blessed are the meek, for they shall inherit the earth." The term "meek" in this context can be understood as being gentle or humble.
- Matthew 11:29: Jesus describes Himself as "gentle and humble in heart," inviting those who are weary to find rest in Him.
- Galatians 5:22-23: The Apostle Paul lists gentleness as one of the fruits of the Spirit, qualities that should be displayed by those who are led by the Holy Spirit.
- Ephesians 4:2: Paul encourages believers to live "with all humility and gentleness, with patience, bearing with one

another in love."
- 1 Peter 3:4: Peter speaks of the "gentle and quiet spirit" that is precious in God's sight, in the context of describing inner beauty.
- 2 Timothy 2:24-25: Paul encourages Timothy to correct opponents "with gentleness," with the hope that God may grant them repentance leading to a knowledge of the truth.

The consistent biblical message is that gentleness is a mark of strength, not weakness. It is a quality that reflects the character of Christ and is to be pursued in Christian living.

Grace

The term "grace" is a significant concept in the Bible and plays a crucial role in Christian theology. In its simplest form, grace can be understood as the unmerited favor or kindness from God.
In the Old Testament, the Hebrew word often translated as 'grace' or 'favor' is 'chen,'(חן) which implies favor, mercy, or kindness. It's used to describe God's favor and compassionate action towards humanity.
In the New Testament, the Greek word for grace is "charis" (χάρις). It carries a broader range of meaning, encompassing concepts like kindness, gift, blessing, favor, and graciousness. It is used in various contexts to express the idea of God's undeserved favor and the free gift of salvation given through faith in Jesus Christ.
Perhaps one of the most well-known New Testament verses on grace is Ephesians 2:8-9: "For by grace you have been saved through faith, and this is not your own doing; it is the gift of God—not the result of works, so that no one may boast."
This verse encapsulates the Christian understanding of grace: salvation is a gift from God, given out of love, and it cannot be earned by human effort or merit. This understanding of grace emphasizes God's initiative and action in the process of salvation.
The concept of grace is fundamental to Christian belief and is often contrasted with the idea of earning salvation through

adherence to laws or good deeds. Instead, Christians believe that they are saved by God's grace, through faith in Jesus Christ.

Hebrew

The term "Hebrew" in the Bible can refer to several related concepts:
- A language: Hebrew is the primary language in which the Old Testament (or Tanakh in Jewish tradition) was written. This ancient form of the language is often referred to as Biblical Hebrew.
- A people: "Hebrews" is used in the Bible to refer to the ancestors of the Israelites, descended from Eber (Genesis 10:24) or more specifically, to the people descended from Jacob, son of Isaac, grandson of Abraham. Abraham is described as a "Hebrew" in Genesis 14:13, likely indicating His lineage and distinguishing Him from the Canaanite peoples. Over time, the term "Hebrews" came to be largely synonymous with "Israelites," especially during the period of the Exodus and settlement in the land of Canaan.
- A cultural or ethnic group: In a broader sense, the term "Hebrew" could be used to refer to the broader cultural or ethnic group of the ancient Israelites, including their descendants, the Jews.

In modern usage, "Hebrew" most commonly refers to the Semitic language spoken by the ancient Israelites and Jews, and which continues to be used as a spoken language today, particularly in the State of Israel.

Jerusalem

Jerusalem, often called "the holy city" in the Bible, has deep Historical and religious significance. The word "Jerusalem" means "foundation of peace," or "city of peace,"(מילשורי) in Hebrew. The city is central to the biblical narrative and is significant in both the Old and New Testaments.

In the Old Testament:
- David and Jerusalem: King David, the second king of the united Kingdom of Israel, established Jerusalem as the nation's capital, and it came to be known as the "City of David" (2 Samuel 5:6-10). It was under David's rule that the Ark of the Covenant was brought to Jerusalem, symbolizing God's presence among the people (2 Samuel 6:12-17).
- Solomon and the Temple: David's son, King Solomon, built the first Jewish Temple in Jerusalem, further solidifying the city's status as the religious center of Jewish life and worship (1 Kings 6:1-38). The Temple was understood to be the dwelling place of God's presence.

In the New Testament:
- Jesus and Jerusalem: Jerusalem plays a significant role in the life, death, and resurrection of Jesus Christ. He was presented in the Temple in Jerusalem as a baby (Luke 2:22-38), visited the city during Passover (Luke 2:41-52), and made several other trips to Jerusalem according to the Gospels. His last visit ended with His crucifixion and resurrection.
- Early Christ ian Church: After Jesus' ascension, the apostles returned to Jerusalem, where the Holy Spirit descended on them during the feast of Pentecost (Acts 2:1-4). The early Christian church began in Jerusalem.

Even beyond its biblical significance, Jerusalem remains a crucial city to this day for Christians, Jews, and Muslims alike due to its rich religious history.

Koine Greek

Koine Greek is the particular dialect of the Greek language that was used in the Hellenistic and Roman periods, from about the 4th century BC to the 4th century AD. Its name derives from the Greek term "koine,"(κοινή) meaning "common," reflecting its status as the commonly spoken language of the time, especially in the Eastern Mediterranean and the Middle East.

The New Testament of the Bible was written in Koine Greek. This was the "lingua franca" or common language across the Eastern Mediterranean during the time of Jesus and the early Christian Church, so it was the natural choice for the authors of the New Testament.

The use of Koine Greek in the New Testament allowed the early Christian message to spread more easily throughout the diverse linguistic environment of the Eastern Roman Empire. Even though the individual authors of the New Testament (like Paul, John, Luke, etc.) may have had different levels of Greek proficiency and style, the use of Koine Greek provided a common linguistic platform for the diverse early Christian communities. Today, studying the New Testament in the original Koine Greek can provide deeper insights into the text, as it allows for a more nuanced understanding of the vocabulary, grammar, and idioms used by the original authors. However, accurate and reliable translations are also available for those who don't read Greek.

Love

"Love" is a fundamental and multifaceted concept in the Bible, serving as the basis for many of its teachings and principles. It is mentioned numerous times throughout both the Old and New Testaments and is presented in various forms such as love for God, love for neighbor, familial love, and divine love.

In the Old Testament, two primary Hebrew words for love are "ahava," (הבהא) which often denotes affection, and "chesed,"(חסד) which conveys steadfast love or loving-kindness, often in the context of God's love for His people. God's love in the Old Testament is shown in His care for Israel, His forgiveness, His steadfast loyalty, and His mercy.

In the New Testament, love becomes central to the teachings of Jesus. Two Greek words for love are often used: "agape"(.ἀγάπη) and "philia."(φιλία) Agape love is selfless, sacrificial, unconditional love—it's the term used to describe God's love for humanity. Philia love refers to brotherly love or friendship.

In the Gospel of John, Jesus states the greatest commandment:

"A new command I give you: Love one another. As I have loved you, so you must love one another" (John 13:34). This instruction encapsulates the call to emulate the selfless and unconditional love of God.

The apostle Paul further emphasizes the supremacy of love in His letters. In 1 Corinthians 13, often referred to as the "Love Chapter," he describes love's qualities: "Love is patient, love is kind. It does not envy, it does not boast, it is not proud. It does not dishonor others, it is not self-seeking, it is not easily angered, it keeps no record of wrongs. Love does not delight in evil but rejoices with the truth. It always protects, always trusts, always hopes, always perseveres" (1 Corinthians 13:4-7).

In the Christian context, the ultimate expression of God's agape love is seen in the sacrificial death of Jesus Christ for the sins of humanity (John 3:16).

In summary, the concept of love in the Bible is multi-dimensional, encompassing God's love for humanity, the love among humans, and the love that believers are called to show towards God. It's characterized by attributes like selflessness, patience, kindness, and endurance.

Parable

In the Bible, a parable is a literary device used by Jesus to teach spiritual and moral lessons through the use of stories or narratives. Parables are fictional or hypothetical scenarios that Jesus presented to his followers, often using everyday situations and familiar imagery to convey deeper truths about the kingdom of God, human nature, and the principles of God's reign.

Here are some key characteristics of parables:

- Symbolic storytelling: Parables typically involve a concise narrative that includes characters, settings, and events. These stories are not meant to be taken as literal historical accounts but are rather fictional or hypothetical scenarios designed to illustrate a spiritual truth.
- Analogical teaching: Parables use analogy and metaphor to draw parallels between the story elements and the spiritual

truth being conveyed. The characters and events in the parable represent concepts or realities beyond the immediate story, allowing listeners to make connections and grasp deeper meanings.

- Thought-provoking and engaging: Parables are intentionally crafted to capture the attention of the audience and provoke contemplation and reflection. They often present unexpected or challenging scenarios that invite listeners to think critically and consider their own attitudes, beliefs, and actions.
- Multilayered meanings: Parables can have multiple layers of meaning, providing insights into various aspects of the kingdom of God, human behavior, or spiritual principles. Jesus often used parables to challenge conventional wisdom, expose hypocrisy, or reveal profound truths about God's character and His relationship with humanity.

The purpose of parables in the Bible was to teach spiritual truths and invite listeners to actively engage with the message. They prompted reflection, encouraged self-examination, and invited a response from the hearers. Jesus used parables to convey complex ideas in a way that was relatable and accessible to His audience, often concealing deeper truths from those who were not genuinely seeking understanding.

Interpreting parables requires discernment and an understanding of the cultural and historical context in which they were given. It is important to consider the broader teachings of Jesus and the overall message of the Bible to properly grasp the intended meaning of each parable.

Pentecost

Pentecost is a significant event in the Christian liturgical calendar, traditionally celebrated 50 days after Easter Sunday. It commemorates the descent of the Holy Spirit upon the apostles and other followers of Jesus Christ while they were in Jerusalem for the Feast of Weeks, as described in the second chapter of the Acts of the Apostles in the New Testament.

Biblical Account:

In the biblical account, the apostles were gathered in a room when a sound like a strong wind filled the place, and "tongues of fire" appeared above each of them. They were then filled with the Holy Spirit, which enabled them to speak in different languages. This event was significant because it equipped the apostles for their mission to spread the "Good News" of Jesus Christ, allowing them to communicate with people from various linguistic backgrounds.

Theological Significance:

- Gift of the Holy Spirit: Pentecost is often referred to as the "birthday of the Church." The Holy Spirit is considered the "giver of life," and its presence empowers the community of believers and individual Christians for service, witness, and worship.
- Unity in Diversity: The gift of tongues symbolizes the Church's universal reach across linguistic and cultural barriers. It's seen as an undoing of the Tower of Babel story in the Old Testament, where humanity's languages were confused.
- Launch of Evangelism: After receiving the Holy Spirit, Peter, one of Jesus' closest followers, steps out and preaches a sermon that leads to about 3,000 people being baptized. This event marks the beginning of the apostles' public ministry and the expansion of early Christianity.

Liturgical Observance:

In the Christian liturgical calendar, Pentecost ends the season of Easter and initiates what is known as "Ordinary Time." Red vestments are often worn to signify the fire of the Spirit, and the use of doves, wind, and fire imagery is common. Various Christian traditions have different ways of observing this day, including special worship services, scripture readings, hymns, and even processions.

Connection to Judaism:

It's worth noting that Pentecost has its roots in the Jewish Feast of Weeks (Shavuot), which occurs 50 days after Passover and commemorates the giving of the Torah at Mount Sinai. The apostles were in Jerusalem to observe this Jewish festival when the events of Pentecost occurred.

Overall, Pentecost is a pivotal moment in Christian history, signifying the coming of the Holy Spirit to empower the Church for its global mission.

Pharisee

A "Pharisee" was a member of an ancient Jewish sect that existed during the Second Temple Period, from around the 2nd century BCE until the 1st century CE.
The Pharisees were known for their meticulous observance of the Torah (the first five books of the Bible) and for their emphasis on following both the written and oral Jewish laws. They believed in the resurrection of the dead and the existence of angels and spirits, which differentiated them from another prominent group of the time, the Sadducees, who rejected these concepts.
In the New Testament of the Christian Bible, Pharisees are often depicted as opponents of Jesus. They are portrayed as focusing on the letter of the law, sometimes at the expense of the spirit of the law, and as being hypocritical.
It's important to note that the New Testament's portrayal reflects a specific Historical and religious context. Historically, Pharisees had a significant role in the development of Judaism. After the destruction of the Second Temple in 70 CE, Pharisaic beliefs and interpretations of the law became foundational in Rabbinic Judaism, the form of Judaism that has continued to modern times.

Piety

Piety, as a concept, is widely present in the Bible, though the specific English word "piety" may not appear frequently due to variations in translation. Nonetheless, piety generally refers to reverence and dedication towards God, shown through actions, attitudes, and lifestyles that align with His commands.
The concept is often demonstrated through characters and teachings in the Bible:
- In the Old Testament, piety is often exemplified by the prophets and individuals who obeyed God's commands, even

under difficult circumstances. For example, Noah showed piety by building the ark in obedience to God's instruction, despite the ridicule he faced from his community.

- The Psalms often reflect a deep sense of piety. King David's psalms, for instance, reflect a heart turned towards God, demonstrating reverence, love, trust, and a thirst for righteousness.
- In the New Testament, Jesus Christ is the ultimate model of piety, perfectly following the will of God the Father. His teachings, such as the Sermon on the Mount (Matthew chapters 5-7), highlight how we should live righteously.
- The apostle Paul's writings in the epistles also emphasize piety. For instance, he highlights the importance of leading a peaceful and quiet life in godliness and dignity (1 Timothy 2:2). While the term "piety" may not always be used explicitly in these contexts, the concept of reverence and respect for God, demonstrated through obedient and righteous living, is a core theme throughout the Bible.

Prayer

The word "prayer" in the Bible refers to communication or conversation with God. It is an integral part of the Judeo-Christian tradition and features prominently throughout the Old and New Testaments.
Prayer can take on various forms and serves several purposes, including:

- Adoration a nd Praise: This involves expressing love and admiration towards God, acknowledging His greatness and goodness. The Book of Psalms is filled with prayers of adoration and praise.
- Confession: This includes acknowledging one's sins and asking for forgiveness. An example is found in Psalm 51, a penitential psalm where King David confesses His sin to God.
- Thanksgiving: Expressing gratitude to God for His blessings and His works. An example can be found in 1 Thessalonians 5:16-18, where believers are encouraged to give

thanks in all circumstances.
- Supplication: This involves making requests or petitions to God. This can be for oneself (personal supplication) or for others (intercession). An example of This type of prayer is seen in Philippians 4:6.

In the New Testament, Jesus teaches His disciples how to pray with the Lord's Prayer (Matthew 6:9-13). This model prayer includes all the aforementioned elements.

It's important to note that while the term "prayer" refers to communication with God, it's often used to refer to a number of related activities, including meditation on God's word, contemplation of His nature, and silent reflection on His works.

Prophecy

In the Bible, prophecy refers to the communication of divine messages or revelations from God to His chosen prophets. It is a means through which God communicates His will, His plans for humanity, and His desires for individuals, communities, and nations. Biblical prophecy encompasses various forms, including predictions of future events, proclamation of God's judgments, warnings of impending consequences, and declarations of God's promises.

Prophets in the Bible were individuals chosen by God to receive and deliver His messages to His people. They acted as intermediaries, receiving direct revelations, visions, dreams, or impressions from God, which they then conveyed to the intended recipients. The prophetic messages were often given in the context of specific historical situations or to address particular spiritual, moral, or social issues.

Biblical prophecy serves several purposes:
- Revelation: Prophecy reveals truths and insights about God's character, His plans, and His redemptive purposes for humanity. It provides a glimpse into the divine perspective and helps people understand God's intentions and ways.
- Guidance and Instruction: Prophecy offers guidance on how to live in alignment with God's will. It provides moral,

ethical, and spiritual instructions, offering clarity on issues such as justice, righteousness, worship, and personal conduct.
- Warning and Correction: Prophecy often includes warnings of impending judgment or consequences for disobedience. It calls individuals, communities, or nations to repentance and offers the opportunity for course correction.
- Encouragement and Hope: Prophecy can provide encouragement, assurance, and hope to those facing challenges, trials, or difficult circumstances. It reassures people of God's faithfulness, His promises, and His ultimate plan for restoration and redemption.

The fulfillment of biblical prophecies varies throughout the Bible. Some prophecies were fulfilled within the historical context in which they were given, while others had a longer-term fulfillment or a spiritual significance beyond their immediate context. Christians often interpret certain prophecies as pointing to the life, death, and resurrection of Jesus Christ or the establishment of His kingdom.

It is important to study and interpret biblical prophecy with care, considering the cultural, historical, and literary context, as well as seeking guidance from trusted sources and the guidance of the Holy Spirit to discern its meaning and application.

Salvation

The term "salvation" in the Bible refers to the act of saving or protecting from harm, risk, loss, or destruction. In a theological context, it typically involves deliverance from sin and its consequences, leading to a state of eternal happiness in the presence of God.
Here are some ways "salvation" is used in the Bible:
- Old Testament: In the Old Testament, the Hebrew word for salvation is often "yeshua (ישוע)," which can mean deliverance, rescue, safety, welfare, victory, and salvation. It is used in a variety of contexts, such as deliverance from enemies or oppression. For instance, in Exodus, the Israelites' liberation from slavery in Egypt is depicted as a form of salvation by God.

- New Testament: In the New Testament, the Greek word "soteria" (σωτηρία) is typically translated as "salvation," and it refers to deliverance, preservation, and safety. It is most often used in the context of spiritual salvation, a central theme in the teachings of Jesus Christ and the apostles. The New Testament presents salvation as a gift from God through faith in Jesus Christ, who, through His death and resurrection, redeems humanity from sin and death (Ephesians 2:8-9).

The concept of salvation is central to Christian theology and is often interpreted as being synonymous with being granted eternal life in Heaven. However, different Christian denominations may have varying interpretations of how salvation is achieved and what it entails.

Samaritan

The term "Samaritan" in the Bible refers to a person from Samaria, a region in the central part of ancient Palestine, situated between Judea to the south and Galilee to the north. Samaritans and Jews in the biblical period had significant religious and cultural differences which often led to tensions and conflict. Both groups traced their heritage back to the tribes of Israel, but after the northern Kingdom of Israel was conquered by the Assyrians in 722 BC, many Israelites were deported and foreign peoples were settled in their place. The Samaritans emerged from these historical circumstances, and their worship incorporated elements that the Jewish people in the southern Kingdom of Judah considered to be foreign and idolatrous.

In the New Testament, the term "Samaritan" is most prominently featured in two places:

- The Parable of the Good Samaritan (Luke 10:25-37):

In this parable told by Jesus, a Samaritan helps a man who has been robbed and beaten, after a priest and a Levite (members of the Jewish religious elite) have passed by without helping. The Samaritan shows compassion and mercy, illustrating the commandment to "love your neighbor as yourself." The parable was notable because it presented a Samaritan, someone whom

Jesus's Jewish listeners might have looked down upon, as the example of neighborly love.
- Jesus and the Samaritan Woman (John 4:4-26): In this narrative, Jesus encounters a Samaritan woman at a well and asks her for a drink, which surprises her because Jews typically did not associate with Samaritans. Jesus then reveals His knowledge of her personal life and declares Himself to be the Messiah, leading the woman to believe in Him.

In both these instances, the use of Samaritans in the narratives serves to challenge societal norms and prejudices, emphasizing the universal love and mercy that should be characteristic of followers of Jesus.

Semitic

The term "Semitic" is not specifically used in the Bible, but it refers to a family of languages and their associated group of people. Semitic languages include Hebrew, Aramaic, and Arabic, among others.

In the context of the Bible:
- Hebrew is the original language of the Old Testament, and the Hebrew people, later known as the Israelites or Jews, are central to biblical narrative.
- Aramaic was the common language spoken in the Near East during the time of Christ and is present in some portions of the Bible, particularly in the book of Daniel and some sayings of Jesus in the New Testament.

"Semitic" comes from the name Shem, one of the sons of Noah in the book of Genesis in the Bible, and traditionally the ancestor of the peoples of the Near East. It is thus used to describe the group of people who speak Semitic languages, including Hebrews, Arabs, Assyrians, and others.

It's important to note that "Semitic" is a linguistic and cultural term, not a racial one. The Semitic peoples are a diverse group, spread across multiple geographical regions and encompassing a variety of ethnic and cultural backgrounds.

Sermon

A "sermon" is a discourse or speech that is generally delivered by a clergy member or religious leader for the purpose of providing religious instruction, moral guidance, or encouragement. In Christianity, sermons are typically based on biblical scriptures and are designed to interpret those scriptures in a way that provides guidance and edification to the congregation. The term "sermon" is derived from the Latin word "sermo," which simply means "speech."
In the context of the Bible, the most famous sermon is the Sermon on the Mount, delivered by Jesus Christ as recorded in the Gospel of Matthew, chapters 5 to 7. This sermon includes some of Jesus's most well-known teachings, including the Beatitudes ("Blessed are the meek, for they shall inherit the earth..." and so on), the Lord's Prayer, and the commandment to "love your enemies." Sermons remain an integral part of many Christian worship services, providing a means for pastors, priests, or ministers to teach biblical truths, offer commentary on current events through a religious lens, and inspire their congregations in their faith journeys.

Sin

The word "sin" generally refers to an act that violates a moral rule or law, often seen from a religious perspective. It is usually associated with any thought, word, deed, or omission against the divine law set by God.
In many religions, sin is regarded as a transgression against divine law or cosmic order. It's often linked to concepts of guilt, condemnation, and punishment. Different religious traditions may have their own specific definitions and categories of sins, as

well as mechanisms for atonement or forgiveness.
In Christian theology, sin is traditionally understood as any act or thought that separates an individual from God. It's often associated with actions that go against the commands and expectations laid out in the Bible. The concept of original sin, which originates in the disobedience of Adam and Eve in the Garden of Eden, is also central to many Christian denominations, suggesting a fundamental state of sin inherited from the first human beings.
It's important to note that interpretations of sin can vary widely among different religious, philosophical, and cultural systems.

Testament

The term "testament" is derived from the Latin word 'testamentum', which means "covenant" or "agreement." This is a translation of the Hebrew word 'berith'(בְּרִית) and the Greek word 'diatheke'(διαθήκη),), both of which are often translated as "covenant, agreement, or will."
In the context of the Bible, a "testament" refers to a covenant or agreement made between God and His people.
- The "Old Testament" pertains to the covenant that God made with the people of Israel, particularly the covenant made with Moses on Mount Sinai (Exodus 19-24). This part of the Bible, which is also the Jewish Tanakh, includes the Torah (the first five books of the Bible, also known as the Pentateuch), the historical books, the wisdom books, and the prophets.
- The "New Testament" pertains to the new covenant established through Jesus Christ, as foretold by the prophet Jeremiah (Jeremiah 31:31-34). This part of the Bible, which is specific to Christianity, includes the Gospels (accounts of the life and teachings of Jesus), the Acts of the Apostles, the Epistles (letters), and the Book of Revelation.

In a broader sense, "testament" can also refer to any proof or evidence that validates a particular fact or claim, or a person's will, the legal document by which they specify how their possessions should be disposed of after their death. It carries the idea of an agreement or contract between two parties, often with implications of a binding and solemn promise. This term is used in the Septuagint, the Greek translation of the Hebrew Bible, to refer to the covenant between God and the Israelites. In the New Testament, "diathēkē" is used to designate the new covenant established through Jesus Christ. The English word "testament" is a direct translation of "diathēkē" and is used to describe the two main sections of the Christian Bible.

The term "testament" was used to describe these sections because it reflects the concept of a covenant or agreement between God and humanity. It symbolizes the relationship, promises, and agreements between God and His people as documented in the respective sections of the Bible.

Walk to Emmaus

The expression "the walk to Emmaus" refers to a story found inthe Gospel of Luke (Luke 24:13-35) in the New Testament of the Bible. This event is said to have happened on the day of Jesus' resurrection.
In this account, two of Jesus' disciples are walking from Jerusalem to the village of Emmaus, which was about seven miles away. They are discussing everything that has recently occurred (the trial, crucifixion, and reported resurrection of Jesus). As they walk, Jesus Himself comes up and joins them on their journey. However, they are kept from recognizing Him.
Jesus asks them what they are discussing, and they tell Him about their hopes that Jesus of Nazareth would have been the one to redeem Israel. They also share the confusing news that some women found His tomb empty that morning. Jesus, still unrecognized by them, explains the Scriptures to them, showing how it was necessary for the Messiah to suffer these things.
As they reach Emmaus, they invite the stranger (Jesus) to stay with them as it is getting late. As they sit to eat, Jesus takes bread, blesses it, breaks it, and gives it to them. At this moment, their

eyes are opened, they recognize Him, and He disappears from their sight. They return to Jerusalem and tell the other disciples about their experience.

In a broader metaphorical sense, the "walk to Emmaus" can symbolize the journey of understanding or faith, where one moves from doubt and despair to recognition and belief, often aided by the interpretation of Scripture and the breaking of bread, symbolizing the Eucharist for many Christians.
In some Christian traditions, "Walk to Emmaus" is also the name of a spiritual retreat designed to strengthen and renew the faith of Christian people and through them, their families, congregations, and the world in which they live. This is done through a structured three-day program of singing, learning, sharing, praying, and participating in small groups and communion.

Index

A
amen, 204
Andrew, 105-106
Apostle Creed, 183-186
Aramaic, 205

B
Bahai, 187, 193-195
baptise, 205
Bartholomew, 110
being on the road
　　to Damascus, 206
bible, 169-171, 207
Buddhism, 187, 198-200

C
Canaan, 207
calming the storm, 43, 46
christian, 208
Church of Christ of Latter-Day
　　Saints (LDS), 187, 200-203
compassion, 209
covenant, 209
crucifixion, 211

D
death and resurrection, 50-51
disciple, 100-104, 126, 211
divinity, 13-17

E
Eucharist, 212

F
feeding the crowd
　　of 5000, 47-48
forgiveness, 212

G
Galilee, 213-215
Garden of Gethsemane, 54-55
Gentile, 213
gentle, 214
God, 13-18, 98-100
Gospels, 177-183
grace, 215

H
healings, 55- 74
Hebrew, 216
Hinduism, 195-197
Holy Spirit, 16

I
Islam, 187, 190-192

J
James the Greater, 107
James the Lesser, 113
Jesus, 13-95
Jeruaslem, 43, 49-50 217,
John, 108
John the Baptist, 115-116
Judiasm, 187, 188-190
Judas Iscariot, 115

K
Koine Greek, 219

L
Last Supper, 41-42
Lazarus, 43, 48-49
Lord's Prayer, 34-38
love, 218
Luke, 122-124

M
Mark, 119-122
Mary, Jesus Mother, 117
Mary Magdaalene, 117-118
Matthew, 100, 110-112
metaphor, 21, 74-95
miracles, 14, 21, 55-74

N
Nicene Creed, 184-186
Nicodemus, 118-119

O

P
parables, 20-31, 219
Paul, 124-125,126
Pentecost, 221
Phillip, 109
Pharisee, 222
piety, 223
prayer, 223
prophecy, 224

Q
questions and answers, 20, 38-39

R
rabbi, 10, 16, 18-20

raising Lazarus, 48-49
resurrection, 13-14
road to Damascus, 206-207

S
salvation, 225
Samaritan, 226
Semitic, 227
sermons, 31-34, 228
Simon Peter, 104-105
Simon the Zealot, 114
sin, 228

T
teachable moments, 20, 41-
temple confrontations, 53-54
testament, 229
    New Testament, 177-183
    Old Testament, 173-177
Thaddeus, 113-114
Thomas, 112-113
Transfiguration,43, 45-45
turning water into wine, 56-57

U
V

W
walk to Emmaus, 52-53, 230
walking on water, 43, 46-47
washing disciples' feet, 42, 43-44
who do you say I am, 39-40

X
Y
Z

Notes

About the Authors

Mark Standley, PhD

Mark is a researcher and writer. His books include subjects on families curating their possessions into a digital future, fishing on kayaks, drones, touring on bikes, learning to become an old man, the teachings of Jesus, and salmon hatcheries in Alaska.

He spends time exploring via RV, bike and kayak with family, friends, and his puppy ,'Chili Dog'. He enjoys volunteer time in church and works at a Christain retreat center. And greatly admires his two adult children.

website: answers.academy

Foreword by H. Fred Brown, JD, M.Divinity

St. Mary's Univ. School of Law, San Antonio, TX. J.D. 1970. Houston Graduate School of Theology, M.Div. 1993. Military: Underwater Demolition/SEAL Team Training Class #27, 1962. (The first East Coast SEAL class) US Navy Amphibious Base, Little Creek, VA. Platoon Commander, 2nd Platoon, Underwater Demolition Team 22, 1963. Mr. Brown brings years of experience and inspiration to his sermons and teachings. Now retired working with family on his mountaintop retreat in West Texas.

www.ingramcontent.com/pod-product-compliance
Lightning Source LLC
LaVergne TN
LVHW020927090426
835512LV00020B/3234